Toronto Architect Edmund Burke

REDEFINING CANADIAN ARCHITECTURE

ANGELA CARR

McGILL-QUEEN'S UNIVERSITY PRESS

MONTREAL & KINGSTON • LONDON • BUFFALO

© McGill-Queen's University Press 1995
ISBN 0-7735-1217-9

Legal deposit first quarter 1995
Bibliothèque nationale du Québec

Printed in Canada on acid-free paper

This book has been published with the help of a grant
from the Canadian Federation for the Humanities, using
funds provided by the Social Sciences and Humanities
Research Council of Canada.

McGill-Queen's University Press is grateful to the Canada
Council for support of its publishing program.

Canadian Cataloguing in Publication Data

Carr, Angela
    Toronto architect Edmund Burke: redefining Canadian
architecture
    Includes bibliographical references and index.
    ISBN 0-7735-1217-9
    1. Burke, Edmund, 1850–1919. 2. Architects – Canada –
Biography. 3. Architecture, Modern – 19th century –
Canada – History. 4. Architecture, Modern – 20th century
– Canada – History. I. Title.
NA749.B87C37 1995   720'.92   C95-900129-8

This book was typeset by Typo Litho Composition Inc.
in 10.5/12.5 Sabon.

*To my parents with
deepest appreciation*

*And in memory of
Janet Boucher and
Mrs Douglas MacLennan*

Contents

Acknowledgments

Research for this book was funded by a Social Sciences and Humanities Research Council of Canada Doctoral Fellowship; the Arthur Caplan Fellowship in Canada-U.S. Relations at University College, University of Toronto; the Kinghorn Travel Scholarship, History of Art Department, University of Toronto; an Ontario Graduate Scholarship; and a University of Toronto School of Graduate Studies Travel Award.[1]

Many individuals across this country, from Halifax to Victoria, generously shared their time and expertise to help make this book possible. First and foremost I wish to express my gratitude to Douglas Richardson, who suggested Toronto architect Edmund Burke as a topic for my doctoral dissertation. During the course of that undertaking, for which he served as my advisor, his guidance and insights were invaluable, as were his many helpful suggestions in editing. To George Baird and Gunter Gad, who willingly agreed to act as readers of the dissertation, and to the other members of the examining committee, my sincere thanks for their astute comments and constructive criticisms. My thanks in particular to Kelly Crossman, whose own writing in the field confirmed the conceptual framework for this study and provided many broader insights on the period. Sincere thanks are also due to McGill-Queen's University Press, in particular the editor, Frances Rooney, who spent many patient hours reviewing the manuscript, and Philip Cercone, Peter Blaney, Joan McGilvray, and Susanne McAdam, who saw this project through to completion.

Instrumental in the successful completion of this work were many architectural historians, archivists, librarians, and others, who, without exception, gave unstintingly of their time and energy to locate the material I required. Among the institutions and individuals I particularly want to thank are the Archives of Ontario, including William Cooper, archivist of the Horwood Collection, Ken Macpherson and Jan Rollins, past and present archivists of the Picture Collection, John Fortier, Map archivist (retired), and Katrin Cooper and Paul Thomas of photographic services, all of whom indulged my year-long occupation of their research facilities and incessant retrieval requests with good humour and solicitous attention. To the Baldwin Room staff and the Art History section of the Metropolitan Toronto Reference Library my thanks for prompt responses to my inquiries and for courtesy throughout our many years of dealings. Acknowledgment is also due to Paul Dilse and Alan Miesner among others at the City of Toronto Archives, whose assistance saved me many hours of research time. I am also indebted to numerous individuals at the United Church of Canada Central Archives and the Pratt Library, Victoria University, Toronto; the Presbyterian Church of Canada Archives, Knox College, Toronto; the University of Toronto Archives; and the Thomas Fisher Rare Book Library at the University of Toronto. In addition Stephen Otto's press kit for the Horwood Collection offered a useful starting point for this study, and additional reference material was supplied by the ever-generous Robert Hill from his forthcoming *Biographical Dictionary of Architects in Canada 1800–1950*. The Architectural Conservancy of Ontario through its Archindont index at the Metropolitan Toronto Reference Library provided an invaluable resource, and Alec Keefer, president of the Architectural Conservancy of Ontario, alerted me to a number of important details of which I might otherwise have remained unaware. My thanks, too, to Garnett Martin, administrator of the Jarvis Street Baptist Church in Toronto, whose knowledge of the history of that structure contributed significantly to my understanding of its development.

Information relating to Burke's Baptist commissions and those he executed for Senator William McMaster was made available by the Canadian Baptist Archives and McMaster University Archives in Hamilton; special thanks in this case to Judith Colwell, archivist of the former collection. Also of great assistance in connection with Hamilton architecture was Nina Chapple, architectural historian with the Planning and Development Department of the Regional Municipality of Hamilton-Wentworth, as well as the staff of the Special Collections Room at the Hamilton Public Library.

In Ottawa the National Archives of Canada was endlessly helpful in providing information from the National Map Collection, National Photography Collection, and Manuscript Division. Also of immense value were the files of the Canadian Parks Service, compiled on a nation-wide basis by architectural historians on its staff. Collections of the National Library of Canada and the National Research Council of Canada included some of the more obscure American architectural publications of the last century, which are otherwise available only through international lending services.

Among the many individuals across this country who went out of their way to assist this project were Donna Beal, Mount Allison University archivist, Keilor Bentley, Director of the Owens Art Museum, and William Black, all of Sackville, New Brunswick; Donald P. Lemon of the New Brunswick Museum in Saint John; Garry Shutlak, Map and Architecture archivist for the Public Archives of Nova Scotia, Halifax; in Montreal, Howard Shubert of the Canadian Centre for Architecture, Jean-Marc Garant of the Archives

Nationales du Québec, Marie Baboyant of the Salle Gagnon, Bibliothèque Municipale du Montréal, P. Lepine, Bibliothèque National du Québec, Eileen Paradis, Bureau du Patrimonie, Giselle Marinier of the Services des Travaux Publics de la Ville de Montréal, and Mrs Burger of the Redpath Library at McGill University; Barbara Salomon de Friedberg and Sylvie Parent of the Ministère des Affaires culturelles, in Quebec city, André Laflamme and Mariette Naud, Archives de la Ville de Québec, and Senette Biellant of the Archives de l'Université Laval; in Ontario, the City Museum, Woodstock; in Winnipeg, the staff of the Public Archives of Manitoba and the Hudson's Bay Company Archives, Giles Bugaliskis of the City's Historical Projects Branch, architectural historian, Randy Rostecki; Betty Barootes, and Margaret Hutchinson, Saskatchewan Archives Board, Regina; John Gilpin and Diana Thomas of the Historic Sites Service, Edmonton, Alberta, the Provincial Archives of Alberta, the City of Edmonton Archives, and Duncan Fraser, Heritage Officer for the City of Edmonton; in Calgary, the Glenbow-Alberta Institute, the City of Calgary Archives, the Canadian Architectural Archives of the University of Calgary, and the Alberta Historical Resources Foundation; the Vancouver City Archives, the Historical Photographic Collection, Vancouver Public Library, and the University of British Columbia Library; and in Victoria, the Provincial Archives of British Columbia, and the City of Victoria Archives.

I also wish to thank the following individuals and institutions in the United States and in the United Kingdom: Robert Bruegmann of the University of Illinois at Chicago, Scott LaFrance of the Chicago Historical Society, John Zukowsky of the Art Institute of Chicago, Karen Herring of Washington, D.C., the staffs of the New York Public Library, the Avery Library, and the New York Historical Society, Michael King and Philip Browning of the Liverpool City Planning Department, the Central Libraries, Liverpool, and the Central Reference Library, Glasgow.

Special thanks are also due to the descendents of Edmund Burke, the late Mrs Douglas MacLennan of Fredericton, New Brunswick, and the late Mrs Janet Boucher of Winnipeg, Manitoba, who supplied the few direct insights I have into the character and personality of my subject.

Finally, but not least, I wish to thank my family, who endured the years of research and writing with patience and understanding, offering support at every stage of the undertaking, and without whose encouragement none of this would have been written.

To all those who have contributed so much to the completion of this project, my sincere thanks.

Chronology

1850   Edmund Burke, eldest child of lumber merchant and builder William Burke and Sarah Langley, born in Toronto 31 October

1852–62   William Hay in practice in Toronto, latterly with Thomas Gundry

1862–69   Gundry & Langley form partnership after Hay returns to Scotland

1863–65   Burke at Upper Canada College following early education at Jesse Ketchum School

1865–72   Burke architectural apprentice with uncle Henry Langley, signs perspectives by 1869

1869–72   Henry Langley sole practitioner following Gundry's death

1873–83   Henry Langley, his brother Edward Langley, a builder, and nephew Edmund Burke form partnership of Langley, Langley & Burke (LLB)

1874–75   Jarvis Street Baptist Church for Senator William McMaster Burke's first important commission at LLB

1874   Burke's membership in Ontario Society of Artists

1880–81   Burke as partner in LLB executes Baptist Theological College in Toronto for Senator William McMaster

1881   Burke and Minnie Jayne Black of Sackville, New Brunswick, married 27 July

1883–92   partnership continues as Langley & Burke (LB) after Edward Langley retires

1886–87   Burke supervising partner for Sherbourne Street Methodist Church

1887   Burke among founders of Architectural Guild of Toronto

1887–89   Burke supervising partner for Trinity Methodist Church

1889   Burke among founders of the Ontario Association of Architects (OAA)

1892–94   Burke sole practitioner after purchasing the practice of W.G. Storm

1892   Burke executes Walmer Road Baptist Church for Rev. Elmore Harris

1893–95   Burke wins the competition for the design of the Owens Art Museum in Sackville

1894   Burke president of OAA

1894   Burke designs innovative scheme for Robert Simpson store in Toronto

1895–1908   partnership of Burke & Horwood (BH)

1895   BH rebuilds Simpson store on a freestanding iron frame

1902   Burke among those who propose grounds plan for Canadian National Exhibition

1905–07   Burke president of OAA

1905   Burke a member of the Civic Guild plan committee

1906–7   Burke an assessor for the Departmental buildings competition in Ottawa

1908–19   partnership of Burke, Horwood & White (BHW)

1908   Burke among founders of Royal Architectural Institute of Canada

1911 on   BHW retained by Hudson's Bay Company to design its flagship stores in western Canada

1913–17   Burke designs architectural portion of Bloor Viaduct

1919   Burke dies at home of pneumonia 2 January; interred at Mount Pleasant Cemetery

1   *Introduction*

> Few men of the present generation of architects have so widely
> held the respect and esteem of their *confrères*, or been more
> closely identified with the building progress of the country.
> Practising continuously for a period of over forty years, dur-
> ing the time when Canada was passing from its more backwards
> state to the present great strides of nationhood, his efforts
> stand out prominently in the modern character of Canadian
> architectural work.
>
> Obituary of E. Burke, *Construction* (January 1919)

Toronto architect Edmund Burke (1850–1919) is known chiefly for
his role in introducing "curtain-wall" construction to Canada and for
his part in establishing a formal professional organization for architects in Ontario. His career covers a critical period at the end of the
last century when the profession sought legal recognition of its status
– a move designed to protect the public from unscrupulous and un-
qualified practitioners while at the same time providing architects
with a standing in the community and suitable financial recompense
for the spiraling demands upon their expertise. But Burke's significance is not limited to these matters alone. In a more general way, his
life reflects the profession's growth from colonial beginnings to a distinct national maturity: it was Canadian practitioners, like Burke,
who accomplished this transition by assimilating modern American
and European traditions in search of forms appropriate to Canadian
needs.

Just twelve years before Burke's birth, Anna Jameson had written
of the province: "Canada is a colony, not a country; it is not yet identified with the dearest affections and associations, rememberances,
and hopes of its inhabitants; it is to them an adopted, not a real
mother. Their love, their pride, are not for poor Canada, but for high
and happy England; but a few more generations must change all
this."[1]

At that time – barely a generation after the War of 1812 and a year
since the 1837 Rebellion – descendents of the United Empire Loyalists
regarded the new institutions of the United States with "repugnance"
and "contempt."[2] In the years that followed, however, geographic
proximity and the vibrant cultural ferment of the United States had an
impact, particularly in the field of architecture. American pattern
books and professional publications flooded into Canadian architectural offices, and those educated in the British tradition of apprenticeship were forced to come to terms with new ideas.

Events taking place south of the border inspired Canadian
architects to establish professional organizations, institute formal
programs of architectural education, and investigate modern technol-

ogies. Kelly Crossman has described these late nineteenth-century developments and the ensuing rise of Canadian nationalism in *Architecture in Transition*. He details the Canadian response to innovations in American architecture and educational practice as well as the reaction to architectural competition from the United States. Burke, who figured prominently in this changing architectural ethos and is singularly representative of the era, offers an appropriate focal point for further investigation.

The primary resource for the study of Edmund Burke was the body of architectural drawings in the Horwood Collection at the Archives of Ontario, as well as a smaller body of works in the Langley Collection of the Baldwin Room at the Metropolitan Toronto Reference Library. I examined all 750 files, some containing as many as a hundred or more drawings potentially related to Burke's career – in the successive offices of Henry Langley; Langley, Langley & Burke; Langley & Burke; Edmund Burke; Burke & Horwood; and Burke, Horwood & White – the effort to attribute both individual drawings and projects to the appropriate partner. In some cases perspective views and other works are initialled by the delineator, but few contract drawings are identified in this way. By 1890 Burke carried responsibility for design in the Langley practice, but the office employed at least half a dozen draughtsmen; the same large staff was characteristic of the Burke & Horwood firm. Conventions of "office style" make it difficult to distinguish individual hands (even the partners sometimes had to rely upon lettering technique rather than draughtsmanship to make such distinctions). Yet differences are apparent among Langley, Burke, Horwood, and van Raalte, the chief draughtsman in the Burke firm in the early years of this century. Analysis confirms that Burke's designs are typically simple and uncluttered, and his buildings – like his draughting style – are economical in detail and practical in preference to ornamental. Horwood, by contrast, had a precious, jewel-like technique derived from the Arts and Crafts Movement, and was given to florid ornamentalism and beautiful (if sometimes costly) materials in the realization of his projects.

Burke's work developed consistently through a variety of building types in all periods, accommodating technological advances almost as rapidly as these appeared and expressing the new aesthetic of a changing society. His works are so extensive, however, that it is necessary to limit the scope of this discussion to pivotal monuments, selecting key works from each stage and addressing them in the context of others of similar building type. To the extent possible, I have maintained chronology within the chapters, and the chapters have been arranged more or less sequentially in accordance with interrelated historical issues.

Burke was born in Toronto on 31 October 1850, and began his articles at the age of fourteen in the office of his uncle, Henry Langley. Langley, who had received his education in turn from William Hay – a Scottish emigrant who came to British North America as clerk of works for the well-known English architect Gilbert Scott – was prominent among the first generation of architects trained in Canada. Langley's productive career was notable both for exemplary training of architectural students and for the design of no fewer than seventy Gothic-revival churches throughout Ontario, though he also worked in the French Second Empire mode then fashionable in the United States. This experience, passed to Burke in the course of his articles, provided a sound if conservative basis for future work.

Burke's professional career began formally in 1872 when he entered into partnership with his uncle, an association that lasted for twenty years, until 1892, when he left to set up his own firm. During that time he was the beneficiary of two important commissions financed by Senator William McMaster; the first, Jarvis Street Baptist Church, was his earliest independent work, and McMaster Hall on Bloor Street (now the Royal Conservatory of Music) constituted a significant transitional development. The endowments were instigated by McMaster's American-born wife Susan Moulton, who was also instrumental in the selection of American precedents for both buildings. As a result the plan for Jarvis Street Baptist Church incorporated an amphitheatre plan, common among evangelical denominations in the United States, while McMaster Hall included a three-storey Romanesque arcade of a type similar to examples the architect saw during a preparatory tour of New England colleges.

As the firm's design partner in the 1880s, Burke was among the first architects in Toronto to adopt the distinctive Romanesque manner of the American architect Henry Hobson Richardson following the latter's death in 1886. Burke's impulse for innovation was also manifest in a number of technically sophisticated church interiors and at least one commercial facade. In many of these instances, too, precedents for Burke's new initiatives appear to have been American.

Works executed by Burke in the period 1892–94, as a sole practitioner, are critical to an understanding of his development. They reveal the architect at the peak of his career, truly independent of his mentor for the first time, and (through most of this period) before the arrival of J.C.B. Horwood, his influential future partner. Burke's commercial designs in this phase disclose a growing awareness of the latest building technologies then burgeoning in the United States. His knowledge came partly from his own travels to the World's Columbian Exposition in Chicago in 1893 and partly from the growing number of American professional journals, notably the *American Architect and Building News* (Boston) and the *Inland Architect and News Record* (Chicago), which recorded the momentous developments taking place in the American Midwest at the end of the last century. Also of major importance was Burke's continuing correspondence with his future partner, Horwood, then completing his studies in New York, who wrote regularly concerning American innovations he observed. As Burke assimilated this information, he revised the traditional approaches, values, and vocabularies of their mutual mentor, Henry Langley, and increasingly investigated new avenues of both formal and rational expression. The most noteworthy example of Burke's new synthesis was the Robert Simpson store of 1894, which featured the fundamentals of a free-standing metal skeleton and brick curtain walls – the first such structure in the city and, to my knowledge, in the country. This landmark monument was the turning point of Burke's career. It not only provided a precedent for the firm's later commercial structures, but also set the stage for his future activities in city planning and public works.

Burke dedicated the last decade and a half of his life to public and professional service. By 1910 his partnership duties were limited almost entirely to management. He became increasingly involved with education and organization for the Ontario Association of Architects, an organization formed partly in response to the growing number of Americans practising in Canada. He was the mainstay of the Toronto chapter, acting as its chairman for five years, while serving on the council of the provincial organization and sitting as president for four years: 1894, 1905, 1906, and again in 1907. In this capacity he chaired the board of assessors for the Departmental buildings (buildings to house government departments) competition in Ottawa in 1906. The following year he participated in founding of a new federal umbrella organization, the Architectural Institute of Canada, of which he became a founding vice-president in 1908. During the same period he also took an active part in city planning initiatives for Toronto, including the Civic Guild scheme to improve the city's traffic flow and the architectural design of the Bloor Viaduct. Having crossed the great divide between the *retardataire* practices of his apprenticeship and the uncharted waters of metal-frame construction, he presided over the transformation of the architect from craftsman to consulting professional. His own search for realization parallels that of the architectural profession, and his preparedness for future challenges was a bench mark against which others measured themselves.

2 Apprenticeship and Draughtsmanship: The Educational Lineage

About sixty years ago most of our best work was done by men who were trained in England, and who brought with them a sincerity and conservative restraint in their work.

The days of handling a large architectural practice in a small professional way are past ... This means that architecture to meet present-day conditions must be a highly organized business, and not a one-man profession as it used to be. There are many in the United States being trained to fulfil these modern requirements in the way of design, but practically none in Canada.

Alfred Chapman, "The Development of Architectural Design in Canada," *Construction* (October 1917)

In 1897 the British architect Leonard Stokes likened the "system of observation" upon which architectural apprenticeship was based to watching a conjurer "bring two live rabbits and a bunch of flowers out of an empty hat" – the better the performer, the more obscure the process.[1] The state of architectural education in Canada during the same period was no less a matter of concern. As late as 1900 in an address before the Architectural League of America, Toronto architect Eden Smith observed that "we have no generally approved and accepted course of training for the architectural student. The usual system of a few years apprenticeship cannot be seriously taken as sufficient."[2] The few programs in Canadian universities were poorly attended because academic qualifications were not required for licensing.[3] Two years later Edmund Burke, who had already served one of his four terms as president of the Ontario Association of Architects, reiterated the apprehension that students in Ontario still entered offices "without or before taking a proper course in the School of [Practical] Science" at the University of Toronto. After two decades of struggle to achieve professional recognition for architects in the province, it was his conviction that architects should refuse to employ students until their formal training was complete.[4]

It may have seemed that opportunities were being allowed to slip away. Burke's own apprenticeship had begun in 1865 at the age of fourteen after only two years of secondary schooling.[5] At that time there were few choices. The first advanced program of architectural study in North America was established only a year later at Massachusetts Institute of Technology, its system based on that of the Ecole des Beaux-Arts in Paris.[6] Toronto had no such facilities until 1889 when the first lecturer in architecture was appointed to the School of Practical Science.[7] A more broadly based program was instituted at McGill several years later.[8] As Burke wryly remarked, "The young men of today [have] greater opportunities by far, with regard to education, than the students in [my] day, when little was thought about the subject. Then, if students read Paley and Ryckman [*sic*], that was about all that was expected of them, aside from looking out of the window when the boss was out."[9]

Architecture in Canada in 1865 was founded almost entirely upon British traditions and methodology.[10] But the unquestioned acceptance of British practice began to wane after Confederation. Then, in the latter half of the 1870s, the United States was galvanized by the Centennial celebrations in Philadelphia.[11] American preoccupations with "national architectural identity" soon spread across the border.[12] The need for Canadian-trained professionals became increasingly apparent.[13] Innovative commercial construction pioneered in the American Midwest demanded a high level of technical expertise, as did Canadian corporate clients, who often selected American architects for major building projects.[14] Associations were formed to promote the architect's professional status, and education seemed to offer the best prospect for credibility.[15]

Burke's career offers a vantage point from which to consider the momentous changes taking place at this period. In his youth Canadian architecture had a distinctly "borrowed" flavour. By the end of his life, largely through his leadership and that of his generation, the profession in Canada entered a new era of self-confidence. And yet Burke was a modest and industrious figure rather than a heroic genius writ large. The contributions he made lie quietly between the lines, the process of change was often a matter of nuance and context rather than boldly recorded fact. It is perhaps the best tribute to Burke that he is so little known, when his name is so consistently recorded at the centre of events that shaped the future of the architectural profession in Canada.

For Burke architecture was a natural choice. His father William was a general contractor and dealer in builder's supplies, his uncle Henry Langley a well-known practitioner of Gothic revival and Second Empire modes.[16] Langley provided Burke's articling experience, and subsequently took him into partnership in 1873.[17] When Burke began, the firm had been in business over ten years, and its lineage could be traced to one of the most illustrious names in British architecture – Gilbert Scott. Its files must have included as comprehensive a set of precedents as any student could have wished, an altogether exemplary opportunity by contemporary standards.

The firm had been founded in 1852 by William Hay, who went to Toronto after serving as Gilbert Scott's clerk of works on the Anglican cathedral at St John's, Newfoundland.[18] Trained in Edinburgh by John Henderson, Hay was familiar with a full array of early nineteenth-century revival styles.[19] But his association with Scott seems to have solidified his affinity for Gothic. Many of his Toronto commissions were conceived in this mode, laying the groundwork for Langley's practice in the years to come.[20] Hay's forms and draughting techniques were based almost exclusively on British models – for clients who shared his affinities. He soon became one of the leading practitioners in the city, alongside Kivas Tully, William Thomas and his sons, and Frederic William Cumberland and his partner William George Storm.[21]

By contrast Henry Langley was born and educated entirely in Upper Canada. After attending the Toronto Academy he began his apprenticeship in Hay's office at the age of seventeen or eighteen, and remained there seven years.[22] When Hay returned to Scotland in 1862, his English-trained associate Thomas Gundry took over and immediately offered Langley a partnership. Langley is reputed to have handled the draughting and design, while Gundry specialized in valuation and estimates.[23] Their partnership which achieved considerable success, continued until Gundry's death in 1869.[24]

Apart from Langley's role as design partner, we can only surmise the range of experience to which he was exposed as an articled student through comparison with contemporary practice elsewhere. In Britain, for example, Gilbert Scott, whose mentorship of Hay had led to the founding of the firm in the first place, reported that his own apprenticeship consisted of thorough instruction in the basics of building and estimating, but that other aspects of his principal's practice were of a most indifferent quality.[25] George Edmund Street is reputed to have supervised his students so closely they never got beyond tracing his drawings. By contrast Richard Norman Shaw thoroughly coached his apprentices in all phases of project execution, and even provided their first independent commission.[26] The evidence preserved in the Horwood collection drawings suggests that Hay was closest to Shaw's model, concentrating on draughting and design, so that Langley was fully prepared for these responsibilities when he entered into partnership with Gundry.

In large North American offices the system was equally idiosyncratic. American architect Henry Hobson Richardson confined himself to freehand, thumb-nail sketches depicting form and massing, while his draughtsmen were charged with the preparation of presentation and contract drawings for his approval.[27] But Charles McKim (of McKim, Mead & White), a one-time Richardson student, shunned the pencil completely. The draughtsman served as his amanuensis while the watchful McKim stood over him, directing the placement of each and every line.[28] In Hay's firm in Canada West, by contrast, the senior partner prepared the presentation pieces, and left the contract drawings and minor commissions to the student. Langley later adopted an even clearer division of labour in his partnership with Burke, placing his junior partner in charge of a draughting room of five and delegating to him almost all the design responsibilities.[29]

Judging by contemporary accounts, Langley's practice must have been an outstanding training ground for draughtsmen. His students consistently assumed a major part of the design work before their articles expired. Their initials on the many perspectives in the Horwood collection of the Archives of Ontario document this fact, and indicate that Langley respected his draughtsmen enough to credit them with these prestigious presentation drawings.[30] Predictably many prominent names of the next generation were Langley old boys who carried on the same tradition.[31] By contrast Gambier-Bousfield, another Toronto architect, complained in 1891:

We have to do all our work for ourselves, for there is little we can trust entirely to our clerks and draughtsmen in the matter either of construction or design, and it is often far easier to do all the work oneself, than to correct the errors of our clerks. The draughtsmen whom we can get hold of are for the most part not properly educated. They have (I say the majority of them), been "*fetched*" up somehow, not trained, and we certainly can not spare the time to teach them.[32]

The pattern of education and contributions made by partners and students at each phase in the firm's development can be traced by an examination of the drawings. Identification is by no means straightforward, because architectural firms large enough to employ a number of draughtsmen, as Langley's did, often sought to minimize variations in drawing style by conforming to a consistent set of criteria formulated by the senior partner. Format and appearance were circumscribed so that "office style" tended to take precedence over individual artistic expression.[33] To a large extent this model applied to the Langley firm, but observable variations in technique suggest some latitude in personal approach and demonstrate the impact of growing educational opportunities in response to international trends in draughtsmanship. The point can be illustrated by examining a series of drawings from each of the firms.

Hay's sections for the Gould Street United Presbyterian Church of 1855 are executed in pen and wash on Whatman paper[34] (fig. 2.1). The flat projection consists of pale, ruler-drawn outlines tinted with pale colour-coded washes – pink representing brick, yellow for wood,

2.1   William Hay. Gould Street United Presbyterian Church (later Catholic Apostolic Church, now demolished), Toronto, 1855. Transverse and longitudinal sections, 23 July 1855. Pen and wash on paper. MTRL-Baldwin Room (BR), Langley Collection (LC):126.

2.2   Henry Langley. McGill Square Church (Metropolitan Wesleyan Methodist Church, now Metropolitan United Church), Toronto, 1870–72. Longitudinal section, c.1870. Pen and wash on paper. MTRL-BR, LC:67.

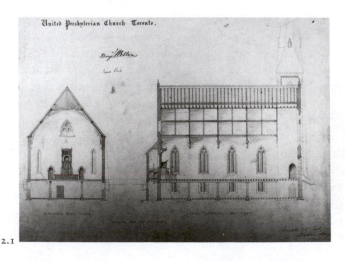

2.1

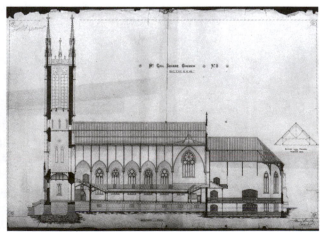

2.2

and grey for stone.[35] Of particular interest are the shadows used to differentiate the planes, especially in the ceiling ribs, a practice long since abandoned in British contract drawings because of the tendency to confuse builders.[36]

By contrast Langley's sections for the McGill Square Methodist Church of 1870 are replete with the "wiry insensitive line" and "acrid washes" Blomfield later described as typical of British draughtsmanship of the 1860s and 1870s (fig. 2.2).[37] The vogue for heavy outlining was inspired by Blomfield's compatriot William Burges, who was fascinated by this feature of medieval design.[38] And the vibrant red used to represent brick (and intended to convey the clearest possible instructions to the builder) contrasts sharply with Hay's pastels. The flat, shadowless forms are unmistakable.[39]

The difference in technique between Langley and Hay is apparent even before Hay turned over the practice to Gundry & Langley. Two elevations of the Yorkville Town Hall of 1859 clearly demonstrate the allocation of responsibilities in the practice. A preliminary study under the signature of William Hay is executed in pencil and watercolour on wove paper (fig. 2.3). Probably intended as a presentation piece, the facade is rendered with graded washes to bring out the three-dimensional quality of the form. The same pastel washes and fine outlines that characterized the earlier sections for the Gould Street United Presbyterian Church are apparent here.

A second elevation, which served as the contract document, shows the tower on the left as it was built (fig. 2.4). Executed on Whatman paper in ink and wash, the drawing is characterized by heavy outlining with areas of flat, unshaded colour. Neither signature nor delineator's initials appear, but the work is in line with what the Langley office produced in the 1870s and 1880s.[40] It seems fair to assume,

2.3 William Hay. Yorkville Town Hall (demolished), Toronto, 1859–60. Presentation drawing, c. 1859. Pencil and wash on paper. MTRL-BR, LC:188.

2.4 William Hay. Yorkville Town Hall (demolished), Toronto, 1859–60. Contract elevation, no signature, drawing style of Henry Langley, c.1859. Pen and wash on paper. MTRL-BR, LC:187.

2.3

2.4

2.5

therefore, that Langley, as Hay's student, worked on contract drawings, having familiarized himself with contemporary British draughting techniques that Hay in turn accepted.[41]

Sections with vibrant washes – such as those for the McGill Square Methodist Church – are characteristic of Langley's contract drawings.[42] Contemporary usage dictated that tint should be applied without mixing (and presumably with as little dilution as possible) in order to maintain consistency in the coding formulas. This, together with the absence of shading, insured that builders might rely upon a uniform diagrammatic motif.[43] It was unnecessary to show such distinctions in competition drawings, however. The sections Langley submitted to the McGill Square competition committee under the pseudonym "York" are marked in sombre brown – in place of the dramatic red brick coding of the contract copy.[44]

Langley's linear style is also present in a perspective of the Metropolitan Methodist Church on McGill Square deposited with the Royal Canadian Academy of Arts in 1880 as the architect's diploma work (fig. 2.5). Executed on paper in pen and wash, the building is outlined against the blank sheet with landscape added at the base to suggest a setting – what Goodhart-Rendel once described as "architectural drawing with pictorial accompaniments."[45] Despite Langley's apparent authorship, however, the initials "F.D." in the centre foreground identify the draughtsman of the diploma piece as Frank Darling, a Langley student from 1866 to 1870.[46] The drawing dates from the time the project was designed; its deposit in Langley's name is a tangible repudiation of the principle of artistic authenticity

2.5   Henry Langley. Metropolitan Methodist Church (now Metropolitan United Church), Toronto, 1870–72. Perspective signed Henry Langley/ Architect/Toronto and initialled "F.D.," c.1870. Pen and wash on wove paper. National Gallery of Canada, Ottawa. Royal Academy of Arts diploma work, deposited by the architect, Toronto, 1880.

2.6   Gundry & Langley. St Patrick's, Dummer Street (now Our Lady of Mount Carmel, St Patrick's Street), Toronto, 1869–70. Perspective signed "E. Burke," c.1869. Pen and wash on paper. Archives of Ontario (AO), J.C.B. and E.C. Horwood Collection (HC):C 11–482–0–1(451)1.

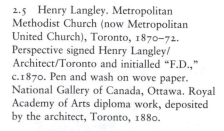

Saint Patrick's-Dummer Street Toronto Ont.

2.6

and an apt demonstration that an architect's creative worth lies in the concept of the building, not in the drawing of it.[47]

Darling was one of Langley's most gifted pupils, and Burke's contemporary in age. He joined the staff a year later than Burke in 1866 after being educated at Upper Canada College and Trinity College. The boldness and facility of his perspective suggest considerable skill and self-confidence for a twenty-year-old. That very year he left for England, where he studied with Sir Arthur Blomfield and George Edmund Street before returning in 1873 to set up his own practice in Toronto.[48] His sojourn overseas must have exposed him to a range of new ideas because Street was a strong opponent of the kind of medievalizing linearism practised in the Langley office. Street had protested Burges' "strong thick lines" before the Royal Institute of British Architects, pointing out that "every artist who was fit to be called an artist drew in his own way," and that "it would be absurd to ask him [any artist] to draw like anybody else."[49] It is no surprise that, upon Darling's return, his mature style bore no resemblance whatever to the one he had so ably emulated as a student.[50]

Virtuoso displays of office style were not necessarily typical of the Langley draughting room. One of Burke's early perspectives – the Roman Catholic church, *St Patrick's, Dummer Street, Toronto* – indicates a different approach (fig. 2.6).[51] Dated about 1869 and executed under the firm name of Gundry & Langley, it depicts a church and rectory in a scenic landscape with cloud-filled sky. The pen-and-wash rendering fills the lunette-shaped sheet, its pictorial qualities a distinct contrast to the diploma piece. Yet the scene is too clinical to pass for art. Langley's hard-edge models are the starting point for this brittle image, but the fully rendered setting suggests some training in pictorial watercolour.[52]

Classes in architectural draughtsmanship and ornamental painting had been offered at the Mechanics Institute since 1863.[53] Records indicate that Burke won second prize in the mathematics section in 1867,[54] and his draughting skills may have been supplemented in the same way although there is no record of his enrolment in the drawing programs. At Upper Canada College he generally excelled in the classically oriented curriculum, but the training was not geared for the exigencies of architectural practice.[55] Evening classes were a necessity for articled students who wished to improve their technical skills.[56]

After seven years of office training Burke's professional career began in earnest. Henry Langley took his brother Edward Langley, a builder, and their nephew Edmund Burke into the partnership of Langley, Langley & Burke in 1873. One year later Burke was elected to membership of the newly formed Ontario Society of Artists.[57] That year he entered an architectural drawing entitled *Chapel etc. Toronto Necropolis* in the society's annual exhibition in which three other architectural firms also participated.[58] This drawing seems not to have survived, but the entry signals the firm's interest in the artistic life of the community and demonstrates a concern for professional excellence, a tradition it maintained well into the twentieth century.[59]

2.7

2.8

2.7   Langley, Langley & Burke. Canada Life Assurance Company Building (demolished), Toronto, 1874. Perspective signed "F. Burke," November 1874. Pen and wash on paper. AO, HC:C 11–41–0–1-(48)1.

2.8   Langley, Langley & Burke. Design for Offices (executed as the Union Loan and Savings, now demolished), Toronto, 1878. Elevation initialled "E.B.," exhibited at the Ontario Society of Artists in 1879. Pen and wash on paper. AO, HC:C 11–643–0–1(623)1).

In the meantime Burke's brother Frank had begun his articles with the Langley firm in 1871.[60] Within three years he was an accomplished draughtsman. Two perspectives from 1874 of the Canada Life Assurance building (fig. 2.7) and Imperial Chambers testify to his skill.[61] Executed in pen and wash on paper, the buildings are viewed as if from the street. Dark, painterly shadows in the windows distinguish Frank's work from his brother's more fastidious approach, and foreshadow a growing artistic emphasis in the 1880s represented in the work of Burke's future partner, John Horwood, who articled with Langley & Burke during that decade.

Two years later, in 1876, the firm's leadership in education and draughtsmanship was recognized when Langley was appointed by the Ontario Society of Artists to the selection committee for the Philadelphia Centennial.[62] The firm sent an unidentified chromolithograph, and a panel of British judges later awarded it one of the four bronze medals presented by the Canadian Centennial Commission.[63] The same year the Ontario Society of Artists established a school of art with a program similar to that of the South Kensington Department of Science and Art in London. Day and evening classes were offered, and Ryerson's Educational Museum provided casts from which the students could work.[64] The firm's interest in the arts and its success at Philadelphia soon engendered an even greater concern for the potentials of architectural design and draughtsmanship.

Langley's firm entered three works in the seventh annual Ontario Society of Artist's exhibition in 1879, including one entitled *Design for Offices*, which marks generational change in the firm's office style and indicates the division of labour among the partners.[65] This may have been a preliminary elevation for the Union Loan & Savings now in the Horwood collection, which bears the same title (fig. 2.8).[66] Initials in the lower right identify the delineator as Edmund Burke. The facade is in flat projection, but intended as a perspective because of the recessions and voids modelled by shadows. Neighbouring buildings are faintly indicated on either side, giving not only a sense of actual size and relative scale, but also of the general context. Otherwise there is no description of natural setting. However, the fine lines and pale watercolour washes mark a significant departure from the canons of the Langley era, as if Burke – a decade after finishing his training – had finally appreciated the merit of each artist's "finding his own line."[67]

Many of the drawings Langley's firm produced, particularly for the larger projects, continued to employ the wiry "medieval" lines of Burges. But increasingly in the 1880s drawings for the smaller residential commissions follow the trend of Burke's *Design for Offices*, indicating perhaps that the younger members of the draughting team were picking up new ideas. The same fine lines and pale washes are evident in a contract document for an unidentified residence dated 1890 bearing the pencilled notation, "Fo. E. Burke" (fig. 2.9).[68] The formal lettering is less conspicuous than Langley's multi-coloured old English script, the borders that framed earlier images are entirely abandoned, and elevations and sections are now crowded onto a single sheet. The change is undoubtedly attributable to the Arts and Crafts Movement, which emphasized the dignity of labour and required that architectural drawings serve first and foremost as convenient working documents.[69]

Younger members of the Langley firm gradually assumed a more prominent role in design under the direction of Burke. A floor plan published in *Canadian Architect and Builder* illustrates the working arrangements in 1890 (fig. 2.10).[70] Each of the partners had his own office (Edward Langley having retired in 1883–84). But Langley's office contained a desk, while Burke's area accommodated both writing desk and drawing board. The junior partner overlooked the draughting room and had direct access to it, which indicates that he must have accepted if not encouraged the new drawing methods in his capacity as design partner. The staff of four or five appears to have produced all drawings in-house under his supervision. By contemporary American standards the draughting room was relatively small, but the direction of future development was set.[71] When Burke left to found his own business in 1892, the office style established in the previous decade at Langley's travelled with him. The firm Burke headed ultimately sustained a large staff of draughtsmen, growing in later years to match its American counterparts with a staff of twenty or more.[72]

Among those in the Langley draughting room during the crucial period of the 1880s was John Charles Batstone Horwood, later to be Burke's partner for over twenty-five years. Horwood was born in Newfoundland in 1864, and like his future associate was the son of a builder. He joined Langley, Langley & Burke as an articled student

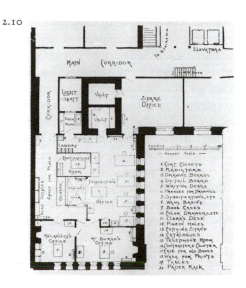

2.10

2.9   Langley & Burke. Unidentified Residence. Miscellaneous elevations and section, marked "Fo. E. Burke" in pencil, 17 March 1890. Pen and wash on paper. AO, HC:C 11–572–0–1(537a)1.

2.10   Offices of Langley & Burke, Canada Life Building, Toronto, 1890. Plan. Photograph by Robarts Library. Thomas Fisher Rare Book Library, University of Toronto (UofT-RB), *Canadian Architect and Builder* (CAB) 3 (November 1890):123.

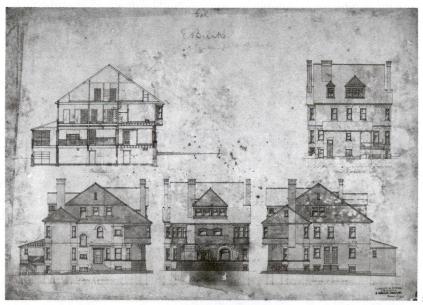

2.9

in 1882 after attending Ryerson's school and Jarvis Street Collegiate Institute.[73] Beyond this nothing is known of his early artistic training. But his exemplary talent reflects the tenor of the times in which refined artistic expression displaced the desiccated archaisms of traditional draughtsmanship.[74]

Horwood's first public showing could have been in the Ontario Society of Artists exhibition of 1885, but it is not possible to link the *House on Bloor Street* and *Study of a Gable*, shown that year by Langley & Burke, definitively to him.[75] Horwood's *Design for a Suburban Residence* entered in 1886 can be identified, however (fig. 2.11).[76] This small-scale pen-and-ink perspective depicts the B. Rosamond house in Almonte from the south, in an oblique view flanked by trees. Large areas of white modelled by horizontal parallel lines express texture and shadow. There is no suggestion of sky, nor any border apart from one below that separates the scene from its caption. (At the time the Royal Academy considered the black-and-white perspective the only acceptable form.) The so-called dazzle technique, which Horwood adopted here, was a concession to modern methods because it was intended to facilitate high quality photolithographic reproduction. Popular first in the United States, it was adopted in Britain only after 1888, according to Goodhart-Rendel.[77] This small work by Horwood – the last to be exhibited by the firm at the Ontario Society of Artists – confirms the direct assimilation of American presentation techniques even before their transference to Britain; it also foreshadows Horwood's later decision to continue his studies in the United States.

The start of Horwood's career also coincided with a sudden burst of organizational activity among architects and related professionals. In 1884 architectural draughtsmen established the Architectural Draughtsmen's Association of Toronto in conjunction with the Canadian (later Royal Canadian) Institute. Meetings were held once a week during which lectures were presented and competitions organized. In February 1887 John Horwood addressed the group on the subject of architectural "style," provoking "considerable discussion." Non-members such as Henry Langley were also invited to lecture, and architects Darling and Burke acted as judges for one of the group's competitions.[78]

A more broadly based group known as the Toronto Architectural Sketch Club was founded in December 1889. Dedicated to the artistic side of architecture, the club was a fitting complement to the scientifically oriented program of architectural study established the same year at the School of Practical Science.[79] Among its members were architects, artists, and draughtsmen; they, too, met to hear lectures and organize competitions twice monthly. Burke addressed the group in 1890, and the following year Murray White, then a student in the Langley office, won the club's competition for *A Staircase in Wood*. The scheme included an ingle and a staircase rising in three stages to a hidden destination on the upper floor. The line drawing (fig. 2.12), published in *Canadian Architect and Builder* (CAB), makes minimal

2.11

2.12

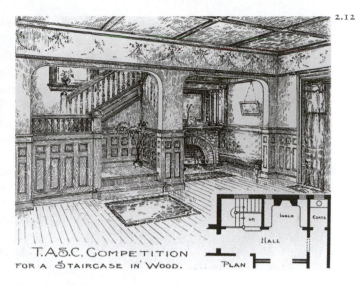

T.A.S.C. COMPETITION
FOR A STAIRCASE IN WOOD. PLAN

2.11 Langley & Burke. Design for a Suburban Residence. Perspective signed "John C.B. Horwood, del.," no date, exhibited Ontario Society of Artists in 1886. Pen on paper. AO, HC:C 11-25-0-2(543)4.

2.12 Murray A. White. "T.A.S.C. Competition for a Staircase in Wood," 1891. Print. Photograph by Robarts Library. UofT-RB, *CAB* 4 (July 1891): after 72.

use of graphics to convey wood textures and shading. Both form and technique accord with the Arts and Crafts interests evident in works by other members of the firm.[80]

Despite the growing number of professional activities available to students and draughtsmen, Horwood decided after completing his apprenticeship to test his skills further afield. He moved to New York in 1890, where he worked as a freelance draughtsman, reputedly for Renwick & Aspinwall.[81] He also worked at the Brooklyn Institute of Arts and Sciences, which established classes in architectural draughtsmanship in 1891.[82] In 1894 Horwood received an award from the institute that financed a grand tour of Europe before his return to Toronto the same year.[83] The sketchbooks from this trip are a far cry from the tradition of measured drawings and architectural orders. Instead, Horwood's vision is one of picturesque landscapes and glowing Mediterranean seas.[84]

Canadian Architect and Builder records details of Horwood's American sojourn. His description of the typical New York job interview for a "migratory" draughtsman speaks of a vast cultural divide:

It is very amusing when seeking for a position to be frequently asked by one's interrogator whether he is a good man or not – a capable one – and should the applicant happen to possess some modesty in regard to speaking of his capabilities – recognized by us as a commendable trait – he must always avoid making a remark which might at all be transposed to mean that he was in some degree doubtful of his ability. Should he be so unwise as to thus commit himself, he would receive no further hearing.

He went on to note how architects roughed out sketches, then passed them to an assistant for scale drawing, and on to an engineer to solve structural problems. Finally an expert draughtsman would finish the drawings. Such was the haste with which everything was prepared that all contract documents had to be traced. "I have never yet seen a set of plans inked in and coloured on paper for contract drawings as is our custom," he wrote.

Horwood's conclusions were mixed. On the one hand he thought the opportunity to concentrate on detail drawing a decided advantage, because

[if] we Canadians spent more time in training ourselves in ornamental work in order to have it, as it were, more at our finger ends, notwithstanding the somewhat limited expenditure of our clients, we would find it easier to occasionally introduce it in our work than when we neglect our education in this respect, and consequently too often pass the matter over by concluding that it is altogether because we do not have the money to spend upon it.

Canadians benefitted from the enterprise and industry of their southern neighbours, but were less self-reliant as a result. Horwood called for the development of mind, character, and individuality, noting that the new style emerging in the United States was the result of "constant and most strenuous efforts in the industrial and commercial spheres, to climb above all other national competitors." The tendency, he said, of Canadians to place a premium on American expertise could only be reversed by thinking more broadly and developing a distinctly national mode of expression.[85]

Despite the fact that most American institutions based their programs on the Ecole des Beaux-Arts, Horwood's approach was exclusively Arts and Crafts. Four years after his return to Toronto he executed a *Sketch of a House on a Fifty Foot Lot* which demonstrates his sophisticated painterly panache (fig. 2.13). Sky and landscape are dotted in behind the picturesque half-timbered residence. The scene is a jewel-like watercolour: the loose casual quality of the brushwork, the colour sense, and the compact format are thoroughly characteristic of Horwood's approach. A result of comprehensive artistic training far beyond the necessities of architectural practice, the work exhibits all the qualities one normally associates with pictorial watercolour. It is scarcely surprising, therefore, that Horwood should have assumed the role of Burke's design partner soon after his return to Toronto.

Horwood's impact upon the firm's draughting room is apparent in a perspective of the Fudger Residence, Toronto, from about 1902, signed by delineator William F. Sparling (fig. 2.14). Sparling, who articled with Burke & Horwood from 1901 to 1906, used a technique that displays the same saturated washes and glowing quality found in Horwood's work.[86] Accompanying the exterior view is an interior of the billiard room – unsigned, but presumably from the same hand (fig. 2.15) – which may have been exhibited by the Toronto Architectural Eighteen Club in 1905.[87] The elevations are rendered in a series of tiny colourful cartouches on a dark background, a format typical of the Arts and Crafts.[88]

Horwood's disposition toward the "art" of architecture was shared

by others in the city. As early as January 1899 the Toronto Architectural Eighteen Club was formed to provide an alternative to what its members considered the narrow educational perspective of the Ontario Association of Architects.[89] Instead of scientific training the Eighteen emphasized the expressive aspects – much as the Sketch Club had done years before. Their position drew upon ideas propounded in England by Richard Norman Shaw and his compatriots.[90] Members included the Arts and Crafts practitioner Eden Smith, as well as John Horwood, C.H. Acton Bond, William Ford Howland, and Charles Langley, all former associates from Langley's draughting room. Later known as the Toronto Society of Architects, the Club was affiliated with the Architectural League of America, and staged six important exhibitions between 1901 and 1912.[91] Initially John Horwood entered several items under his own name, while the firm of Burke & Horwood appeared separately. This reflected Horwood's close involvement with the group, and the fact that Burke's philosophical and political links lay with the Ontario Association of Architects. But the practice was not repeated, and in 1905 Burke took steps to reconcile the two groups, a goal that was not achieved for many years.[92]

The strong Arts-and-Crafts flavour of the Langley office and Burke's new firm sharply contrasted with the approach Murray White brought back with him from Chicago about 1907. Son of a Woodstock architect, White studied with the Langley firm from 1889 to 1893 – and won the Sketch Club's "Staircase" competition. When his articles ended he moved to the American Midwest, where he remained for fourteen years. At the time the Beaux-Arts rage was at its peak as American architects educated in France introduced the atelier system for their pupils and Beaux-Arts societies sprang up in major cities.[93] Conventions of sciagraphy (three-dimensional shading), symmetrical planning, and classical or Renaissance ornamentation became standard for all monumental public works.

One unlabelled rendering, *Music Academy Project*, signed in the lower left by Murray White is said to have been offered as evidence

2.13   Burke & Horwood. Sketch of a House on a Fifty Foot Lot. Front and side elevations, initialled "J.C.B.H.," 3 October 1898. Watercolour on cardboard. AO, HC:C 11–869–0–1(804a)2.

2.14   Burke & Horwood. Fudger Residence, Toronto, 1895–97. Perspective, delineated by W.F. Sparling, c.1902. Watercolour on paper. AO, HC:C 11, perspectives.

2.15   Burke & Horwood. Billiard Room in a House in Rosedale. Elevations, no signature, no date. AO, HC:C 11, perspectives.

2.14

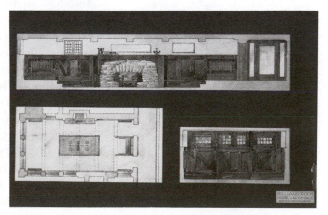

2.15

2.16

2.17

2.16   Murray A. White. Music Academy Project. Perspective rendered by "H.D. Jenkins," c.1907. Watercolour on paper. AO, HC:C 11, perspectives.

2.17   Burke, Horwood & White. Hudson's Bay Store, Calgary, 1911–18. Perspective initialled "L.R.," exhibited at the Canadian National Exhibition in 1913. Watercolour on paper. AO, HC:C 11, perspectives.

of his architectural skills when he applied to join the Burke & Horwood firm (fig. 2.16).[94] The name "H.D. Jenkins" appears in the middle foreground, indicating the piece was finished by an expert renderer. Unlike conventional Beaux-Arts competition drawings, which consisted of plan, elevation, and section, the building appears in perspective with a rather low viewing angle that emphasizes the monumentality of the structure.[95] Not only does the facade speak to the eclectic traditions of the Beaux-Arts, so does the draughtsmanship. The outline of the structure is framed in, possibly traced to avoid erasures, and then the illusion of modelling in the round is created using carefully graded washes, as John Harbeson later described in a popular manual he published on the subject.[96] The effect is controlled and serene, especially by comparison with Horwood's florid ornamentalism.

White's influence guided much of the firm's perspective work well into the twentieth century. Renderings of the various Hudson's Bay Company stores – represented here by the Calgary example – appeared regularly in public showings such as the Canadian National Exhibition (fig. 2.17).[97] This example, exhibited in 1913, is based on a Beaux-Arts precedent, Selfridge's store in London, and the draughting follows the same closely controlled formula noted above.[98] In this instance, however, the work is significantly larger (about three feet by five), truly a *pièce de résistance*. Such a striking rendering undoubtedly served as an eloquent advertisement for the firm's skills. But the sophistication and intricacy of these works often necessitated the assistance of freelance specialists in rendering – in this instance an individual identified only as "L.R."[99] Times changed, the office quadrupled in size, yet the firm's determination to maintain its tradition of fine draughtsmanship continued with new ideas incorporated as required.

In 1908 William S. Maxwell had suggested that a synthesis of Arts and Crafts and Beaux-Arts could "develop [Canadian] architecture along lines which recognize our country and its traditions and associations."[100] Horwood's son, Eric, was trained at Toronto's School of

Practical Science and at the Ecole des Beaux-Arts in Paris, bringing together the two traditions represented by the surviving partners, Horwood and White. The firm continued until Eric Horwood's retirement in 1969. Ten years later he donated his collection of drawings to the Archives of Ontario.[101] They chart not only the careers of the respective partners but also Canada's historic path from British colonial outpost to independent Dominion. Changes in technique document a shift from exclusive trans-Atlantic ties to a strengthening of North American contacts. The drawings reveal a rejection of the comfortable conventions of the past, a drive to explore new ideas, and a dedication to education and excellence that was to propel the Canadian architectural profession vigorously into the twentieth century.

3 Ecclesiastical Architecture: The Triumph and Demise of the Amphitheatre Plan

[If] it becomes necessary to increase the capacity of an auditorium, so that the greatest possible number can see and hear a single speaker within its walls ... we are almost obliged to adopt one form, and that is the general shape of the old Greek theatre.

There is no one style of architecture that is suited more than another to religious uses. That a church should give the impression of being a church is undoubtedly true, but the effect should be produced by the absolute fitness of every part to the particular ceremonies for which it is intended.

J.A.F., "Modern Church Building – Part 2," AABN (March 1879)

Because ecclesiastical architecture was the mainstay of Henry Langley's practice, Burke's early design experience was concentrated in this area, providing a thorough preparation for his first independent commission.[1] When Burke began his articles in the mid-1860s, Gothic revival was the usual choice for most Toronto churches, the tradition having been established by the Anglican church under the influence of two important ideological developments in Britain.[2] The first, initiated in the 1830s and 1840s by British architect and theorist Augustus Welby Pugin, promoted what he called "pointed" or "Christian" architecture in preference to the Baroque classicism of Wren's auditory churches. Pugin, a Roman Catholic convert, revered Gothic as a national ecclesiastical tradition, predating the Protestant break with Rome. Most emphatic and influential was his assertion of a connection between architectural style and ethical standards in society. Equally resounding in its impact upon his contemporaries was his quintessential formulation of structural rationalism – that there should be no features about a building not necessary for convenience, construction, or propriety, and that all ornament should enrich essential construction.[3]

Similar principles were espoused by the Anglican High Churchmen of the Cambridge Camden Society whose views were published in *The Ecclesiologist*.[4] They recommended specific medieval churches as precedents and selected basilical forms in which the chancel was clearly expressed on the exterior. While the former were designed to facilitate the movement of religious processions, the latter articulated the location of the altar where the ritual of the Mass was performed.

Ecclesiology was introduced in British North America in 1845 when Bishop John Medley retained English architect Frank Wills to

3.1

design Christ Church Anglican Cathedral in Fredericton, New Brunswick, according to the fourteenth-century British precedent of St Mary's, Snettisham, which had been specifically approved by the ecclesiologists.[5] Two years later William Hay, who trained Burke's uncle Henry Langley, arrived at St John's, Newfoundland to act as Gilbert Scott's clerk of works on St John the Baptist Anglican Cathedral, a scheme the ecclesiologists considered learned but lifeless (fig. 3.1).[6] After finishing a portion of the design Hay moved on, settling in Toronto in 1852, where he became a well-known practitioner of the Gothic revival.[7]

Hay's awareness of contemporary British developments is demonstrated by the fact that he wrote an obituary of Pugin in 1853.[8] Medieval plans Pugin prescribed as most suitable for Roman Catholic ritual were the same forms the ecclesiologists saw as symbolic of and liturgically appropriate to the Church of England.[9] Both Pugin and the ecclesiologists thought the aisleless preaching hall or auditory church preferable for evangelical sects, who emphasized the sermon rather than the sacraments.[10] But Hay and his fellow Toronto architects cheerfully ignored these niceties, combining Gothic revival exteriors with auditory plans whenever necessary.[11] Even after the secularization of the Clergy Reserves in the 1850s when Anglicanism was eclipsed by the so-called nonconformist sects, Gothic continued to signify "church" regardless of denomination. It was not until the 1870s that the auditorium plan and the Romanesque revival of American architect Henry Hobson Richardson offered a solution better adapted to the needs of evangelical sects.

Comparison of Hay's well-known Roman Catholic landmark – St Basil's Church adjoining St Michael's College begun in 1855 – with a contemporaneous commission for the Gould Street United

3.1   Sir George Gilbert Scott. (Anglican) Cathedral of St John the Baptist, St John's, Newfoundland, 1848–50 and 1880 on. Exterior view, c.1892. Photograph. National Archives of Canada (NA):C21331, from St John's, Newfoundland in 1892, 13.

3.2   William Hay. St Basil's (Roman Catholic) Church and College of St Michael, Toronto, 1855 on. View from southwest by Maclear, Toronto, 1855. Lithograph. MTRL:T-10002.

3.3   William Hay. St Basil's Church, Toronto, 1855. View of original interior, no date. Photograph. University of St Michael's College Archives, Toronto.

3.2

3.3

3.4

3.5

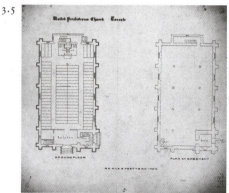

3.4   William Hay. Gould Street United Presbyterian Church (later Catholic Apostolic Church, now demolished), Toronto, 1855. Elevation, no signature, c.1855. Pen on paper. MTRL-BR, LC:127.

3.5   William Hay. Gould Street United Presbyterian Church (later Catholic Apostolic Church, now demolished), Toronto, 1855. Plan of ground floor and basement, no signature, c.1855. Pen on paper. MTRL-BR, LC:125.

Presbyterian Church confirms this flexible approach to church design. For St Basil's Hay proposed a modest Early English parish design in white brick (fig. 3.2).[12] The rectangular plan provided for a side tower and spire, as well as a small chancel at the north end that made a structural distinction between sanctuary and church in accordance with the requirements of Roman Catholic ritual.[13] The form was basilical, divided by wooden columns into a nave and flanking aisles. An open trussed-roof, since replaced by mock-Gothic vaults executed in plaster, constituted one of the city's early expositions of Puginian and ecclesiological principles (fig. 3.3).[14]

Almost identical to St Basil's on the exterior was Hay's Gould Street Presbyterian Church of 1855 (fig. 3.4). Likewise executed in brick, its main facade was pierced by triple lancets instead of a rose window.[15] Only the aisleless interior with a panelled plaster ceiling born on timber ribs offered a clue to the evangelical practices of its congregation (fig. 2.1). A central pulpit occupied the body of the church, and what appeared from the exterior to be a chancel served to enclose a stairwell leading to the robing rooms below (fig. 3.5).

Long after Hay returned to his native Scotland, Langley continued to combine Gothic revival exteriors with a variety of internal schemes, a practice Burke also adopted in his earliest ecclesiastical works.[16] Henry Langley's most important commission of this type, undertaken in 1868, just three years after Burke began his articles, was the Wesleyan Methodist Church on McGill Square in Toronto (fig. 3.6). Initially Langley was the runner-up in a competition won by William George Storm, but the cost of Storm's design was nearly double what had been anticipated. As a result the decision was declared invalid and the job assigned to Langley.[17] His plans proposed a veritable cathedral of Methodism in fourteenth-century French Gothic style, a conventional basilical design (to all appearances) complete with shallow transepts and semicircular apse, executed in white brick.

The importance of preaching for the Methodists was reflected in the configuration Langley designed for the Metropolitan's interior, which was quite different from that expressed on the outside. An almost square auditorium occupied the body of the church, and the floor canted a full eighteen inches for better viewing of the central pulpit (fig. 3.7).[18] Straight benches divided into three blocks occupied the main floor with the front rows encircling the podium. Slender iron columns carried an elliptical gallery that included accommodation for the choir and pipe organ behind the pulpit. The same columns also supported a canopy of Gothic arches, while the apsidal space traditionally occupied by the sanctuary housed lecture halls and Sunday school rooms (fig. 3.8).[19]

The Sunday school on the main level adjacent to the auditorium was intended to "bring the Sabbath school into more close connection with the church."[20] In the 1860s Methodists on both sides of the Atlantic, and particularly bishop John Heyl Vincent in the United States, took the view that basement schoolrooms did not offer sufficient opportunity for the minister to address the children's meeting.[21]

Vincent edited a whole series of publications on the subject of Sabbath schools, including *Sunday-School Advocate*, *Sunday-School Journal*, and *Sunday-School Classmate*, which reflected the broad commitment of evangelism to spiritual education and community service. He was a prime mover in a precedent-setting design for the First Methodist Church in Akron, Ohio (fig. 3.9). There, a schoolroom shaped like a semioctadecagon was added to an existing church in 1870 (fig. 3.10). What made the so-called Akron plan unique was a movable wall system that could be thrown open to allow the minister or superintendent of the school to address all the classes from a central point.[22] Langley's design for Metropolitan Methodist must have been one of the earliest in Canada to respond to the Sunday school movement by integrating the accommodation into a space traditionally alloted to the chancel.

When completed Metropolitan was said to be the largest Methodist church in the world and representative of the Wesleyan determination to build large expensive churches in key cities.[23] Its size reflected the rate of growth of the denomination since the 1840s and the abrupt displacement of Anglicanism by a more generalized "Protestant culture" centred on education, moral crusades, and evangelical worship.[24] Yet the first Methodist publications were quite reserved in their directions to church builders, the *Doctrines and Discipline of the Methodist Church of Canada*, of 1874, providing only that churches should be built "plain and decent, and not more expensive than absolutely necessary." Plans adapted, as Metropolitan Methodist was, to the needs of the preacher were not uncommon in both Britain and the United States.[25] In such churches an auditorium with galleries was usually the best way to accommodate large numbers within earshot of the pulpit, and an array of classrooms, community halls, and meeting

3.6   Henry Langley. Metropolitan Wesleyan Methodist Church (now Metropolitan United Church), Toronto, 1870–72. Exterior view from the northwest, c.1872–73. Photograph by William O'Connor. AO:Acc. 3621, S-14179.

3.7   Henry Langley. Metropolitan Wesleyan Methodist Church (now Metropolitan United Church), Toronto, 1870–72. Original interior, c.1873. Albumen stereograph by J. Esson of Preston. MTRL:T-31199.

3.8   Henry Langley. Metropolitan Wesleyan Methodist Church (now Metropolitan United Church), Toronto, 1870–72. Plan of the ground floor, no date. Pen and wash on paper. MTRL-BR, LC:60.

3.7

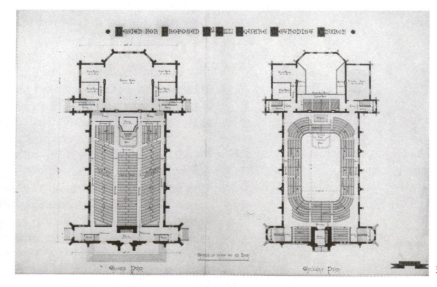

3.8

3.9

FIRST M. E. CHURCH, AKRON, OHIO.

3.10

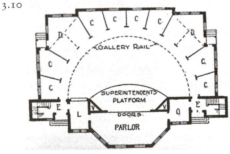

rooms of various kinds adjoining the church proper facilitated the broader missionary goals of the congregations.

Purists of architectural expression would have objected to Langley's design primarily because of the discrepancy between outer appearance and actual function. This discrepancy had been problematic since the 1840s when evangelical sects first adjusted Gothic revival forms to suit their own liturgical purposes, and a pertinent discussion was eventually published in *Canadian Architect and Builder* in the 1890s with reference to a design exhibited that year at the Royal Academy:

At first sight this appears to be a pretty little Anglican church with an apsidal chapel. The plan, which is inserted on a smaller scale, shows that what appears to be a chancel is in reality the infants' department at the entrance end of the church, the opposite end from the pulpit and choir. Is this good designing or not? It is an adaptation of an old external form to an internal use to which the old form is perfectly suited. Instead of looking upon it as a chancel clapped on to the wrong end of the church, we may consider it as an expansion of the apsidal baptistry which was common at the entrance end and was like this devoted to the young. Nevertheless the design is disturbing. The natural man abhors it but has no arguments. The truth probably is that whereas the chancel was the glory of a church, this infants' department is a mere adjunct, to be connected with the church occasionally by opening folding doors, and the real centre of interest, the pulpit and its surroundings, has probably no external expression but a flat wall ... so that the design is in reality, turned round, proving once more the futility of imitation, even the cleverest.[26]

Not only did Pugin's principle of "truth" in architecture imply a considered use of materials; it also demanded a form of expression that did not contort conventional meanings. Architectural expression in the ecclesiastical sphere was circumscribed by the same competing theoretical interests that defined nineteenth-century architecture in general – on the one hand nostalgia for ancient forms and a belief that Gothic was the only true Christian architecture, on the other an expectation more familiar to twentieth-century minds that practicality should be the sole determinant of form.

For Burke, who had begun his career as a draughtsman in 1865, early drawings indicate that he had ample opportunity to examine the nuances of the Gothic "problem." His rendering from 1869 of the Roman Catholic church of St Patrick's, Dummer Street (fig. 2.6), discussed in the second chapter, explores Early English motifs.[27] A second unsigned work, depicting the Anglican church of St Peter's, Carlton Street (fig. 3.11), studies the wedge-shaped compositional arrangement of St Michael's, Longstanton, a thirteenth-century precedent, again among those recommended by the Cambridge Camden Society (fig. 3.12).[28] Porch, nave, and chancel are distinct in accordance with ecclesiological precepts, while the red-brick fabric with white-brick dressings is a judicious exercise of a technique known as "constructional polychromy."[29]

3.9   First Methodist Church, Akron, Ohio, 1866. Exterior view, no date. Print. McMaster University, Hamilton: M. Simpson, *Cyclopedia of Methodism* (Philadelphia, 1880), opposite 9.

3.10   First Methodist Church, Akron, Ohio, 1866. Plan of Sunday School, c.1870. UofT-Architecture Library: F.E. Kidder, *Churches and Chapels* (New York, 1910).

3.11 Gundry & Langley. St Peter's, Carlton Street, Toronto, 1864–66. Perspective, no signature, July 1869. Pen and wash on paper. AO, HC:C 11–481–0–1(452a)1.

3.12 St Michael's, Longstanton, Cambridgeshire, England. Early English. Engraving by J.K. Colling. MTRL: R. and J.A. Brandon, *Parish Churches* (London, 1848), before 33.

Among Burke's early renderings was another from 1872 depicting the chapel of the Toronto Necropolis, the first he is known to have exhibited. The drawing is lost, but the building with its low walls, high angular gable, and squat bell-tower (fig. 3.13) recalls an Anglican church William Hay executed in Brampton twenty years before (fig. 3.14).[30] Hay's church was described in a contemporary article as early Decorated Gothic with "no gingerbread work, no gimcrackery, no useless pinnacles to give a trumpery effect."[31] The Necropolis chapel shares the same simplicity, its chief ornamental feature consisting of two large bar-tracery windows in the north and south facades, and internally a high roof of exposed timber.[32] Burke's familiarity with Gothic revival having been established by his early studies, he was able to undertake a knowledgeable exploration of new ideas upon his admission to partnership in 1873.

Most church commissions with which Burke was concerned during his career were for Methodist and Baptist rather than Roman Catholic or Anglican congregations. This was partly a consequence of his own religious affiliation and partly because evangelical denominations grew rapidly from the mid-1840s to become by century's end the largest religious block in the province.[33] Among the adherents were many *nouveau-riche* entrepreneurs whose fortunes grew out of a new economic mercantilism and who owed no loyalty to traditional Tory institutions and interests. Their churches, with the emphasis upon preaching rather than the sacraments, did not provide for kneeling communicants or processions. The main concern, as with Langley's Metropolitan Methodist Church, was for audibility and visibilty reflected in interiors where the pulpit was located at the centre front while banked floors transformed the body of the church into an auditorium.[34] At the same time, however, evangelical congregations were loathe to relinquish Gothic revival for church exteriors, despite objections by Protestant theorists that medievalism smacked of "popery."

3.15

3.13

3.14

NEW CHURCH AT BRAMPTON.

3.13   Henry Langley. Chapel of the Toronto Necropolis, Toronto, 1872. View from the south, 1955. Photograph by J.V. Salmon. MTRL:T-33180.

3.14   William Hay. Anglican Church, Brampton, 1853. MTRL-BR: *Anglo-American Magazine* 4 (January 1854): after 20.

3.15   Langley, Langley & Burke. Jarvis Street Baptist Church, Toronto, 1874–75. View from the southwest, no date. Photograph by Josiah Bruce. AO:Acc. 13222–39.

It is in the context of liturgical requirements and the traditional spirit of Gothic revival that Burke's earliest independent work must be considered. Jarvis Street Baptist Church was begun in 1874 just a year after his admission to the partnership of Langley, Langley & Burke (fig. 3.15). A significant undertaking that sought a more truthful revelation of the plan in the elevation, Jarvis Street Baptist Church is lavishly executed in Queenston stone, its cost funded by Senator William McMaster, a dry-goods entrepreneur, whose family remained Burke's

3.16 Langley, Langley & Burke. Jarvis Street Baptist Church, Toronto, 1874–75. Plan of ground floor and gallery, c.1874. Pen and wash on paper. AO, HC:C 11–618–0–1(599)1.

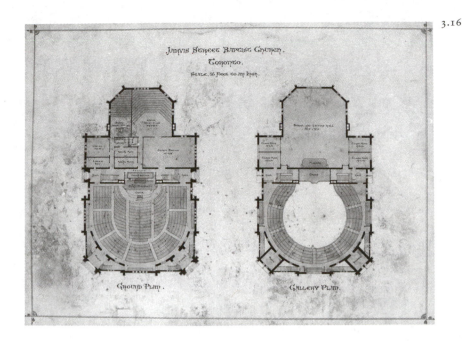

loyal patrons throughout his career. A tall Early English spire canted on the diagonal accentuates the corner location, while two massive gables of equal dimensions – forms traditionally associated with nave and transept – articulate a nearly square auditorium. A third gable combined with a semicircular apse at the rear of the structure houses the church parlour and infants' class, clearly identifying the separation between church proper and Sunday school from the outside.[35]

The main floor at Jarvis Street Baptist is arranged as an amphitheatre – the first of its kind in the city – with the last six rows banked in a semicircle around a block of seating at the centre (fig. 3.16), the latter being reserved for elders of the church. Above is a horseshoe-shaped gallery supported on iron columns, with access provided by stairways flanking the tower. The columns also carry a *faux*-Gothic ceiling – the same structural methodology and conventional stylistic vocabulary as Langley's Metropolitan Methodist. But the amphitheatre plan (based on American precedents) and its clear expression on the building's exterior are important innovations.[36]

Often billed as the first ecclesiastical amphitheatre construction in Canada, Jarvis Street Baptist Church was contemporaneous with a similar scheme by Montreal architect Joseph Savage for Zion Tabernacle in Hamilton (fig. 3.17).[37] Savage had spent a number of years in Delaware where he may have seen American examples of this type. But Savage's plan, published in the *Canadian Methodist Magazine* in 1875 (fig. 3.18) with two more conventional schemes by Langley, Langley & Burke, was part of a series requested by the Committee on Church Architecture to establish further standards for Methodist churches in the province. Savage's auditorium measured seventy by eighty feet and included a canted floor with a central pulpit

3.18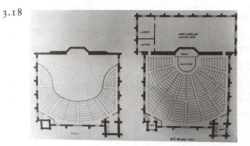

3.17

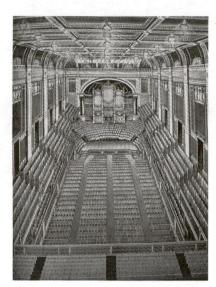 3.19

3.17   Joseph Savage. Zion Tabernacle (demolished), Hamilton, 1874. Exterior, 1875. Print. The United Church of Canada, Victoria University Archives, Toronto: *Canadian Methodist Magazine* 1 (1875):382.

3.18   Joseph Savage. Zion Tabernacle (demolished), Hamilton, 1874. Plan, 1875. Print. The United Church of Canada, Victoria University, Toronto: *Canadian Methodist Magazine* 1 (1875):382.

3.19   Tremont Tabernacle (formerly Tremont Theatre, status unknown), Boston, Massachusetts, after 1843. Interior view, no date. Print. McMaster University, Hamilton: W. Cathcart, *Baptist Encyclopaedia* (Philadelphia, 1881), 1163.

encircled by banks of seats arranged in pie-shaped segments, the aisles radiating from front to back, unlike the plan at Jarvis Street.[38]

While Savage's Zion Tabernacle achieved recognition in the publication by the Methodists, Burke's Jarvis Street Baptist Church is more widely remembered, perhaps because of the fine quality of execution or because of its association with such well-known names as the McMasters, Reverend John Castle, and later Reverend T.T. Shields, whose break with the Baptist convention initiated a controversy that continues to this day. From the outset no expense was spared at Jarvis Street, later described as "one of the finest churches on this side of the Atlantic."[39] The result was sufficiently lavish to offend the sensibilities of some local Baptists like the founder of Canada Packers William Davies, who wrote:

There has been built in this city recently a large Baptist Chapel, gothic, brown stone, spire pointing upward if not heavenward, marble baptistry &c &c cost $100,000 & odd, & the organ $7000 besides, & I believe it is all paid for, but it has been built regardless of the needs of the city. This congregation were in part of the city which was thickly populated but they had an old-fashioned building. One of the members, a MLC, say a Senator, very wealthy, married an American, natural result they soon had an American minister, *then this new building also American*, then the Lady & the minister lay their heads together & get a professional singer a sort of *prima donna* & she is paid $300.00 per year and many are very hurt about it. It has been sanctionned by a large majority & the result will be I expect some of *their* best people will leave. This building was erected to the N.E. of its former site which has left the S.W. part of the city without any Baptist church, while they have gone into a district that was pretty well served. There appears to have been a spirit of centralization & aggrandizement about it which is hateful.[40]

American ideas introduced by McMaster's wife Susan Moulton ruffled feathers, as did her role in the installation of the Philadelphian, John Harvard Castle, as minister. Burke, however, remained a protégé of Mrs McMaster (who introduced him to his future wife Minnie Black), and a loyal member of the Jarvis Street congregation throughout his life. Yet his affiliations were no bar to dealings with men like William Davies or more radical members of the denomination such as the pre-millenialist Elmore Harris, a scion of the Massey-Harris empire, both of whom were later to commission churches themselves.[41]

Because Burke consulted the Reverend Castle about the design of a later commission for the McMasters, it seems likely that Castle was also instrumental in the planning of Jarvis Street and that the concept was based on contemporary examples in the United States. The amphitheatre-auditorium format shares a common heritage with the galleried meeting houses of New England, but finds its closest parallel in early octagons and theatres used for evangelical meetings in the heart of major American cities.[42] British commentators had repeatedly noted the suitability of theatre design for preaching to large groups of people, but the idea reached its culmination in North America – with New York's Broadway Tabernacle of 1836 and Boston's Tremont Tabernacle of 1842 (fig. 3.19).[43] The former was a Congregational meeting house on Broadway, which took the form of a galleried rotunda topped by a flat dome born on giant columns. The Tremont example in Boston was actually built as a theatre, and later taken over by a Baptist congregation for prayer meetings. Such precedents were undoubtedly known to Burke, although the main publication on the subject, F.E. Withers' *Churches and Chapels*, followed somewhat later.

ROMANESQUE: THE NEW BEHEMOTH

A number of British publications of the 1830s dealing with Norman architecture are credited with a Romanesque revival that is now generally overlooked. Theorists appear to have been influenced by German *Rundbogenstil* (round-arched style) of the late 1820s as well as other European models.[44] British architectural critic, the Reverend J.L. Petit, suggested that a new type of architecture for the Church of England might be based on Romanesque or Byzantine sources. His ideas were roundly condemned by the ecclesiologists, who asserted that Gothic was the only true Christian architecture.[45] But British architects Wyatt & Brandon had already adopted the round-arched style at St Mary's, Wilton, 1840–46, as had J.W. Wild for Christ Church, Streatham, 1840–42. John Gibson did the same in his Central Baptist Chapel of 1845–48 in Bloomsbury Street, London, indicating an acceptance of the mode for nonconformist chapels.[46] Later in the century the motif evolved into the neo-Renaissance forms Sedding used for the Church of the Holy Redeemer, Clerkenwell, in 1887 and the Italo-Byzantine of John Bentley's Westminster Cathedral of 1895–1903.[47]

In the 1870s one British commentator suggested that denominations not governed by the traditions of the Church of England might facilitate the exploration of a new style.

> With Nonconformist places of worship there is not the same restriction, and it certainly seems a pity to continue building chapels exactly like churches, when, if they were made to embody the peculiar characteristics of the worshippers, they might pave the way to what so many people are crying out for – an abiding nineteenth-century style – for no lasting style will ever be attained that does not faithfully express the wants of the age.[48]

Writing in the same journal, Maurice B. Adams added a more conservative corollary of the type that might have explained a hybrid scheme like Jarvis Street Baptist: "If Gothic architecture be thought more suitable than a classical treatment, by all means use it, only let it be true to the spirit of the style." He stipulated that traditional symbols should never be adapted to purposes for which they were not originally intended.[49]

In the United States, meanwhile, German *émigrés* like the architect Leopold Eidlitz introduced ideas similar to those of his employer, Richard Upjohn, and contemporary James Renwick (the two great Gothicists of their generation), both of whom adopted the round-arched style for a number of evangelical commissions.[50] However, the Romanesque revival only gained general acceptance after America's leading architect, Henry Hobson Richardson, developed his own distinctive idiom in Trinity Episcopal Church, Boston, of 1874–77 (fig. 3.20). Having investigated round arches in his early work, Richardson combined elements from French and Spanish sources to create one of the most influential North American syntheses – which was widely imitated only after his death in 1886. Trinity Church with its granite and brownstone exterior is remarkable as much for its massive presence as for its stylistic innovation. The squared cruciform interior, open to the full height of the crossing tower, was specifically designed with galleries in the transepts to accommodate the congregation within sight and sound of the pulpit (fig. 3.21).[51]

As historian Thomas Tallmadge has pointed out, the influence of Trinity Church was immeasureable, particularly in the field of evangelical architectural design. While few architects followed Richardson's design as far as the inclusion of the great tower, Trinity spawned a generation of "ugly ducklings, many of them, hatched out under the beautiful swan mother." Tallmadge described how

> almost every town in the land has one of these Romanesque Revival Churches ... Its material is red brick and its trimming red sandstone carved with the familiar Romanesque detail. In place of the thin, narrow, pointed arches of the preceding era, the windows and portals are broad and squat, and have round arched heads. A tower with a dome-like cupola has supplanted the thin spire. In general appearance obesity has succeeded emaciation, and floridity, anaemia. The interior was as startlingly unlike its elder

3.20   Gambrill & Richardson. Trinity Episcopal Church, Boston, 1872–77. Exterior view, 1877. Photograph. UofT-Robarts Library (RL) *American Architect & Building News* (*AABN*) 2 (3 February 1877): after 36.

3.21   Gambrill & Richardson. Trinity Episcopal Church, Boston, 1872–77. Plan of ground floor, no date. UofT-Architecture Library: F.E. Kidder, *Churches and Chapels* (New York, 1910).

3.20

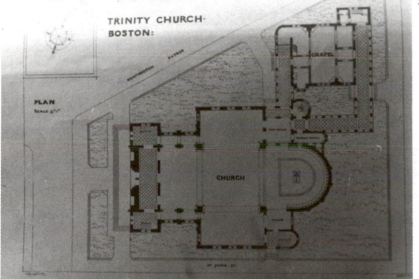

3.21

brother as the outside. Instead of being long and narrow, it was short, almost square, and the pulpit, organ, and choir – hardly a chancel under the circumstances – were tucked into one corner. The floor was sharply bowled, and the pews were all curved, which was inevitable in a cat-a-corner church.[52]

In this type of church, the amphitheatre plan and the adjoining Sunday school were often linked by means of "a huge gate or portcullis," as Tallmadge described. A by-product of the Akron design, fully three-quarters of all Protestant churches built in the United States between 1875 and 1900 are said to have been influenced by this idea.[53]

3.22

3.22   William Thomas & Sons. Cooke's Presbyterian Church (demolished), Toronto, 1858. Exterior view, no date, c.1859. Stereograph by Armstrong, Beere & Hime. MTRL:T-30684.

3.23   William George Storm. Carlton Street Methodist Church (demolished), Toronto, 1874. Exterior view, no date. Photograph. The United Church of Canada, Victoria University Archives, Toronto.

3.24   William George Storm. New St Andrew's Presbyterian Church, Toronto, 1874–75. Exterior view, no date. Photograph by Josiah Bruce. AO:Acc. 13222–96.

In the boom of evangelical church building that overtook Toronto in the 1870s, city architects were slow to adopt novelties like folding partitions, but Sunday schools were often located on the main level behind the church auditorium. As for the "round-arched style," it made an early appearance in the city with the St Andrew's (Presbyterian) Church of 1832 on Adelaide Street and in Cooke's Presbyterian Church of 1857 by William Thomas (fig. 3.22).[54] Two decades later, in 1874, William G. Storm developed a somewhat more substantial Romanesque motif for Carlton Street Methodist Church (fig. 3.23), and the following year reworked the powerful "Norman" theme he and Cumberland had devised in 1856 for University College, creating a Scottish variant for the Church of St Andrew at King and Simcoe (fig. 3.24).[55]

Langley's office was slow to change stylistic motifs, despite its adoption of the advanced amphitheatre plan for Jarvis Street Baptist. In 1878 the firm built a new church at the corner of Carlton and Jarvis Streets for the more conservative members of the Old St Andrew's congregation (fig. 3.25).[56] Still expressed in Gothic vocabulary, its facade is framed by asymmetrical towers that enclose stairways to a gallery – the precise format used in the firm's later Romanesque churches. Broad gables positioned like those of the Jarvis Street Baptist Church mark the location of an amphitheatre with school rooms at the rear, while reddish-grey Credit Valley freestone with Ohio stone dressings gives a massive rough-hewn appearance typical of many later monuments.[57] Langley's chief competitor, E.J. Lennox, adopted a similar rugged Gothic for his Bond Street Congregational Church of 1879 (fig. 3.26), its plan later a precedent for the architect's Broadway Tabernacle of 1887, one of the city's early Richardsonian Romanesque churches.[58]

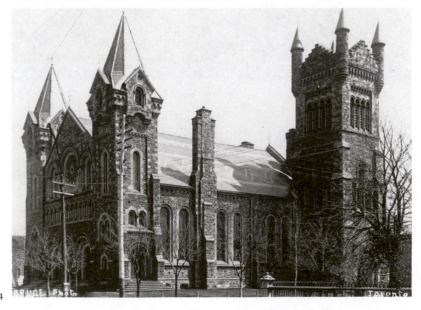

3.24

3.23

3.25   Langley, Langley & Burke. St Andrew's Presbyterian Church (now Estonian and Latvian Lutheran Church), Toronto, 1877–78. Exterior view, no date. Photograph by Josiah Bruce. AO:Acc. 13222–62.

3.26   E.J. Lennox. Bond Street Congregational Church (demolished), Toronto, 1879. Exterior view, no date. Photograph by Josiah Bruce. AO:Acc. 13222–7.

3.27   Langley & Burke. Beverley Street Baptist Church (now Chinese Baptist Church), Toronto, 1886–87. Exterior view, 15 February 1954. Photograph by J.V. Salmon. MTRL:S1–485.

3.25

3.26

3.27

3.28   Langley & Burke. Sherbourne Street Methodist Church (now St Luke's United Church), Toronto, 1886–87. Exterior and interior views, no date. Photograph. The United Church of Canada, Victoria University Archives, Toronto.

3.28

3.29

3.29   E.J. Lennox. Broadway Tabernacle (demolished), Toronto, 1887. Exterior view, c.1899. Photograph. MTRL: T.E. Champion, *Methodist Churches of Toronto* (Toronto, 1899), opposite 177.

In 1886 Langley & Burke explored round-arch forms in the design of Beverley Street Baptist (fig. 3.27). A mission of Jarvis Street Baptist Church erected on land donated by William McMaster, the once-remote location is now in the heart of Toronto's Chinatown. Although the building's High Victorian polychromy is hidden by a recent coat of white paint, the interior retains its original banked auditorium furnished with folding opera chairs that eliminated the class distinctions of pew rentals. Also intact despite alterations in the colour scheme is an elongated U-shaped gallery faced by elegant ornamental ironwork and supported on cast-iron columns.[59]

Later the same year Langley & Burke rebuilt Sherbourne Street Methodist Church (fig. 3.28) at the corner of Carlton Street in what must be one of the earliest Canadian manifestations of American-style Richardsonian Romanesque.[60] The architects were appointed to the project after the building committee turned down a more expensive proposal by William George Storm. Its congregation included affluent men such as Joseph Flavelle, A.E. Kemp, and H.H. Fudger, all of whom later retained Burke to design their residences. As the partner responsible to meet with the building committee, Burke was undeterred by a $30 thousand limit placed on the cost of the project. He finished this grandiose monument in a mixture of rough grey Credit Valley stone with brownstone dressings.[61] Broad facing gables – with the chequerboard pattern Richardson favoured – again mark the location of the auditorium. The interior space is covered by an elliptical barrel vault spanning some seventy-five feet, its arches corbelled into the outer wall, while at the western end a curved balcony is carried on

3.30

3.30 Langley & Burke. Trinity Methodist
Church (now Trinity-St Paul's United
Church), Toronto, 1887–89. Exterior view
from the east, c.1898. Photograph. AO:
Artwork on Toronto (Toronto: W.H. Carré,
1898), 93.

metal columns. A virtuoso performance of technical skill typical of
Burke's thinking and approach, the result prompted John Ross
Robertson, who resided in the neighbourhood, to describe it as one of
the handsomest churches in central Toronto.[62]

The following year, 1887, E.J. Lennox – one of Richardson's few
genuinely skilful imitators – followed the lead already established by
Langley & Burke. His Broadway Tabernacle at the intersection of
College and Spadina was marked by a high tower with a thoughtful
Romanesque exterior of red brick banded with basketweave detail on
a battered rusticated stone foundation (fig. 3.29). The plan is said to
have been an amplified version of the auditorium at Bond Street
Congregational, this time accommodating 2000 adherents. Surviving
descriptions indicate that an octagonal dome rested on immense
columns, which rose from the floor through the gallery to the roof,
a structural methodology clearly less advanced than Burke's at
Sherbourne Street.[63]

While Lennox worked on Broadway Tabernacle, Langley & Burke
began yet another design for a large church, half a mile to the north,
on Bloor Street one block west of Spadina. The trustees of what was
then Western Methodist decided to build for the rapidly growing population in the Annex. Lennox had planned a temporary wooden structure for this site, but his mandate ended in a dispute over fees. As a
result the building committee turned to Langley & Burke for the permanent building. Among the committee were Timothy Eaton and
W.J. Gage, both highly successful businessmen, who carried the project forward with all possible speed.[64]

From the outset Burke was responsible for the design of what was
later known as Trinity Methodist Church. He developed a monochro-
matic Romanesque scheme in rustic Credit Valley stone ornamented
with simple pinnacles and dressed-stone voussoirs over the main
doors (fig. 3.30). On the inside a cruciform auditorium with abbrevi-
ated transepts projecting barely three feet on each side could seat
seventeen hundred (fig. 3.31). Pews were arranged in an amphitheatre
format with an upstairs gallery carried on metal columns surrounding
three sides of the hall. Massive arches supported by sixty-thousand-
pound wood trusses span a remarkable seventy-eight feet, while at the
centre of the ceiling is a large square lantern that suffuses light
throughout the interior. The result was an elegant fusion of sophisticated technology and the latest in American style.[65]

Among other round-arched schemes the firm undertook at this time
was the College Street Baptist Church, its decorative brick and brownstone exterior in sharp contrast to the plainness of Burke's Trinity design (fig. 3.32). A lot at the corner of College and Palmerston was purchased in 1888 with the intention of erecting a church for 900. Plans
called for Credit Valley stone to the level of the imposts, entrance
arches decorated in terra cotta, and a massive square tower roofed in
red clay tiles, which still marks the building's location for blocks in
either direction. From the outside the church appears to consist of
a broad longitudinal nave, but the interior houses an amphitheatre

3.31   Langley & Burke. Trinity Methodist Church (now Trinity-St Paul's United Church), Toronto, 1887–89. Interior view, c.1910. Photograph. MTRL:T-10827.

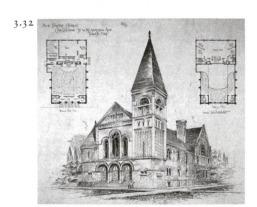

3.32   Langley & Burke. College Street Baptist Church (now Overcomers Church), Toronto, 1888–89. Perspective and plans, delineated by John Horwood, c.1888. AO, HC:C 11–546–0–2(580)1.

with a horseshoe-shaped balcony carried on metal columns.[66] The apparently joint project is a composite of ideas from Langley's Metropolitan Methodist, Burke's amphitheatre plan, and the ornamental-design talent of John Horwood, whose perspective of this building appeared in *Canadian Architect and Builder*.

Dunn Avenue Methodist Church, with a capacity of 2000, was typical of the outlying districts of the city where evangelical congregations were also growing at an enormous rate. Langley & Burke began the drawings in 1889 shortly after the trustees had purchased a new site on King Street West. It seems likely that Burke was instrumental here, too, because his own firm was retained for alterations in 1896. Yet the initials on the drawings read like a who's who of Langley students: John Horwood, Murray A. White, and C.H. Acton Bond.

The exterior followed what was by now a well-rehearsed pattern, with the auditorium identified by two great gables flanking a tall corner tower, while school rooms were situated behind a separate gable at the rear (fig. 3.33). Brick was combined with brownstone dressings on a foundation of quarry-faced Credit Valley stone. But unlike contemporary schemes in the city, the standard Romanesque formula was detailed with Gothic arches.[67] On the inside, however, the format was similar to Trinity Methodist with a canted amphitheatre of semicircular pews surrounded on three sides by a U-shaped balcony. Massive wooden trusses again supported four monumental arches that spanned the hall while the lantern of the earlier example was replaced by a simple panelled ceiling (fig. 3.34).[68]

3.33   Langley & Burke. Dunn Avenue
Methodist Church (later Parkdale United
Church, now demolished), Parkdale,
1889–90. Exterior view, c.1899.
Photograph. MTRL: T.E. Champion,
Methodist Churches of Toronto (Toronto,
1899), opposite 246.

3.34   Langley & Burke. Dunn Avenue
Methodist (later Parkdale United Church,
now demolished), Parkdale, 1889–90.
Interior view, c.1899. Photograph. MTRL:
T.E. Champion, *Methodist Churches of
Toronto* (Toronto, 1899), opposite 246.

3.33

3.34

Langley's firm continued to build large Romanesque churches well
into the 1890s, including one as far afield as Winnipeg. And Burke
& Horwood, who undertook major churches in London and
Woodstock, Ontario, perpetuated the style.[69] By the early twentieth
century Richardsonian Romanesque and the auditorium plan were a
spent force. Burke's firm favoured the Arts and Crafts mode for
smaller chapels, while neo-Gothic assumed importance for the larger
churches.

Amid this liturgical revisionism one last unique exposition of the round-arched style was undertaken by Burke & Horwood for the King Street East Methodist Church in 1902 (fig. 3.35).[70] With funding from the Methodist Social Union, the Hart Massey estate, and the Sherbourne Street Methodist congregation, an existing stucco chapel was refaced with a block-like facade vividly striped in cream and red brick. The architects abandoned the revivalism of earlier examples for an uncompromising exterior of narrow buttresses banded in polychromy, a combination related in spirit if not in detail to examples of South Italian Byzantine style published by the architectural writer James Fergusson.[71] Chosen to reflect the building's dual function as chapel and community centre, the exterior recalls the deliberate austerity of early Methodist meeting halls in Britain.[72]

THE ARTS AND CRAFTS INFLUENCE

In the second half of the nineteenth century there were two developments in English domestic architecture which spilled over into North American ecclesiastical works: the Arts and Crafts Movement, which sought to reinstate craftsmanship and local building vernaculars, and the eclecticism of Richard Norman Shaw, who experimented with Old English, Queen Anne, Scottish baronial, and Dutch motifs. Conceptually opposed but nevertheless interrelated, artisan philosophy and the eclecticism commonly misnamed Queen Anne revival soon spread to North America.[73]

In 1883, a decade and a half after British architect Richard Norman Shaw had resurrected Old English vernacular for residential works, Massachusetts-born William Le Baron Jenney used similar motifs from colonial models for American ecclesiastical architecture. His St Paul's church in Riverside, Illinois, was built with exposed timbers

3.35   Burke & Horwood. King Street East Methodist Church (now Riverside Church), Toronto, 1902. Perspective, no signature, no date, c.1902. Watercolour on paper. AO, HC:C 11, perspectives.

3.35

and rubble masonry infill chosen specifically for economy and suitability in a suburban setting (fig. 3.36).[74] The result was a picturesque hall church with transepts and apse that fell somewhere between Shaw's manorial borrowings and Arts and Crafts vernacular.

North American architects had previously seen merit in exploring inexpensive wood construction for churches when they adopted the "Hyperborean" Gothic proposed by the ecclesiologists as combining structural expression with appropriate religious symbolism.[75] The Langley firm had a long history of such churches to its credit, including the Anglican church of St Thomas, Brooklin, Ontario (1869–70), an outstanding example in board and batten.[76] Twenty years later, in 1889, Langley & Burke published a *Sketch for a Village Church*, which included a perspective as well as plans and elevations for a church with an adjoining school (fig. 3.37).[77] The foundations were quarry-faced ashlar, while the building itself consisted of a steeply pitched roof descending almost to the level of the stonework. Facing gables were half-timbered and stuccoed, the pattern a decorative appliqué characteristic of American imitations of Old English style, rather than an archeological recreation of the type represented by Strickland & Symons' design of 1888 for St Simon's (Anglican) Church in Rosedale – where the English-trained architect, William L. Symons, instilled a genuine Elizabethan flavour (fig. 3.38).[78]

In the United States vernacular revivals also brought about a renewed interest in the colonial shingled structures of New England. From this followed a development in domestic architecture that modern writer Vincent Scully has dubbed "Shingle style."[79] On occasion the same impulse, too, found its way into ecclesiastical work with examples such as John Wellborn Root's Lakeview Presbyterian Church in Chicago of 1887–88 (fig. 3.39).[80]

Burke experimented with Shingle-style ecclesiastical structures after

3.36   William Le Baron Jenney. St Paul's Church, Riverside, Illinois, 1883. Perspective, c.1883. Art Institute of Chicago (AIofC): *Inland Architect & News Record* (*IANR*) 1 (January 1883):23.

3.36

3.37

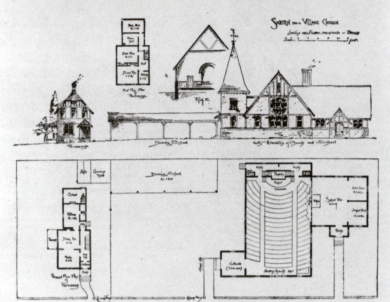

3.37   Langley & Burke. Sketch for a Village Church. Perspective, elevations, and plans, 1889. UofT-RB: *CAB* 2 (January 1889): before 12.

3.38   Strickland & Symons. St Simon's Anglican Church, Toronto, 1888. Exterior view, c.1889. Photograph. MTRL:T-10809.

3.38

entering practice on his own. In 1893 he was retained to build a small chapel in the Quebec town of Maskinongé, where two hundred disaffected Catholics had been received into the Baptist convention in 1891. Bringing together church and parsonage in a single structure, Burke chose clapboard and cut shingles for the exterior, articulating the building's purpose by means of a small conical tower aligned with the gable end (fig. 3.40).[81] Eminently well suited to the rustic surroundings and modest means of the congregation, the building apparently served its purpose for the best part of a generation.[82]

3.39

3.40

3.39 John Wellborn Root. Lakeview Presbyterian Church, Chicago, 1896. Exterior view, 1896. Photograph. AIofC: *IANR* 17 (May 1891).

3.40 Edmund Burke. Baptist Chapel (status unknown), Maskinongé, 1893. Elevations and plans, 1893. Pen and wash on paper. AO, HC:C 11–14–0–1(16)3.

Other Arts and Crafts works were more imposing. When the Reverend Elmore Harris left Bloor Street Baptist Church in 1889 to establish a new chapel (now known as Walmer Road Baptist Church) he retained Langley & Burke to plan a structure with seating capacity for six hundred. Accordingly, a scheme described as "red brick with Elizabethan detailing" was prepared, which was very much in keeping with the half-timbering and shingled gables of neighbouring Annex houses (fig. 3.41).[83]

Three years later two members of the Harris family provided $70,000 for a major addition to the original structure. Once again the architects were Langley & Burke, the project (completed in ten months) one of Burke's last undertakings while still a member of the Langley firm. The stylistic choice was unusual, combining battered foundations of Credit Valley brownstone with reddish-brown pressed brick detailed in an astylar medieval blend including lancet windows (fig. 3.42). Portions of the massing of the facade recall Richardsonian Romanesque, but on the long flank, half-timbered stucco was originally planned to fill the section beneath the eaves, blending with the Elizabethan motif of the 1889 chapel. It was an inspired synthesis – the lightness of stucco and shingle counterposed with fortress-like masses of stone – to produce what was then Canada's largest Baptist church.

On the interior an elegant horseshoe gallery supported on wooden columns with stairs curving down to the pulpit on either side encircles the pressed brick auditorium with its lighter, buff-brick dado (fig. 3.43). The ceiling is open-beam construction with tinted plastered panels – all in a manner sympathetic to the hallmark natural materials and vernacular methods of the Arts and Crafts Movement.[84]

3.42

3.41

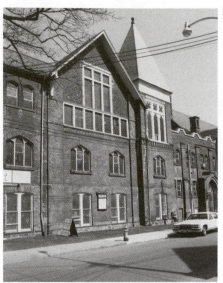

3.43

3.41   Langley & Burke. Walmer Road
Baptist Church, Toronto, 1889. Exterior
view, 1994. Photograph by Angela Carr.

3.42   Langley & Burke. Walmer Road
Baptist Church, Toronto, 1892. Exterior
view, 1892. Photograph. Canadian Baptist
Archives (CBA), McMaster University,
Hamilton: *Christmas 1892 Souvenir: The
Opening Services of the Walmer Road
Baptist Church, Toronto*, 2.

3.43   Langley & Burke. Walmer Road
Baptist Church, Toronto, 1892. Interior
view, 1900. Photograph. CBA: cover from
Walmer Road Pulpit 3, 9 (1900):no. 30.

A few years after the completion of Walmer Road Baptist, in
1896–97, Burke & Horwood were called upon to design a new
church for another Baptist congregation in the west end of the city.
Their original building was a modest rough-cast mission hall on
Tecumseh Street, which benefactor William Davies (whose views on
McMaster's Jarvis Street Baptist Church have already been noted)
offered to rebuild in memory of his daughter. The ample brick structure, with its unusual angular battered buttresses and a half-timbered
gable, designed for Memorial Baptist Church, is now cloaked by a
thick layer of stucco (fig. 3.44). But the angled buttresses still evident
on the exterior were characteristic of designs by Burke & Horwood
at this particular period. British Arts and Crafts architect, Charles
F.A. Voysey, focused attention on this element of Early English vernacular in his house designs which were first published in 1886. But
churches of the medieval period had also been built in this way, judging by a rendering of Baginton Church, Warwickshire (fig. 3.45) in a
well-known British publication by Raphael and J. Arthur Brandon.[85]

Fourth Avenue Baptist Church in Ottawa, commissioned in 1904
by the Reverend William Wardley McMaster, great-nephew of
Senator William McMaster and son of J. Short McMaster, also features angled buttresses. The client took serious interest in the scheme,
and the architects responded by producing one of their most unusual
designs to date. Returning to the eclectic medievalism of Walmer
Road, Burke & Horwood erected a red brick church with battered
buttresses trimmed in rustic stone (fig. 3.46). The tower, with a chim-
ney hidden in its tapered profile, recalls the pyramidal elements of
Walmer Road Baptist. Inside, walls are finished with face brick, and
stained beams support the roof (fig. 3.47).[86]

3.44

3.44   Burke & Horwood. Memorial
Baptist Church (now Ukranian Baptist
Church), Toronto, 1896–97. Exterior view,
1957. Photograph by J.V. Salmon.
MTRL:SI–4025A.

3.45   Baginton Church, Warwickshire,
England. Exterior view, Early English.
Engraving. MTRL: R. and J.A. Brandon,
Parish Churches (London, 1848), opposite
113.

3.45

The choice of material in Fourth Avenue Baptist may have been influenced by the ideas of American architect Ralph Adams Cram,
whose book, *Church Building*, had just been published in 1901. Cram
and his partner Bertram Grosvenor Goodhue were instrumental in
founding the Boston Society of Arts and Crafts in 1897,[87] yet Cram
unequivocally condemned the practice of building churches in a style
"of the chaotic, fantastic, would-be picturesque horror that owes its
existence to the deadly shingle, the seductive wood-stain, cheap col-
ored glass, and 'the art movement.'" He suggested that brick could be
employed if stone was not available, as long as it was the rough-
surfaced, red variety laid up in common mortar. He added that red
brick "with plenty of stone worked in for quoins, string courses, and
trimmings, is used admirably in England."[88]

Such theoretical tracts were by no means definitive, as Burke &
Horwood demonstrated the following year in their plans for a small
church in Preston, Ontario (fig. 3.48). Erected on battered foundations, the half-timbered, stuccoed chapel is sheltered beneath a steeply
pitched bell-cast roof.[89] The design ignores Cram's interdictions on
the subject of picturesque churches, adopting the despised practice of
"treating a small church like a cottage, of trying to obtain an effect of
'cosiness,' which is quite the most wrong-headed scheme that has
offered."[90]

Burke, Horwood & White also developed a half-timbered scheme for Vancouver's Mount Pleasant Baptist Church of 1909 (fig. 3.49). In keeping with its suburban location, the mock-Tudor superstructure is planted atop a rusticated stone foundation contiguous with a castellated bell-tower. It bears some similarity to two schemes already published by Cram for All Saint's Church, Ashmont Square in Boston and the church at Cohasset, Massachusetts (fig. 3.50).[91] But Cram's projects reserved the half-timbering for the residential facilities, executing the church itself in modern neo-Gothic. By contrast, the Vancouver example by the Toronto firm combines rustic stone and

3.46

3.47

3.46   Burke & Horwood. Fourth Avenue Baptist Church, Ottawa, 1904. Exterior view, 1994. Photograph by Angela Carr.

3.47   Burke & Horwood. Fourth Avenue Baptist Church, Ottawa, 1904. Interior view, 1994. Photograph by Angela Carr.

3.48   Burke & Horwood. King Street Baptist Church, Cambridge (Preston), 1905. Exterior view, 1989. Photograph by Angela Carr.

3.49   Burke, Horwood & White. Mount Pleasant Baptist Church, Vancouver, 1909. Exterior view, 1988. Photograph. City of Vancouver Archives, Vancouver (CVA):CH P167, negative 6.

3.48

3.49

half-timbering in a single structure. Such a synthesis suggests that the ecclesiastical architecture of Burke, Horwood & White was governed less by theoretical purity than by economics and the need for stylistic consistency with neighbouring residential structures.[92]

NEO-GOTHIC AND RALPH ADAMS CRAM

In some respects the American architect and theorist Ralph Adams Cram took up where the ecclesiologists left off, asserting that Gothic was "the one style in which we can work." But instead of Early

English or Decorated, he chose Perpendicular of the early sixteenth century as his starting point, believing that a new development could be built upon the foundations of the old. He described his methodology as art rather than archaeology, echoing the approach of British architects George F. Bodley and Henry Vaughan – who employed Gothic as a matter of course for ecclesiastical projects throughout their late nineteenth-century careers. In a single terse paragraph Cram dismissed "the fancied necessity of getting rid of all obstacles to direct vision, together with the very absurd theory that a square plan rather than a long one gives the best acoustics," blaming such ideas for "the shapeless and ignorant edifice that has usurped the place of the really Gothic, and Catholic church."[93]

Taking the essence of what Cram had said about the requirements for Anglican edifices, Burke, Horwood & White adapted the principles for a series of town churches erected for evangelical denominations in the second decade of the twentieth century. First Baptist Church in Vancouver is a case in point. Executed between 1909 and 1911, the rustic granite exterior returns to the traditional longitudinal format with a Sunday school at right angles in an adjacent structure (fig. 3.51). Before a disastrous fire in 1931, the interior consisted of an auditorium with tripartite seating like Langley's Metropolitan Methodist, and a U-shaped balcony on the upper level (fig. 3.52). The plan fused the traditions of the evangelical hall church with Cram's more conventional ideas. At the same time, open wood trusses were in line with Cram's admonition that "the roof must, of course, be wholly of wood."[94]

Similar examples were built in Peterborough for Murray Street Baptist Church and Trinity Methodist on Rubidge Street. Both are quarry-faced ashlar and combine modern methods with the medieval

3.50   Cram, Goodhue & Ferguson. Church at Cohasset, Massachusetts, 1902. Exterior view, 1905. Photograph by Robarts Library. UofT-RB: *CAB* 18 (February 1905):19.

3.53   Cram, Goodhue & Ferguson. Project for St Alban's Cathedral, Toronto, 1912. Perspective, 1912. Photograph from microfilm by Robarts Library. University of Guelph, Guelph: *Construction* 5 (January 1912):50.

3.50

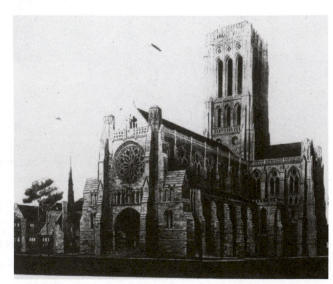

3.53

3.51

3.51   Burke, Horwood & White. First
Baptist Church, Vancouver, 1909–11.
Exterior view, c.1911. Photograph. AO, HC:C
11, Additional 5.

3.52   Burke, Horwood & White. First
Baptist Church, Vancouver, 1909–11.
Interior view, c.1911. Photograph. AO, HC:C
11, Additional 5.

3.52

ones Cram preferred. Consistent with this generalized return to traditional forms, the Rubidge Street congregation also decided to purchase straight pews for their church.[95]

The widespread acceptance of Cram's ideas in Canada did not preclude criticism when his firm undertook All Saints (Anglican) Church in Halifax in 1906 and the Cathedral Church of St Alban the Martyr in Toronto in 1911 (fig. 3.53).[96] At the fourth annual convention of the Royal Architectural Institute of Canada in 1911, one speaker expressed his admiration for Cram's work as an exponent of English Gothic, but "hoped that the Bishop of Toronto would engage a Canadian if not an English architect" to undertake the St Alban's project. "It seemed a pity," the commentator went on, "that in a country of this size its professional men could not be looked upon with confidence in every respect."[97] Richard C. Windeyer had supplied the original plans for St Alban's in 1883, but the work had been abandoned after completion of the choir amid controversy about the quality of the design. Nearly three decades later Canadian architects borrowed profusely from their southern neighbours, but were unrelenting in their opposition to the admission of American competitors. Yet British participation was accepted, particularly after the election of 1911 when the Tories returned to power. Their traditional Imperial loyalties and historic resistance to the United States seem to have engendered a toleration for British architects where there was little for Americans.[98]

Despite the tenor of the times, Burke's ecclesiastical works chart a shift from British-influenced models to predominently American precedents, beginning in 1874 with his amphitheatre design for Jarvis Street Baptist, and followed twelve years later by his adoption of Richardsonian Romanesque for Sherbourne Street Methodist. His stylistic and planning innovations were accompanied by new structural technologies, which facilitated vast unsupported spans in place of the metal columns of Langley's designs – apparently a Canadian first. Burke's firm also adopted the American practice of using Arts and Crafts motifs in church architecture. Leaving aside the precedents of his apprenticeship, Burke demonstrated his willingness to confront these challenges with a zeal that marked him as a new breed of architect.

4   *Residential Architecture: Human and Climatic Considerations*

> Canadian work is greatly influenced by the English, who excel in home building. Yet there is a gradual development in the direction of our own necessities which will evolve sooner or later a local style embracing the practical and aesthetic in one harmonious ensemble.
>
> "The Small House," *Construction* (March 1914)

In an address to the Toronto Architectural Sketch Club in 1892 on the elements of building construction, Burke managed to quantify almost in passing his conception of Canadian cultural identity, at least in the field of architecture. Having cited the English book *Building Construction* as an admirable reference text,[1] he started to describe how Canadian framing methods differed:

Much of the splicing, cogging, jointing and morticing dealt with in Mitchell is practically obsolete in this country, much better results being obtainable by the use of wro't iron bolts, straps and stirrups, the use of which avoids the inevitable weakening of the parts which should be the strongest. The high rate of [Canadian] wages is also prohibitive, as the making of the joints illustrated would consume an immense amount of time, which in these days is, indeed, money.[2]

Burke's reservations about the traditional mortice-and-tenon system used in Britain then led him to an even more revealing critique of the American balloon frame. "A great deal of the common class work of to-day is to be deprecated – there is too much tendency to "knock things together," superinduced by the craze for cheapness and inordinate haste, after the example set by our restless cousins to the South who use the almighty nail and trust it implicitly."[3]

In light of Burke's usual restraint and gentlemanly demeanour this was perhaps an uncharacteristically frank revelation of his opinions. But this self-assurance of the prudent middle course based on practical considerations is somehow piquantly Canadian, and reflects Burke's approach to architecture in general and to residential structures in particular. The diversity of forms dictated by the tastes of individual clients has at its core a quiet mediation between British and American models that takes account of Canadian climatic conditions and market factors.

Specific technical problems posed by Canada's harsh environment preoccupied Burke more than the philosophical debates over "national style."[4] He warned about the placement of gutters behind parapet walls, stating that "the only successful roof in our climate is that which permits the snow and ice to have free escape to the ground."[5] Battened walls were preferable for warmth and dryness, and solid backing of slate and tile roofs prevented condensation in winter. While such comments may be prosaic, Burke took into account contemporary Canadian realities, both climatic and educational. In the face of the "positively bad or absolutely uninteresting" state of Canadian architecture at the end of the nineteenth century,[6] his emphasis on standards of design and workmanship provided a starting point upon which aspirations for a national style could be built.[7]

Rational methodology guided Burke's theories on house planning as well. In another lecture delivered to the Architectural Sketch Club in 1890, Burke suggested that British and American planning practices were different because of divergences in the labour market. "Careless and diffuse" room arrangements he thought more common in Britain, where design deficiencies could be redressed by household help. In the United States and Canada on the other hand, a "lack of means ... conduced to more careful and scientific planning," with labour-saving appliances to assure the efficiency of the household. On the question of regional differences Burke observed that in the northern portions of the continent climatic conditions necessitated "a more compact form of planning for easier heating," since houses with wings were prone to roofing problems and snow traps. Cross-border variations in planning methodology reflected climatic adaptation rather than deliberate assertions of cultural identity, while similarities were a factor of common economic conditions not philosophic continentalism.[8]

Among the points Burke emphasized was the notion of "scientific" planning, which he explained using a quotation from American writer C. Francis Osborne, whose *Notes on the Art of House-Planning* he particularly recommended: "We must understand the special wants and natures of the clients; and so must often, to be thoroughly successful, stand for the time being in the relation of father-confessor, to whom must be unfolded all the inner life of the family, the tastes and even the peculiarities of each member of it, in order that the house may be molded to them, and not they to the house."[9] Burke then went on to speak of "smooth-working of domestic machinery" resulting from a careful consideration of the purpose the house is expected to serve – "that it must be fit to live in, and secondly, with the maximum of convenience and comfort compatible with the means available."[10]

Born of the British picturesque aesthetic,[11] practical planning found its way into American theory in the 1850s. Authors like Andrew Jackson Downing, known for his tracts on house designs, equated fitness with the ordering of the plan, while Horatio Greenough, an early proponent of functionalism, suggested that instead of forcing every sort of building into one general form, builders should "begin from the heart as the nucleus, and work outward."[12] Burke aligned himself with the exponents of functional-organic theory – and hence with those who pioneered innovations not only in house planning, but also in the field of commercial architecture.[13]

Despite his obvious affinity for American planning precepts Burke was not adverse to British sources when they suited his purpose. He referred to Robert Kerr's "aspect compass," which allowed architects to calculate the hours of available sunlight in summer and winter according to the room's directional exposure – an important consideration before electrical lighting was widely available (fig. 4.1). He also admired the plan of Richard Norman Shaw's artist's house, in which the dining room and kitchen were located on the main floor, while the studio and drawing room occupied the level above.[14] Many of the house designs executed under Burke's supervision drew upon Shavian themes with mixtures of brick, shingle, and half-timbering where previously residential structures had been uniformly stone or brick. The resulting hybrid of British and American ideas was characteristic of Burke's transitional synthesis, and reflected the general trend toward the end of the century.

EARLY MODELS AND SHAVIAN FREE STYLE

Britain's role in supplying stylistic models and trained professionals in the early nineteenth century had an impact on early residential designs. When William Hay arrived in Toronto in the 1850s, his knowledge of Gothic revival was as eagerly accepted for domestic architecture as for ecclesiastical structures.[15] A ubiquitous successor to earlier revival modes, its vocabulary was considered appropriate for Oaklands, a house commissioned in 1860 by Senator John Macdonald for a site well outside the city on the crest of the St Clair hill (fig. 4.2). Now De La Salle School, Oaklands exhibits the asymmetrical and additive planning, the steep gables and picturesque profile typical of the revival style. An extensive addition on a grander scale by Gundry & Langley in 1869 doubled the size of the original

4.1 Aspect Compass. Photograph by Robarts Library. UofT-RB: *CAB* 3 (May 1890):55, from R. Kerr, *The Gentleman's House.*

4.2 Gundry & Langley with additions by Langley, Langley & Burke. Oaklands (now De la Salle School), Toronto, 1860, and 1874. Exterior view, 1990. Photograph by Angela Carr.

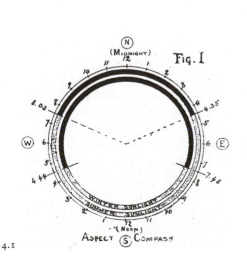

4.1

4.2

4.3

4.4

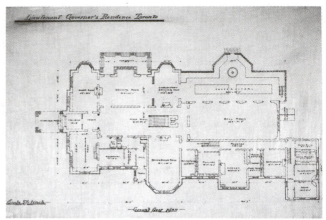

4.3   Gundry & Langley. Government House (demolished), Toronto, 1866–70. Exterior view, no date. Photograph by Josiah Bruce. AO:Acc. 13222–28.

4.4   Gundry & Langley. Government House (demolished), Toronto, 1866–70. Plan of Ground Floor, 1869. Pen and wash on paper. AO, Department of Public Works (Ontario):RG 15–13.

and added the dramatic tower that still dominates the vista.[16] This mode remained a staple of the Langley repertoire well into the 1870s.[17]

An alternative to the British-influenced Gothic revival also adopted by Gundry & Langley was the French Second Empire fashion inspired by the New Louvre in Paris (1852–57). Its pavilions and mansards were widely copied in the United States and later in Canada.[18] By the 1870s imposing facades layered with architectural orders were evidently considered ideal for high-budget public works in both jurisdictions. But smaller residential structures could not accommodate this treatment. The mansard was frequently the principal marker in residential works – often coupled with Italianate details such as brackets, pedimented dormers, and ample symmetrical planning.

Gundry & Langley's Government House of 1866–70, which stood at the corner of Simcoe and King Street West, was the firm's finest residential example of Second Empire (fig. 4.3), its large entrance hall and expansive interiors well suited for entertaining (fig. 4.4).[19] The style's popularity in the United States seems to have been another point in its favour, for Langley himself later described Government House as "designed in the modern French style of architecture which has been adopted largely in American cities and is rapidly getting into favour in England."[20]

Despite the shift in thinking implied by the taste for Second Empire, eclecticism inspired by the British "Queen Anne" movement also had a significant impact upon the firm's Toronto works, occasionally with some American permutations not anticipated by British precedents.[21] In 1888–89, for example, Langley & Burke designed a residence on Jarvis Street for grain merchant James Carruthers (fig. 4.5). Described by G. Mercer Adam as "one of the most modern and ornate in the neighbourhood," it included stone, brick, terra cotta, tile, and half-timbering in the uppermost gable. These in turn were integrated with rusticated voussoirs over the principal windows and a curiously insubstantial spindlework porch, which framed the main door.[22]

4.5   Langley & Burke. Carruthers House (demolished), Toronto, 1888–89. Exterior view, 1891. Photograph. MTRL: G.M. Adam, *Toronto, Old and New* (Toronto, 1891), 145.

4.6   Langley & Burke. Robert Simpson House (demolished), Toronto, 1883. Perspective and plans, no date. Heliotype Printing, Boston. Photograph by Robarts Library. UOFT-RL: *AABN* 19 (20 February 1886):no. 530, after 90.

4.6

4.5

Rugged stone details drawn from Richardsonian Romanesque combined with wooden spindles of American Shingle style imbued the house with a "modern" flavour that respected the existing character of one of the city's most prestigious residential streets.[23]

By contrast to the Carruthers house, works for other clients with whom Burke can be closely identified show great restraint and simplicity. The Robert Simpson house of 1883 on Bloor Street East at the head of Church Street preceded the Carruthers project by five years

4.7   Richard Norman Shaw. Leyswood (demolished), Sussex, 1868. Perspective and plans. UofT-Sigmund Samuel Library: *Building News* (31 October 1871).

4.8   Gambrill & Richardson. William Watts Sherman House, Newport, Rhode Island, 1874–76. Exterior view and plan with additions of 1887. Photograph. Library of Congress, Historic American Buildings Survey (HABS), Washington, DC:RI, 3-NEWP, 68–2, 413470.

(fig. 4.6). Haddon Villa, as it was known, differed from the urban fabric on Jarvis Street, which consisted of largely homogeneous brick and stone residences.[24] Its ground floor was executed in rusticated random ashlar, the upper storey in red brick, with a band of decorative terra-cotta tiles separating the two. Projecting beneath the eaves were half-timbered gables drawn from the Old English motifs of Richard Norman Shaw.[25] Simpson, for whom Burke later designed the first Chicago-style department store in Canada, was ready to experiment with innovative ideas even at this early date. On the fringes of Yorkville, free from the contextual hinderances of the old neighbourhoods, this new mode reminiscent of genteel country squirarchy and unpretentious affluence emerged – the multiplicity of materials a by-product of free-wheeling "Queen Anne" eclecticism.

Richard Norman Shaw is closely identified with "Queen Anne," which architectural historian Mark Girouard describes as "a kind of architectural cocktail, with a little Flemish, a squeeze of Robert Adam, a generous dash of Wren and a touch of Francois Ier."[26] Far from being a literal transcription of the red-brick house with white-painted window bars that characterized domestic architecture of the late seventeenth century in Britain, the nineteenth-century movement espoused a more generalized eclecticism citing the reign of Queen Anne as a period when vernacular forms developed without reference to specific style. The advantage according to J.L. Petit was that motifs could be selected according to their propriety for a particular purpose, and domestic structures could be harmonized with the character of the owner – factors which led to the mode's designation as "free style"

4.8

4.7

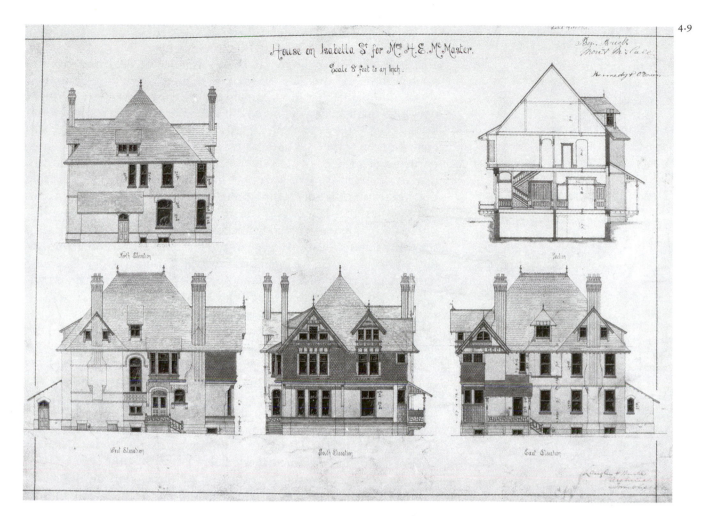

4.9   Langley & Burke. Helen E. McMaster House (now Jesuit Fathers residence), Toronto, 1884–85. Elevations and section. Pen and wash on paper, 8 Sept. 1884. AO, HC:C 11–515–0–2(480)8.

4.10   Richard Norman Shaw. Detached Villas, Bedford Park, Turnham Green, London, 1877. Elevation, sections, and plans. UofT-Sigmund Samuel Library: *Building News* (23 November 1877).

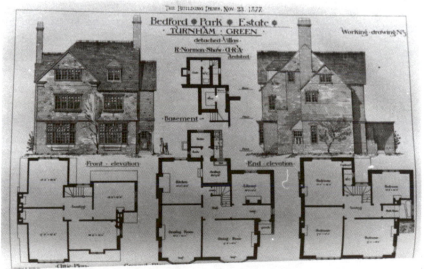

or "free Classic."[27] Shaw's *oeuvre* was soon to demonstrate the breadth these principles offered the architect.[28]

Shaw's works were known in North America through architectural publications like *Building News*, but "Queen Anne" made its first splash in Philadelphia in 1876, when the British government erected two Old-English half-timbered buildings at the Centennial Exhibition. The same year Henry Hudson Holly wrote that he considered "Queen Anne" a natural building style for North America, particularly in light of its originality, relation to site, and truth to materials. *American Architect and Building News* concurred, saying that "Queen Anne" might turn out to have done a good service in calling attention to qualities and constructive possibilities otherwise lost in the unthinking acceptance of conventional forms.[29] For a time in the United States the movement inspired a reprise of colonial vernacular equivalent to Shaw's manorial revival.[30] But by 1883 American writer Montgomery Schuyler could only deplore the "frantic and vociferous mob" who had turned "Queen Anne" into a comprehensive name that covered "a multitude of incongruities."[31]

That very year the Langley firm commenced the Simpson house, its half-timbered gables not unlike Shaw's influential neo-Tudor Leyswood, Sussex, of 1868 (fig. 4.7). Toronto's fire-control by-laws prohibited bare wood except in gables and cornices, so tile-hung elements were, for the most part, avoided in favour of stone and brick.[32] In addition Shaw's asymmetrical "agglutinative" planning based on medieval precedents was discarded in favour of a compact rectangle closer in concept to Henry Hobson Richardson's Watts Sherman house of 1874 at Newport, Rhode Island (fig. 4.8) – the type of planning, Burke later observed, best suited the North American climate.[33]

Burke's role in guiding the choice of the manorial theme can only be surmised, but his seniority would have placed him in charge of the draughting room by 1883.[34] Although surviving drawings by Langley & Burke for the Simpson house bear the hallmarks of Horwood's hand, Horwood had been articling barely a year, and was probably acting under direction.[35] A number of the houses along Shavian lines were executed for prominent Baptists, with whom Burke came into contact as a result of his religious affiliations. These clients apparently shared a taste for practical, unpretentious design.[36]

The same ideas appeared again in 1884–85 when Langley & Burke planned a new house at 94 Isabella Street for Helen E. McMaster, widow of Arthur R. McMaster (fig. 4.9). A long-time protégé of the McMaster family, Burke is likely to have supervised the project. The dense assemblage of gables and chimneys (with cut shingle in the upper storey) was a natural successor to the Simpson house a year earlier. Shingle was an economical material, which once set in mortar complied with city by-laws. The result is remarkably like Shaw's tile-hung house designs of 1877 for the picturesque "countrified" setting of London's Bedford Park (fig. 4.10).[37] It was one of the earliest examples of its type in the city, and its shingle motif soon became standard for many suburban districts like the Annex to the north and west of the city core.[38]

An article in the *Globe* newspaper in August 1890 explains the importance of Shavian motifs in changing the character of Toronto's residential neighbourhoods. Citing the need for houses which reflected the owner's individuality, the writer bemoaned the constraints imposed by the city's fire limits control by-law, noting the exclusion of wood, "which lends itself most readily to artistic treatment": "Those who have seen the beautiful houses of wood construction in the smaller cities of the Eastern and middle States must look with regret on the everlasting rows of brick here in Toronto."[39]

By introducing shingle laid in mortar for the upper storey, architects could relieve the monotony of the city's incessant brick facades. Examples pictured included residences for Walter J. Curry at 27 North Street, H.F. Dwight at 107 St George Street, and one half-timbered specimen executed in 1889–90 for Walter J. Massey at 486 Jarvis Street by American architect William Young (fig. 4.11). The *Globe* might just as appropriately have illustrated the brick-and-shingle design Langley & Burke had executed a year earlier a block further north on the opposite side of the same street for proprietary medicine dealer J.H. McKinnon (fig. 4.12).[40]

4.11

4.11   William Young. Walter J. Massey House (demolished), Toronto, before 1890. Exterior view, 1891. Photograph. MTRL: G.M. Adam, *Toronto, Old and New* (Toronto, 1891), 121.

4.12   Langley & Burke. J.H. McKinnon House, Toronto, 1888. Exterior view, 1990. Photograph by Angela Carr.

4.12

Outside Toronto Langley & Burke undertook a more grandiose design of similar type for Bennett Rosamond of Almonte.[41] Rosamond was a second-generation mill owner who later became County Court judge and member of Parliament for Lanark.[42] In keeping with his position he planned to spend $20,000 – a not insignificant sum at that time.[43] How Rosamond knew of Langley & Burke is not clear, but the commission was one of those that followed Burke when he left Langley's practice in 1892.[44]

Horwood's perspective of the Rosamond house exhibited in 1886 includes Shavian half-timbered elements, but final drawings also called for cut-wood shingles on a foundation of rusticated random ashlar (fig. 4.13). The layout, illustrated in Burke's house planning lecture of 1890, adheres to his injunction against rambling picturesque plans (fig. 4.14). At the core of the structure is a large hall with fireplace, the front entrance protected from drafts by a porch and vestibule. Main rooms face south on the side of the house to gain the exposure dictated by Kerr's "aspect compass." Unhindered by city by-laws and the confines of suburban lots, it is significant that the firm's materials and planning methodology remained substantially unchanged.

Two years later Langley & Burke undertook another important commission, also described in Burke's lecture of 1890, the D.E. Thomson house on Queen's Park Crescent (fig. 4.15). Thomson, a prominent Baptist, was among the executors of the will of Burke's long-time patron, Senator William McMaster. More lavish still than the Almonte work, the ground floor was rustic random ashlar while an overhanging second storey combined half-timber and brick infill. Gables faced in shingle or tile with elaborately carved bargeboards lent a decidedly Jacobean flavour to the whole.[45]

Visitors entered the Thomson house from the south side where an enclosed porch offered maximum protection from prevailing winds (fig. 4.16). The vestibule then connected with a large L-shaped hall adjoining the drawing room. On the south side was a library, and at the rear, with a south-eastern exposure for the best natural light, was the dining room. On the cooler north side the kitchen was separated from the dining room by a pantry to conceal the culinary work-area from view.[46]

Among the more impressive features of the Thomson house was its large entrance hall containing a fireplace and seating accommodation (fig. 4.17). Modelled on the manorial living halls of Robert Kerr's *Gentleman's House* revived in the work of Richard Norman Shaw and Henry Hobson Richardson, the Thomson hall was far more than a mere access corridor.[47] Its large floor area added to the size of the drawing room for formal entertaining, a fireplace on the north wall ensuring that it was adequately heated in the winter. Wood panelling, unglazed brick, leaded windows, and low ceilings contributed to a rustic, informal quality typical of the Arts and Crafts.[48] Along the rear wall a staircase rose in four easy flights designed to hide the upper landing from view.[49]

4.13

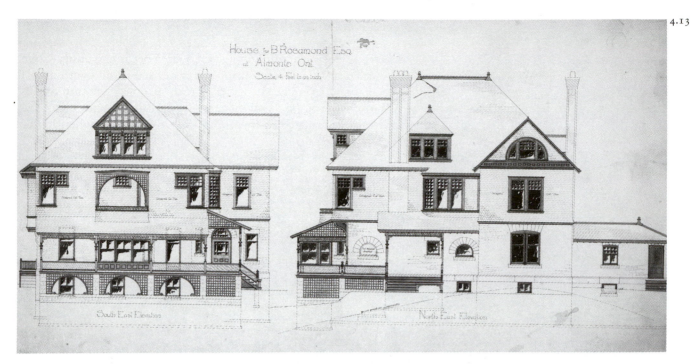

4.13   Langley & Burke. Bennett Rosamond House, Almonte, 1886–87. Elevations, no date. Pen and wash on paper. AO, HC:C 11–25–0–2(499)3.

4.14   Langley & Burke. Bennett Rosamond House, Almonte, 1886–87. Plan of ground floor, 26 April 1887. Pen and wash on linen. OA, HC:C 11–25–0–2(499)9.

4.14

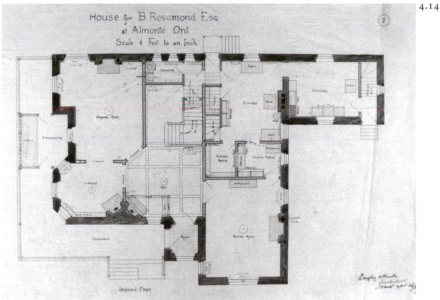

When Burke launched his own firm in 1892 Shavian motifs continued to figure prominently in his residential works.[50] A house in the Annex planned that year for C.J. Holman is typical (fig. 4.18). Holman, a prominent lawyer and Baptist, was also an executor of McMaster's estate along with Thomson.[51] The three-storey structure at 75 Lowther Avenue incorporates a familiar selection of materials – rusticated random ashlar on the ground floor, shingle on the second

4.15

4.15 Langley & Burke. D.E. Thomson
House (demolished), Toronto, 1888.
Exterior view, no date. Photograph. AO,
HC:C 11–36–0–1(45)1.

4.16 Langley & Burke. D.E. Thomson
House (demolished), Toronto, 1888. Plan
of ground floor. Photograph by Robarts
Library. UOFT-RL: CAB 3 (May 1890):56.

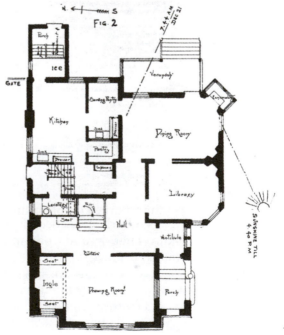

4.16

4.17 Langley & Burke. D.E. Thomson
House (demolished), Toronto, 1888.
Perspective of staircase hall. Pen on paper.
AO, HC:C 11–36–0–3(579)1.

4.17

level, and half-timbered gables, all scaled to fit the narrow suburban lot.[52]

Two projects Burke & Horwood prepared for the T.M. Harris house of 1902 show the range of choices the partners could offer their clients. Now the University of Toronto's Centre for Industrial Relations, at 123 St George Street, the built version is similar to the Helen McMaster residence – the ground floor in stone and brick, the upper storey shingle (fig. 4.19).[53] By contrast, Horwood exhibited a scheme under his own name that took the form of a chateauesque fantasy in the style of New York architect Richard Morris Hunt (fig. 4.20).[54] Its florid ornamental quality typical of his artistic *persona* is an interesting contrast to what seems to have been his partner's more practical and occasionally austere approach.

For his part Burke always emphasized issues of a logical or scientific nature, a philosophy of professional education shared by his associates in the Ontario Association of Architects.[55] In an 1891 competition staged by the *Canadian Architect and Builder* for the design a city house on a thirty-foot lot, judges Frank Darling, Norman Dick, and Edmund Burke complemented the winner on his "painstaking effort and careful attention to every detail necessary for the working of the domestic machinery," a formulation typical of Burke. The winning elevation was considered less satisfactory, however, because "so much wooden construction and tile-hung work on the first floor would send the officials into a fit." Even hypothetical designs had to take no less account of fire control regulations than of aesthetic issues. Another entrant was advised to "study the methods of good draughtsmen and

4.19

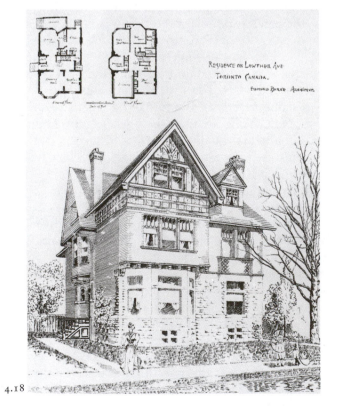

RESIDENCE ON LOWTHER AVE
TORONTO CANADA.

EDMUND BURKE ARCHITECT.

4.18

4.20

4.21

4.18 Edmund Burke. C.J. Holman House (now the Women's Missionary Society of the Regular Baptists of Canada), Toronto, 1893. Elevation and plans. MTRL: *CAB 6* (December 1893): after 130.

4.19 Burke & Horwood. T.M. Harris House (now the Centre for Industrial Relations, University of Toronto), Toronto, 1902. Exterior view. MTRL-Special Collections: Toronto Architectural Eighteen Club, *Catalogue* (Toronto, 1902), 83.

4.20 Burke & Horwood. Project for the T.M. Harris House, Toronto. Perspective drawing. MTRL-Special Collections: Toronto Architectural Eighteen Club, *Catalogue* (Toronto, 1901), 53.

4.21 Burke & Horwood. H.H. Fudger Residence, Toronto, 1895–97. Exterior view, 1920. Photograph by Peake & Whittingham, Toronto. AO:Acc. 9257, S14127.

4.22 Burke & Horwood. H.H. Fudger Residence, Toronto, 1895–97. Dining room interior, 1920–23. Photograph by Peake & Whittingham, Toronto. AO:Acc. 9257, S14126.

4.22

... English house design and the more sober efforts of educated men in the eastern states in lieu of designs from cheap American publications which are designed to catch the eye of the jig-saw carpenter."[56]

In the closing decades of the century British methods and precedents continued to predominate. H.H. Fudger, one of three business associates who purchased the Robert Simpson store following the retailer's death, commissioned a residence at 40 Maple Avenue in Rosedale in 1895 (fig. 4.21).[57] Its intricate Flemish gables recall the "scrolled" silhouette of Richard Norman Shaw's Albert Hall Mansions of 1879 in London.[58] Extensive alterations to the interior carried out by Burke & Horwood in 1902–3 continued to reflect the English Arts and Crafts flavour, with wood panelling, truth to materials, and sensible, liveable designs (fig. 4.22).[59] The hall, library, and living room were enlivened with medieval inglenooks, and staircases rose in short easy stages to the upper floors, in keeping with the firm's approach of the past two decades.

RESORT ARCHITECTURE AND THE SHINGLE STYLE

The architecture of the summer resort, by contrast to the British-based precedents used in Burke's town houses, was a peculiarly American phenomenon. Author Henry Cleaveland wrote that rural life was not only healthy, but "its moral influences ... much better than those of the city, [just] as its air is more salubrious."[60] This type of rustic Romanticism and a widespread belief in the edifying effects of natural environment contributed greatly to the popularity of resorts and of their domestic counterpart – the summer cottage.[61] In the first quarter of the nineteenth century, wood-frame resort hotels sprang up along the eastern seaboard of the United States, to be superseded in later years by private seasonal residences.[62] By the 1870s this tourist trend had spread to the Maritimes, the St Lawrence River valley, and the Great Lakes basin.[63]

Burke's sortie into resort architecture began in 1886 when Langley & Burke prepared a set of cottage designs for the newly incorporated Toronto and Lorne Park Summer Resort Company.[64] The summer amusement park near Port Credit had been operating since 1879, and was easily accessible by railway, steamer, and carriage.[65] Its Norway pines were said to be "famous for their health-giving properties," and the moral rectitude of the park's users was assured by strict observance of the Sabbath and a ban on intoxicating liquors. The natural beauty of the location offered "a most desirable retreat for all who may wish to enjoy a restful and charming summer home."[66] Half-acre lots were sold to buyers who had a choice of seven different cottage plans.[67] Burke even built one for himself, and later became a company director.[68]

Purchasers of the lots contracted to erect "a neat and respectable house or cottage costing not less than $400."[69] Twenty-seven summer residences were built between 1886 and 1891, of which fourteen are reportedly still in year-round occupation following renovation.[70]

4.23 Langley & Burke. Lorne Park Advertisement. Perspective, c.1890. Pen on paper. AO, HC:C 11–593–0–1(568)1.

4.24 Langley & Burke. Cottage at Lorne Park for E. Burke, Port Credit, 1889. Elevations and section, 2 March 1889. Pen and wash on paper. AO, HC:C 11–554–0–1(520)1.

4.25 Andrew Jackson Downing. Cottage Design XIII, 1850. UofT-RL: A.J. Downing, *Architecture of Country Houses* (New York, 1850), 127.

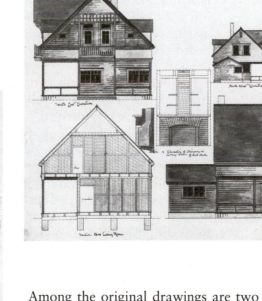

4.24

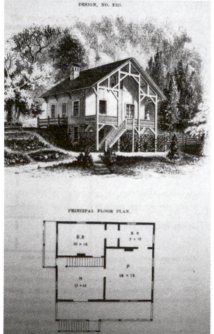

4.25

Among the original drawings are two standard designs; one with a corner tower, the other a front gable motif to which a variety of appurtenant wings could be attached (fig. 4.23). All were in wood, an inexpensive and plentiful material suitable to their rustic and seasonal nature.[71] Each was a storey and a half or two storeys, block-boarded and shingled, with no fewer than four bedrooms. Plans were extremely simple, often symmetrical, and based on the subdivision of a rectangle. Broad verandas and spacious balconies – both standard elements in tropical bungalows, plantation houses, and resort architecture – were billed as "a feature of Lorne Park."[72] Open loggias designed to catch the onshore evening breeze were framed with elaborate lattice and spindle work derived from contemporary American examples.

Unfettered by by-law restrictions the Lorne Park development drew upon the traditions of the North American rustic cottage. As early as 1842 Andrew Jackson Downing had endorsed the use of wood for a "Cottage Villa in the Bracketed Mode" and proposed that an ingenious architect might produce an American *Cottage Style*, by carefully studying its capabilities.[73] At the time wood construction was standard for resort architecture in the United States, and because of its availability, economy, and convenience was the material of choice for many other types of structures.[74] This very ubiquitousness prompted Downing to identify wooden architecture as "the American style."[75]

Burke's cottages were constructed on isolated stone piers, the main floor first with corner posts and studs mounted on top of the planking (fig. 4.24).[76] Then the flooring for the upper storey was completed, and a second set of posts and studs erected. A pitched roof reinforced with collar beams closed off the structure. Horizontal cross-ribs lent stability to the walls, but there was no angular bracing.[77] Cladding consisted of blocked boards, shingle, or board-and-batten mounted in panels between the corner posts, so that the surfaces were patterned horizontally or vertically in combination with a variety of shingle textures.[78] Blocked boarding and shingle were borrowed from the colonial tradition of British North America and New England, while board-and-batten was a more recent American development linked to the balloon frame.[79]

Parallels between Lorne Park and its American counterparts did not end with methods and materials. In 1850 Downing had published a design for a symmetrical "Cottage" which was to be "doubly covered" with jointed inch boards and cut shingle (fig. 4.25).[80] Cleaveland later codified the definition, citing as typical the "veranda or gallery, covered by the projecting roof, and supported by the open framework."[81] This motif formed the basis of at least six Lorne Park designs, the galleried gables and extended verandas lending a decidedly open character to these manifestly impermanent and seasonal dwellings.[82] A common idiom in American resort towns like Ocean Grove, New Jersey, such chalets were customarily ornamented with jigsawn bargeboards, lattice, or spindle work.[83] Lattice and spindle predominated at Lorne Park, with occasional "Oriental Chippendale" motifs for variety (fig. 4.26).[84] Pattern books such as Comstock's *Modern Architectural Designs and Details* (1881) and *Palliser's New Cottage Homes and Details* (1887) disseminated various versions of these schemes, which the authors thought equally suitable for summer mountain homes in the Adirondacks and winter houses in Florida.[85]

The regularized planning that was a feature of the chalet mode was in sharp contrast to the mid-century practice of adapting cottage designs "exactly as may be required, to the peculiarities of the site, usually both irregular in outline upon the ground, and in its style

4.26   Langley & Burke. Sketch for a Railway Station at Lorne Park, Port Credit. Elevation, section and plan, no date. Pen on paper. AO, HC:C 11–596–0–1(569).

4.27   Langley & Burke. Summer Cottage at Lorne Park, c.1887. Port Credit, 1887. Perspective, delineated by E. Wilby, c.1887. Pen on linen. AO, HC:C 11–692–0–1(575)1.

4.28   Langley & Burke. Cottage at Lorne Park for Robert McCausland, Esq., Port Credit, 1888. Perspective, and plans, 20 May 1888. Pen on paper. AO, HC:C 11–590–0–1(573).

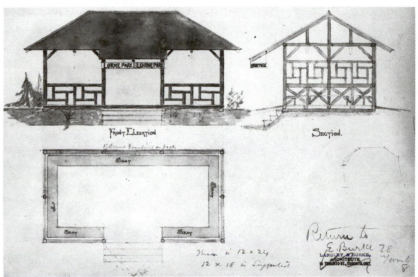

4.27

4.26

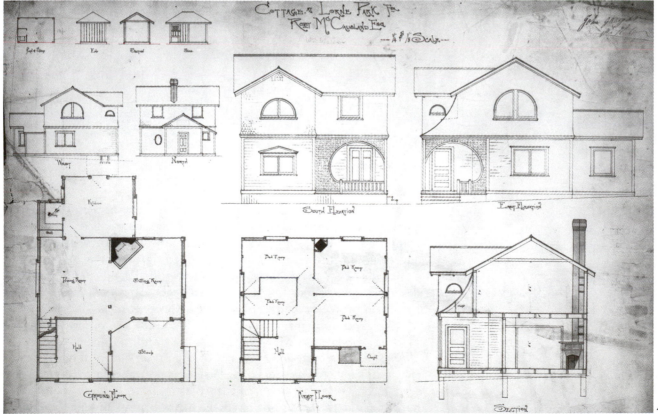

4.28

4.29 Edmund Burke. Cottage at Lorne Park for J. Short McMaster, Port Credit, 1894. Elevations, January 1894. Pen and wash on paper. AO, HC:C 11–20–0–1(22)2.

4.30   Edmund Burke. Cottage at Lorne Park for J. Short McMaster, Port Credit, 1894. Plans, January 1894. Pen and wash on paper. AO, HC:C 11–20–0–1(22)4.

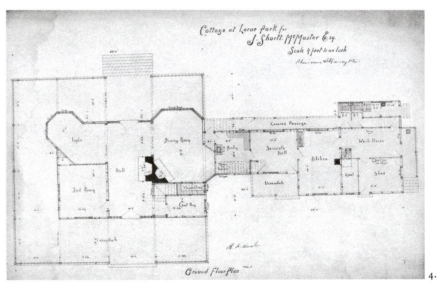

[conforming] less to set rules of art than to general picturesqueness and fitness with the scenery around, and the materials of which it is composed."[86] At Lorne Park the picturesque aesthetic was acknowledged only in the veneration of unspoiled nature, or with the occasional medieval turret translated into wood (fig. 4.27).[87] Just two designs incorporated the unstructured space of a living hall and the free-form profile of American Shingle style; one, of 1888, for Robert McCausland, probably by Horwood (fig. 4.28), the other, by Burke, in 1894, for J. Short McMaster (figs. 4.29 and 4.30).[88]

As a planned community in which the preservation of natural setting assumed significance, Lorne Park was patterned after contemporary garden suburbs such as Bedford Park.[89] Its central "common" harks back to the traditions of village life in Britain and New England where shared lands were set aside for the benefit of all inhabitants. Similar arrangements in the industrial garden cities of Bournville of 1879 and Port Sunlight of 1888 were financed by manufacturers to combat the evils of urban concentration. Improved transportation facilitated an exodus from crowded and uncomfortable cities to rustic retreats that were forerunners of the modern suburb.

SHINGLE STYLE IN EASTERN CANADA

Burke's exploration of American models did not cease with Lorne Park. One year after he entered practice on his own he designed a small, economical residence for a school principal in Grande Ligne, Quebec.[90] Drawings from November 1893 record a modest two-storey structure topped by a gambrel roof, and covered in cut, wooden shingle (fig. 4.31).[91] Inspired perhaps by the shingled gambrel of the Fairbanks house of 1636 in Dedham, Massachusetts (fig. 4.32), the scheme seems to have been drawn from American colonial examples such as those recommended by Boston architect Robert S. Peabody in 1877.[92] Similar forms were also published by Portland architects Stevens & Cobb (fig. 4.33) in a book entitled *Examples of American Domestic Architecture* (1889), which was in the library of W.G. Storm when Burke assumed the practice in 1892.[93]

Some years later Burke & Horwood again used shingled motifs in a series of commissions on the Canadian east coast. Intentionally rustic and redolent of the colonial past, Shingle style was a sophisticated successor to the wooden resort architecture of the first half of the century. Common in Newport, Rhode Island, and other areas along the New England coast, it was readily accepted in the Canadian Maritimes because of the area's geographic and historic ties to the eastern seaboard of the United States.

Burke's links to the Maritimes were forged in 1881 with his marriage to Minnie Black of Sackville, New Brunswick. Years later, after he won the competition to build the Owens Art Museum at Mount Allison University, his partnership was retained for a series of private residential commissions in Sackville and Halifax.[94] The list of patrons includes artist John Hammond, Mrs Burke's brothers F.B. and J.W.S. Black, and Doctor Paisley, all of Sackville, as well as F.W. Green and George S. Campbell, both of Young Avenue in Halifax. Like the Grande Ligne house, these works, all of which predate 1904, are unequivocal in their adoption of American Shingle style.

Chronologically, the Hammond house of 1896 on the campus of Mount Allison University in Sackville is the first commission to have been executed (fig. 4.34).[95] Landscape artist John Hammond had been appointed director of the Owens Art School in Saint John in 1892, and moved to Sackville with the school the following year.[96] In 1899 photographs and plans of a large Shingle-style residence described as the "Hammond house" were published in *Canadian Architect and Builder*.[97] The exterior is a composite of shingled

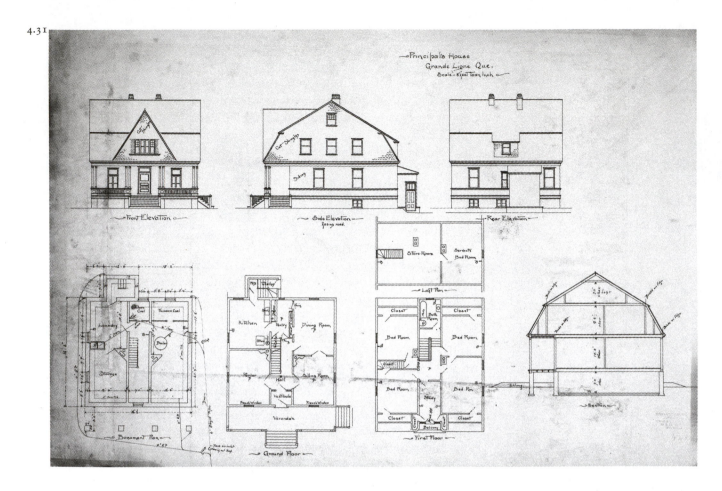

4.31 Edmund Burke. Principal's House, Grande Ligne, Quebec, 1893. Elevations. Pen and wash on paper. AO, HC:C 11-12-0-1 (14)1.

tion of "olive coloured" rubble, an assemblage of disparate units meandering from corner tower to angled bay and bellcast-gambrel. In plan the interior is more cohesive, however, with a large central hall flanked by main reception rooms and the artist's studio at the rear (fig. 4.35).[98] To the south is a kitchen wing, again separated from the dining room by a pantry.[99] The result, unlike the open interior spaces and vast living halls of contemporary American designs, is compact – almost formal in its configuration – a concession, apparently, to the rigours of the Canadian climate.[100]

Among works that followed was a modest cottage in Middle Sackville for Minnie Burke's brother Frank Bunting Black (fig. 4.36).[101] Constructed of blocked boards in the lower storey, the upper level is sheltered by a high pitched roof lit by an unusual pair of shingled turrets. This unique design is related to earlier rustic motifs the firm considered at Lorne Park and for cottages on Toronto Island and elsewhere.[102]

A more elaborate scheme for Captain J. Walter Black, brother and business partner of Frank, was built on an adjacent property.[103] The residence (before a later addition) was a foursquare, hipped-roof design with a single central dormer on each attic face to light the third storey (fig. 4.37). Architectural historian Alan Gowans has described this type of house as fundamentally classical in its cubic symmetrical proportions – a form commonly adopted by mail-order suppliers or prefab houses in the United States as a vernacular version of Shingle style – described in one catalogue as "thoroughly American in architecture ... a house anyone will be proud to identify as 'My Home.'" [104] In this case a two-storey bay enhanced the design as did the striking reddish-brown shingles in the upper storey – the result a sophisticated successor to the resort architecture of Lorne Park.

The last of the Shingle-style commissions in Sackville was a house at 50 York Street built for Doctor Paisley (4.38). [105] Completed prior to 1904 and standing just south of the university, it too bears certain similarities to motifs later popularized by mail-order companies. [106] Twin bays extending through two storeys ripple below a high gable in a manner that invites comparison with the W.G. Low house of 1887 at Bristol, Rhode Island, by McKim, Mead & White (fig. 4.39). Unlike the American example, however, the bays interrupt the shingled facade, instead of undulating beneath it. A final stroke of panache appears in the graceful bellcast over the porch – an elegant culmination of the firm's works in this area.

During the same period the firm also planned two residences on Young Avenue in Halifax. The street, dedicated in 1896, must have been among the earliest examples of controlled development in Canada. Having expended "large sums of money" on building and grading to provide suitable access to a park at the end of Young Avenue, the city council was determined to regulate the surrounding neighbourhood. Not only was the approach to the park to be beautified, but a sewer system and water supply were to be installed at municipal expense. Standards were maintained by enacting a local by-law that provided in part:

No person or persons, company or corporation, shall erect any building or any lot abutting on Young Avenue (so called) or within one hundred and eighty feet of the said Avenue, in the city of Halifax, without first submitting the plans, erections, locations, specifications thereof, and of the material of which said building is to be constructed, and the cost of the said building, to the city council of the said city, and declare the object for which such building is intended ... and no single modern dwelling house shall cost less than five thousand dollars, and no single brick or stone dwelling shall cost less than six thousand dollars. [107]

The by-law also reserved the city's right to expropriate any buildings not in conformity with the stipulated use.

By 1902 there were eight houses on Young Avenue – among them those of city alderman Alfred Whitman and city engineer F.W. Doane. [108] Ample setbacks assured a vista of verdant lawns, and shade trees lined the sidewalk. As one local journalist observed, "Citizens building there must be pretty well fixed financially," and the street was too unique to "fairly be compared with others." [109] Indeed few cities at this date appreciated how much effect legislation might have

4.32 Fairbanks House, Dedham, Massachusetts, 1636 on. Exterior view, 1881. Gelatine print. UofT-RL: *AABN* 10 (26 November 1881): after 260.

4.33 Stevens & Cobb. House of John Calvin Stevens, before 1889. Exterior view. UofT-RL: J.C. Stevens and A.W. Cobb, *Examples of American Domestic Architecture* (New York, 1889), plate vii.

4.32

4.33

in regulating land development, a realization that only dawned with the town planning acts in the early years of the new century.

Among those who moved to Young Avenue shortly after its dedication was Frederick W. Green, local manager of the Confederation Life Association.[110] In 1899 he retained Burke & Horwood to plan a house at the corner of Coburg Road and Oxford Street in Halifax, but

4.34

4.34   Burke & Horwood. Hammond House, Sackville, 1899. Exterior view, 1988. Photograph by Angela Carr.

4.35   Burke & Horwood. Hammond House, Sackville, 1899. Plan of ground floor, 1899. AO, HC:C 11(954a)4.

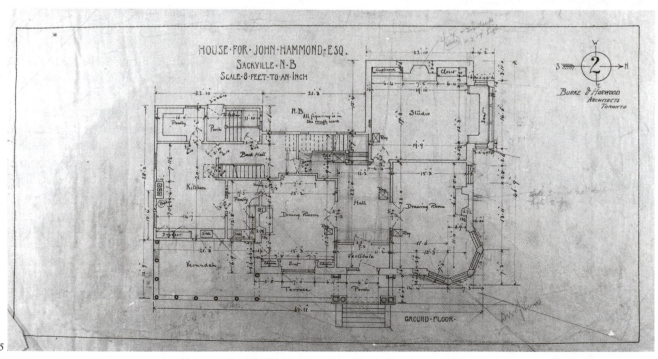

4.35

4.36   Burke & Horwood. Frank B. Black House (now David Silverberg residence), Middle Sackville, before 1904. Exterior view, 1988. Photograph by Angela Carr.

4.37   Burke & Horwood. Captain J. Walter Black House (now Arthur Moyter residence), Middle Sackville, before 1904. Exterior view, after alterations, 1988. Photograph by Angela Carr.

4.38   Burke & Horwood. Doctor Paisley House (now Dr Marion Trenholme residence), Sackville, before 1904. Exterior view 1988. Photograph by Angela Carr.

4.39   McKim, Mead & White. Low House (demolished), Bristol, Rhode Island, 1887. Exterior view, no date. Photograph by Cervin Robinson. HABS:RI, I-BRIST, 18–1.

4.36

4.37

later acquired a lot on the west side of Young Avenue at Atlantic Street in 1899 (fig. 4.40).[111] A large gable and two-storey bay dominate the design, which is covered in cut shingles of various sizes and shapes.[112] Subsequent overpainting has destroyed neither the membranous quality of this fabric nor the lively sense of texture it lends to the surface. Picturesque details such as a belvedere topped by a bellcast roof and a lattice-work veranda complement the simple geometry of the exterior while the interior is deliberately compact.

The residence of George S. Campbell of G.S. Campbell & Co. steamship agents on the opposite side of the street is similar (fig. 4.41). In 1902 Horwood had prepared a number of other proposals, including an all-brick scheme, but Campbell selected the three-storey frame design finished in dark brown shingles. All but one of the elevations consists of a single broad gable with elongated bays.[113] Its brownstained shingles now hidden beneath a layer of homogeneous white siding, the house has lost its original rustic flavour, and the view of the outer harbour it once commanded is obscured by mature trees. But its picturesque garden setting still gives a sense of the pastoral suburbia its legislators were so determined to assure.

In Halifax just as in Toronto, by-laws played a significant role in regulating the materials and motifs chosen by architects. Important, too, was the client's taste, more so perhaps in houses than in any other type of structure; for, as Osborne remarked, "We may, indeed, liken a man's house to his coat, in that the more perfectly it fits the owner the less likely it is to fit anyone else."[114] Burke bemoaned the nuisance of clients, "who have practically no individual tastes or preferences, and who can only explain their requirements by referring to Mr So and So's house as something like what they want."[115] The adaptation of form to function in residential works implied for Burke the fusion of British stylistic precedents and American planning methods. Such a combination, in his mind, represented nothing more or less than a solution appropriate to the problem at hand – the guiding principle implicit in all his works.

4.38

4.39

4.40   Burke & Horwood. Frederick W. Green House, Halifax, 1899. Elevation, 1899. Blueprint and wash on paper. AO, HC:C 11–844–0–1(814a)4.

4.41   Burke & Horwood. George S. Campbell House, Halifax, 1902. Photograph. MTRL-Special Collections: Toronto Architectural Eighteen Club, *Catalogue* (Toronto, 1904), 33.

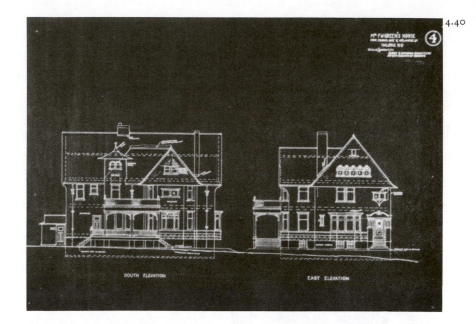

4.40

4.41

5 Institutional Projects: Beauty Grows upon Utility

> We can also make the building fit the practical requirements
> of the organization to be housed, and give the building a
> character that more or less suggests its utilitarian purpose. We
> realize to-day, as we never realized before, the importance
> of this element of giving expression to the innermost character
> of the function a building serves rather than giving it a con-
> ventional, and to a certain extent meaningless architectural
> expression.
>
> Alfred Chapman, "The Development of Architectural Design
> in Canada," *Construction* (October 1917)

Among the many building types with which Burke and his predeces-
sors were concerned, institutional commissions were the least common, probably because of the magnitude of the projects and the
scarcity of public and private endowments. When Ontario was settled
at the end of the eighteenth century, the government declined to enact
poor law legislation and relied on private charities administered by
the churches to care for society's disadvantaged. Toronto General
Hospital only received permanent government funding in the 1870s,
after being closed for an entire year in 1867.[1] Not until the latter half
of the nineteenth century did the proliferating community mission activities of evangelicalism spawn a number of sectarian educational
colleges, the Young Men's Christian Association, and the Women's
Christian Temperence Union – organizations intended to curb vice
and provide a positive foundation for the spiritual growth of the
country's youth.

William Hay's major institutional works were limited to Toronto
General Hospital on Gerrard Street East, of 1855–56, (fig. 5.1), and
the House of Providence on Power Street, of 1855–58, (fig.5.2), the
former replacing a structure built in 1829, the latter a private Roman
Catholic institution to shelter the sick, elderly, and homeless.[2] Both
were practical symmetrical, three-storey buildings with mansarded
pavilions – *Anglo-American Magazine* described Toronto General
Hospital as "old English style" modified to suit the Canadian climate,
with facilities that included running water supplied by reservoirs in
the towers. The addition of water reservoirs (a motif that may have
been borrowed from a scheme by Wyatt & Brandon for St Aidan's
College, Birkenhead [fig. 5.3] published in the *Builder* of 1850) was
a sensible innovation Hay and his successors repeated in many later
examples.[3] Gundry & Langley used a similar idea for Hellmuth
Ladies College in London, Ontario, of 1868 (fig. 5.4), combining both
mansard and Gothic tower. *Canadian Illustrated News* described the

Boys' Home in Toronto, of 1871 (fig. 5.5) more simply as a "plain and substantial" Gothic building in red and white brick with stone dressings.[4]

Burke's institutional commissions were often funded by private patrons or groups connected with the evangelical movement, and while there is consistency among some of the projects, the majority simply reflect the eclecticism of the period and a prudent suitability for the purposes intended. For example, the Toronto Baptist College (later McMaster University) was endowed by Senator William McMaster in 1880 to train students for pastoral, evangelical, missionary or other denominational work. Encouraged by his American-born wife Susan Moulton McMaster, this project succeeded Jarvis Street Baptist Church as part of an initiative to strengthen and centralize the Baptist presence in the province.[5] Langley, Langley & Burke were retained to prepare plans for the new college on Bloor Street West just north of the University of Toronto campus.[6] Advice was provided by the Reverend John Castle, the American incumbent at Jarvis Street Baptist Church whose appointment Mrs McMaster had proposed. Together, Burke and Castle toured similar institutions in the United States to gather ideas for the project.[7]

Toronto colleges were mostly High Victorian Gothic in recognition of the historic link between institutions of learning and the religious community.[8] American models were more diverse, including classical revival, Italianate, Renaissance, and Second Empire as well as the perennial Gothic mode.[9] Among the institutions Burke visited with Dr Castle, stylistic variety was especially marked. Newton Theological Institution at Newton Center, Massachusetts, founded in 1825, housed 700 students in a collection of vernacular, mansarded structures, while the Episcopal Theological College at Cambridge, Massachusetts, of 1866–71, by Ware & Van Brunt was High Victorian Gothic. Brown University at Providence, Rhode Island, on

5.1 William Hay. Toronto General Hospital (demolished), Toronto, 1855–56. Exterior view, 1854. AO:S 1183.

5.2 William Hay. House of Providence (demolished), Toronto, 1855–58. Exterior view, 1855. Lithotint by Courtois. MTRL-BR: John Ross Robertson Collection 308.

5.2

5.1

5.4

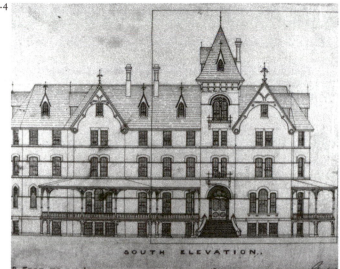

5.3

SOUTH ELEVATION.

5.3 Wyatt & Brandon. St Aiden's College, Birkenhead, 1850. Exterior view, 1850. Engraving. UofT-Sigmund Samuel Library: *Builder* 8 (6 April 1850):163.

5.4 Gundry & Langley. Hellmuth Ladies College (demolished), London, 1868. Exterior view, 1870. MTRL-BR: LC:205.

5.5 Gundry & Langley. Boys' Home (demolished), Toronto, 1871. Exterior view, 1871. AO:S 1182.

5.5

the other hand, combined High Victorian Gothic with classical and vernacular structures.[10]

Burke's synthesis at McMaster Hall is more complex than any of these examples. An irregular facade, animated by corbelled brick oriels and narrow Romanesque arches extending through several storeys, is crowned by a spiky Gothic silhouette (fig. 5.6).[11] Remarkably comparable in feeling to the "indigestible" and "carbolic" Gothic of St Paul's School, Hammersmith, which British architect Alfred Waterhouse was about to undertake in 1881–85, Burke's design also embodies a freewheeling eclecticism associated with the "Queen Anne" movement that Waterhouse emphatically rejected.[12]

Among the more unusual elements of Burke's scheme are the round arches uniting the top three floors of the structure. Examples had appeared in published sources as early as the 1850s, and became entrenched in commercial vocabulary two decades later.[13] But institutional buildings often adhered to the Gothic tradition as was the case with the Chicago Baptist Union Theological Seminary of 1869 (fig. 5.7).[14] Within five years, however, the Romanesque hybrids of American architect Henry Hobson Richardson had created a taste for round arches of every description combined with angular dormers and picturesque towers. Canadian acceptance of the motif is clear by the end of the 1880s in examples like George Durand's Upper Canada College of 1887–91 (fig. 5.8).[15] But in 1880, when Burke was planning McMaster Hall, the idea was a novelty in Canada, and its extension through several floors almost unprecedented.[16] Clearly, therefore, the red-brick-and-sandstone facade testifies to a precocious understanding of nascent developments south of the border.

Despite the building's medieval profile, the plan of McMaster Hall is symmetrical around a central axis (fig. 5.9). A round-arched porch connects with a corridor that bisects the building, providing access to

5.7

5.8

5.7   Chicago Baptist Union Theological
Seminary, Chicago, 1869. Exterior view
1881. McMaster University, Hamilton:
W. Cathcart, *Baptist Encyclopedia*
(Philadelphia, 1881), 212.

5.8   George Durand. Upper Canada College
(demolished), Toronto, 1887–91. Exterior
view, c.1905–15. Photograph. NA:PA 68100.

stairwells, a service wing at the rear, and a transverse passageway connecting all the ground-floor rooms. On the main level are six classrooms, four on the west side, two on the east. A chapel and library, originally at the east end, are identified on the exterior by angular projections that disrupt the regularity of the facade. On the upper floors were generous accommodations for forty-seven students – two bedrooms grouped with a sitting room occupying the same area alloted to a classroom on the main level.

In 1887, after the Toronto Baptist College received its charter as a university, William McMaster died suddenly; he was followed three years later by the Reverend John Castle.[17] A generous endowment assured the survival of the institution, and in 1893 a major new addition was contemplated. Burke, now in practice on his own, threw himself into the project with vigour.[18] Plans were drawn for a new wing to the west of the college (fig. 5.10). The project – later shelved – included a low cubic chapel in Romanesque style adjacent to the main structure (fig. 5.11). Its compact, well-proportioned geometry resembled a scheme recently prepared for McMaster's sister institution in Woodstock (of which more will be said shortly).

Eventually, in 1900, the long-anticipated expansion of McMaster University began with the addition of Castle Memorial Hall, housing a library and assembly room, to the east of the original building.[19] Although its broad, uniformly rough-hewn stone facade was intended to harmonize with the stone dressings of the main structure (fig. 5.12), the result is an unexpected contrast with the predominating darkened brick in the gaunt, angular main building.[20]

Prior to the establishment of the more central Toronto Baptist College, the denomination's educators had set up the Canadian Literary Institute in Woodstock, in 1857. Later known as Woodstock College, it provided higher education to Baptists throughout the province and to others wishing to study in a "Christian setting."[21] The first buildings were destroyed by fire in 1861 and rebuilt the following year in a neoclassical vernacular by local architect David White.[22] In

5.6   Langley, Langley & Burke. McMaster
Hall (now Royal Conservatory of Music),
Toronto, 1880. Perspective, possibly
J.C.B. Horwood, c.1880. Pen and wash on
paper. AO, HC:C 11–632–0–2(622)1.

5.6

5.9 Langley, Langley & Burke. McMaster Hall (now Royal Conservatory of Music), Toronto, 1880. Floor plans, 1880. Pen on paper. AO, HC:C 11–632–0–1(611)18.

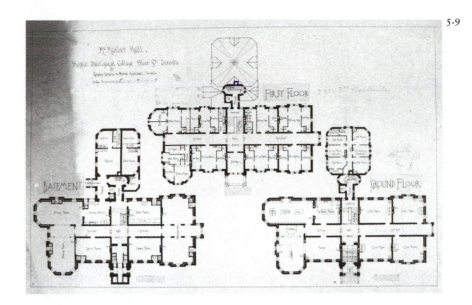

1871 the Langley firm planned additions to these old structures, and in 1886 was again retained to design a new dining hall and art room complex for the growing community of scholars.[23]

A perspective by Horwood from 1886 records a two-storey, round-arched building (fig. 5.13) sandwiched between existing neoclassical blocks. Its red brick facade was dominated by a large Romanesque doorway while a clerestory on the upper level lighted the college's art rooms. Ornamental brickwork contributed to the texture of the exte-

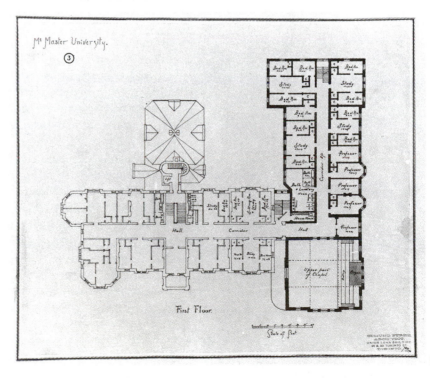

5.10 Edmund Burke. McMaster University (now Royal Conservatory of Music), Toronto, 1880. Plan of projected addition, 5 January 1894 (not built). Pen and wash on paper. AO, HC:C 11–8–0–1(2)3.

5.11   Edmund Burke. McMaster University
(now Royal Conservatory of Music),
Toronto, 1880. Projected perspective, no
date. Pencil and wash on paper. AO, HC:C
11–8–0–1(2)6.

5.11

McMaster University.

rior; inside, cast-iron columns supported the wooden floors of the
upper gallery. By this time the acceptance of American Romanesque
revival was unequivocal, and its aesthetic assimilation was parallelled
in the technical field by a willingness to experiment with new materials and methods.[24]

Among the improvements at Woodstock College was a sub-surface
drainage system Edmund Burke described in the first article he published in the newly founded *Canadian Architect and Builder*.[25] He
detailed how a British cleric had invented a method of expelling
household wastes into the ground through a system of porous tiles in
1864. A similar scheme installed at the college dealt with waste water,
but did not provide for water-closets. As Burke pointed out, however,
the same technology could have been adapted for that purpose. This
practical, unglamourous approach underscores Burke's affinity for
the technical aspects of his calling, in contrast to his partner's preoc-
cupation with artistic excellence.

The patronage of another educational institution came Burke's way
in 1892 when he assumed the practice of the late William George
Storm. Among Storm's long-time clients was The Law Society of
Upper Canada, the professional licensing organization for the province's lawyers, which was and is headquartered in the east wing of
Osgoode Hall in Toronto.[26] When the Law Society decided to make
alterations to its offices in 1893, Burke and a number of other architects were invited to make submissions.[27] His successful scheme
involved the addition of a skylight to the stairhall of the east

5.12 Burke & Horwood. Castle Memorial Hall, McMaster University (now Royal Conservatory of Music), Toronto, 1900–2. Exterior view, 1902. Photograph. MTRL-Special Collections: Toronto Architectural Eighteen Club, *Catalogue* (Toronto, 1902), 95.

5.13 Langley & Burke. Woodstock College (demolished), Woodstock, 1857. Perspective of the dining hall addition, initialled by J.C.B. Horwood, 1886. Pen on paper. AO, HC:C 11–526–0–3(595)1.

5.12

5.13

5.14

5.14   Edmund Burke. Osgoode Hall,
Toronto, 1829 on. American Room, 1894.
AO, HC:C 11, Additional 5.

5.15   Edmund Burke. Owens Art Museum,
Sackville, New Brunswick, 1893–95.
Exterior view, no date. Photograph. Mount
Allison University Archives, Sackville:
Picture Collection, Folder 87, no. 000038.

wing as well as the replacement of various windows, doors, and balustrades.[28]

Following the completion of the Osgoode Hall renovation project, which required careful blending with the existing Palladian design, Burke was also retained for an addition to the law library. Assisted by draughtsman Melville P. White, whose brother, Murray A. White, later became a partner in the firm, Burke planned a lavishly panelled and galleried annex known as the American Room (the room containing volumes concerned with U.S. law) in one of the building's existing light wells (fig. 5.14). Ornamented by a coved plaster ceiling and stained glass skylight, the Renaissance-style saloon was still in the planning stages when Horwood returned from New York in 1894.[29] Horwood's affinity for Italianate ornament and his knowledge of structural ironwork (an undoubted asset he had learned in the U.S.), metal technology, and the cabinetmaker's art were combined to create what is still a fitting complement to Cumberland & Storm's masterfully executed central block of 1856–60.

Burke devised an equally refined and innovative scheme in 1893 for a museum at Sackville's Mount Allison University after the university made a successful bid for the art collection of Saint John shipbuilder John Owen. Land adjacent to the campus was acquired for the purpose, and a competition held in which six sets of plans were received

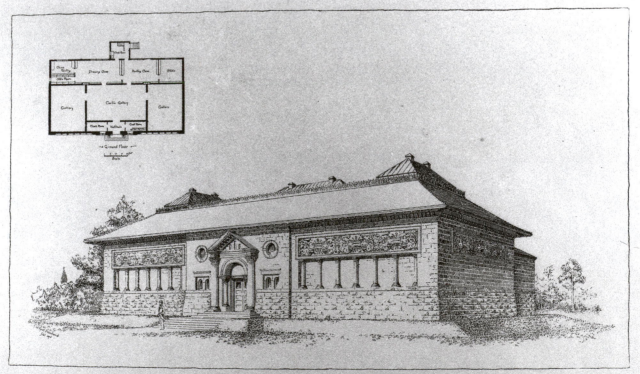

ART INSTITUTE, MOUNT ALLISON LADIES' COLLEGE, SACKVILLE, N.B.
EDMUND BURKE, ARCHITECT, TORONTO.

5.15

from four architects. The committee considered the two designs judged to be the best and recommended the adoption of one bearing the motto "Unique." As it turned out, this was Burke's submission.[30]

The architect evidently heard about the competition from his father-in-law, a member of the university's board of regents. Determined to make a good showing, Burke conceived an elegant Beaux-Arts scheme inspired by recent developments in the United States (fig. 5.15). Newly established American architectural schools adopted many ideas from the Ecole in Paris,[31] and academic vocabulary was also taken up by American firms like McKim, Mead & White of New York, who introduced the new vogue in 1883 with Henry Villard's Renaissance *palazzo* on Fifth Avenue. By 1891 the same architects had also completed plans for the Walker Art Gallery at Bowdoin College in Brunswick, Maine, and the Howard Whittemore Memorial Library in Naugatuck, Connecticut. Rotch & Tilden's I.D. Farnsworth School of Art of 1888 in Wellesley, Massachusetts (fig. 5.16), was a related and still earlier example of Beaux-Arts as was the Robbins Memorial Library of 1890 at Arlington, Massachusetts by Cabot, Everett & Mead. The ultimate triumph of the Ecole in America came in 1893 – the very year Burke undertook his commission – when the Court of Honour at the World's Columbian Exhibition in Chicago was laid out according to its principles of design (fig. 5.17). For two decades thereafter Beaux-Arts remained one of the most influential forces in American architecture.[32]

The Owens Art Museum in Sackville is built on a hillside overlooking the town. Its hermetic stone exterior of olive-coloured sandstone from the Cumberland basin is relieved only by blind colonnades, terra-cotta reliefs, and a central door framed by an aedicule – a severity reminiscent of the mausoleum at Halicarnassus. Rusticated foundations with an angular batter emphasize the ground-hugging profile that originally sheltered beneath a broad bellcast roof crested with wrought iron. Galleries lit by skylights were symmetri-

5.16 Rotch & Tilden. I.D. Farnsworth School of Art, Wellesley, Massachusetts, 1888. Exterior view, 1888. UofT-RL: *AABN* 23 (28 April 1888): no. 643.

5.17 Court of Honour, World's Columbian Exposition, Chicago, 1893. Exterior view, 1893. Photograph by H.J. Woodside. NA:PA 16048.

5.16

5.17

5.18   Burke & Horwood. Men's Residence
Building, Mount Allison University,
Sackville, New Brunswick, 1899–1900.
Exterior view, no date. Photograph.
Mount Allison University Archives, Sackville:
Picture Collection, Folder 92, no. 000083.

5.19   Burke & Horwood. Jarius Hart Hall,
Mount Allison University, Sackville, New
Brunswick, 1909. Exterior view, south side,
no date. Photograph by Mackiel. Mount
Allison University Archives, Sackville: Picture
Collection, Folder 80, no. 000969, acc.
7767/7.

5.18

5.19

cally arranged in the body of the structure while art classes were
housed at the rear, where large windows overlook the campus.[33]

Encircling the facade of the museum are a series of decorative terra-
cotta panels, which bear the names of famous artists. This takes a leaf
from Henri Labrouste's Bibliothèque Ste-Geneviève in Paris, which in
turn was reprised by Shepley, Rutan & Coolidge in their 1892 design
for the Art Institute of Chicago.[34] Unprecedented in any of Burke's
previous work, his abrupt shift to Beaux-Arts models indicates how
deeply his visits to the United States had affected him.[35] The choice
of stylistic vocabulary was an astute one, fixing upon the very associations that were to dominate American museum architecture for the
next two decades.

Other commissions executed for Mount Allison University take a
very different path. In sharp contrast to the museum's smooth-dressed
texture was the rugged, red Sackville Freestone used by the same firm
for two residence buildings on campus. Burke & Horwood were retained to reconstruct the first of these on the foundations of an earlier
structure destroyed by fire in 1899 (fig. 5.18). The firm erected a four-
storey, quarry-faced sandstone building with projecting pavilions decorated by brick-lined Romanesque arches. Two asymmetrical towers
with exaggerated bellcast roofs were added to house water reservoirs,
but their location (apparently determined by the original foundations)
impaired the regularity of the building's profile.[36] The result was a
cocktail of astylar practicality and eclecticism that lacked the conceptual cohesiveness of Burke's decade-old Toronto Baptist College.

Burke & Horwood continued to work intermittently in Sackville,
adding a brick extension to the rear of the original wood-frame college building in 1903–4.[37] Then in 1906–9 the firm undertook a second residence known as Jarius Hart Hall (fig. 5.19). This time the

functional astylar design made the most of the rustic red sandstone fabric.[38] In a series of picturesque freehand drawings that bear the hallmarks of Horwood's hand, the four-storey, L-shaped block appears with its quarry-cut profile punctuated by oriels, angled bays, and contrasting rusticated reveals. A high cottage roof covered with oxidized sheet copper complements the rough-textured red of the walls. And careful integration with the hilltop setting contributes to what *Allisonia* described as the "unexpected beauty of Hart Hall."[39]

The Mount Allison commissions traversed the spectrum from Beaux-Arts to freehand vernacular, and the Toronto works of the same period reflect an equally significant transition from historicist themes to a more liberal interpretation of architectural expression. In the closing years of the century, the firm returned again to Romanesque. When the Toronto Conservatory of Music announced plans for its first building at the corner of University Avenue and College Street (opposite Queen's Park) in 1897, Burke & Horwood were the architects of the unusual round-arched design executed in purple brick with red-brick quoins and reveals (fig. 5.20).[40] Consisting of a concert hall as well as an adjoining block of practice studios and offices, the music-hall portion resembled a chapel, its front gable facing the street. A corbel-table outlined the ridge, and at the centre was a large round-arched window framed by prominent brick reveals, the leaded panes subdivided by arcs of Tuscan tracery. On either side were a pair of oculi circled by brick reveals and accented by prominent keys.

On the west, adjoining the concert hall of the Music Academy, was a three-storey brick ell housing offices and classrooms, its symmetrical cubic form topped by an overhanging hipped roof typical of domestic Italianate models. The chief ornamental feature was a bandcourse demarcating an attic lined by small round-arched windows. On the outer flank was a pavilion with continuous Romanesque arches running through the lower two floors, the same motif later repeated in the Sackville residence of 1899, already described.

Recalling the styles of the mid-century inspired by German *Rundbogenstil*, such motifs were variously identified in the North American context as Lombard, Romanesque, Italianate, and Byzantine. European *émigrés* like Leopold Eidlitz had introduced the round arch in the United States in the 1850s. His contemporary and competitor James Renwick chose Romanesque for the Smithsonian Institution of 1846, in Washington, its vocabulary evocative of monastic repositories of ancient learning (fig. 5.21). Horwood, who had worked in Renwick's office during his tenure in New York, was undoubtedly familiar with this early scheme, and may have thought its associations with Italy appropriate for an institution founded on principles established by the first Academy of Art in Florence in the sixteenth century.[41]

Rather more exotic was the chateauesque motif Burke & Horwood adopted for the Toronto Bible Training School of 1898 on College Street (fig. 5.22).[42] Established by the Reverend Elmore Harris, who

5.20

5.20 Burke & Horwood. Conservatory
of Music (demolished), Toronto, 1897 on.
Exterior view, no date. Photograph by
Micklethwaite. NA:RD 339.

5.21 James Renwick. Smithsonian
Institution, Washington, 1846. Exterior
view, 1860s. Photograph. HABS:Z62–12780,
413470.

5.21

5.22

5.22   Burke & Horwood. Bible Training School (demolished), Toronto, 1898. Exterior view, no date. Photograph. (AO: Acc. 15081–37).

5.23   Richard Morris Hunt. William Kissam Vanderbilt House, New York, 1879–81. Exterior view. Photograph. HABS:Z62–592225, 413470.

had commissioned Walmer Road Baptist Church some years earlier, the school prepared the laiety for foreign and home missionary work that emphasized a more fundamentalist stance than was accepted by the liberal sectarian colleges.[43] Stylistically the building reflected Horwood's fascination with the ornamental architecture of New York (fig. 5.23).[44] A similar project for the T.M. Harris house on St George Street entered under Horwood's name in the first exhibition of the Toronto Architectural Eighteen in 1901, was rejected by Mrs Harris in favour a comfortable Arts and Crafts scheme, perhaps in recognition that what passed for picturesque in a college might appear pretentious in a private residence.[45]

Despite its facade, the Bible Training School was by no means exclusively French in derivation. Attached to the chateauesque front was a longitudinal extension arranged like a church with a nave and transepts. A series of half-timbered dormers ornamented the exterior (fig. 5.24), while on the inside a central corridor provided access to a lecture hall in the body of the building. Walls were of brick, and an open-timber roof lent an air of rustic medievalism to the interior (fig. 5.25). In the transepts were classrooms linked to the main lecture hall by folding doors. Even more than the Walmer Road Church, this structure brought together a seemingly irreconcilable collection of motifs drawn from the Beaux-Arts and the Arts and Crafts – a synthesis of the type William S. Maxwell believed should encompass "that which is good and suitable in Great Britain [while leaving] ourselves open to the many excellent influences which emanate from France and other countries."[46]

In sharp contrast to the florid vocabulary of the Bible Training School was the Dominion Meteorological building of 1906–9 on

5.23

5.24

5.25

5.24   Burke & Horwood. Bible Training
School (demolished), Toronto. Exterior
view from the side, no date. Photograph. AO:
Acc. 15081–40.

5.25   Burke & Horwood. Bible Training
School (demolished), Toronto. Interior
view, no date. Photograph. AO: Acc.
15081–38.

Bloor Street near McMaster Hall (fig. 5.26).[47] Now the Admissions
Office for the University of Toronto, the conventional three-storey
structure was intended as a successor to Cumberland & Storm's
Royal Magnetic and Meteorological Observatory of 1855, which
occupied a site required by the University of Toronto for a new
physics building.[48] As a guide the federal Department of Works
forwarded plans by Chief Architect David Ewart from its Dominion
Observatory, of 1899, in Ottawa.[49] Burke & Horwood in turn
adopted the rough-hewn masses of Ewart's design right down to the
tower resembling a medieval battlement. The scheme went to observatory officials for approval, and the project finally proceeded early in
1908 at an estimated cost of $90,000.[50]

Boulders and quicksand impeding the progress of the excavation
for the foundations of the new observatory added $300 to the cost of
the work. A further problem arose when consultants discovered that
a taller tower would be required for the successful operation of the tel-
escope. Neither issue significantly delayed completion of the project,
however. The structure was finished the following year – its exterior
in the same olive-coloured Miramichi sandstone as the Owens Art
Museum in Sackville. This time, however, rusticated rather than
dressed stone was used throughout, the angled batter at the base of
the tower enhancing the already cyclopean sense of mass. A single-
storey Romanesque arch and sculpted tympanum bearing the coat of
arms of Canada marks the entrance while floral capitals with impish
gargoyles frame the door (5.27). Yet the overall sense of the building
is not ornate: the square-headed windows are simple in comparison
to the Italianate embellishments of Cumberland & Storm's work, al-

though modillions at the cornice-line indicate some reference to the predecessor. Like Burke's design for Trinity Methodist Church and Horwood's for Jarius Hart Hall in Sackville (undertaken as the observatory commission ended), the structure's expression consists almost entirely in the fortresslike quality of its rugged exterior.[51]

A further distinction is apparent between the ponderous Dominion Observatory and a curtain-walled scheme for the Royal College of Dental Surgeons (now the School of Architecture and Landscape Architecture of the University of Toronto) by Burke, Horwood & White in 1908 (fig. 5.28). Located at the corner of College and Huron Streets, the four-storey commercial *palazzo* is faced in red brick with grey stone dressings. Originally eight bays by six before an extensive addition by Molesworth, West & Secord in 1919, the former Dental College consists of an elevated basement ornamented with channelled brickwork, the upper termination of which is marked by a stone bandcourse that meets the main door-frame at the level of the imposts. This lower level is in turn surmounted by two floors faced in brick – forming a base for a superstructure of piers extending through the upper storeys to an overhanging cornice.[52] Verticality is balanced by horizontal layering in a manner reminiscent of New York's commercial vernacular after its exposure to ideas from Chicago.[53]

Again, decorative details are few on the former Royal College of Dental Surgeons. *Diamante* blocks mark the voussoirs over the door, and flanking pilasters are ornamented with stylized geometric tassels, anticipating by well over a decade the angularities of Art Deco

5.27

5.26 Burke & Horwood. Dominion Meteorological Building (now Admissions Office, University of Toronto), Toronto, 1906–10. Exterior view, no date. Photograph by Peake & Whittingham, Toronto. NA:PA 68098.

5.27 Burke & Horwood. Dominion Meteorological Building (now Admissions Office, University of Toronto), Toronto, 1906–10. Detail of front door, 1924. Gelatin silver print. MTRL: Acc. X65–80.

5.26

(fig. 5.29). The pattern – so remarkably advanced for its period – must have been inspired by the machine-cut ornament of Frank Lloyd Wright, as are the toothed mullion heads below the cornice that obviously resemble those of Wright's Unity Temple of 1907.

The interior of the former Dental College was fireproofed with cast-iron framing encased in concrete.[54] Economic and practical, the modern post-and-lintel system meant that large areas of glass could be introduced throughout the structure without any sacrifice of safety. The building's laboratories and offices benefitted from natural light that provided optimal working conditions for the students (fig. 5.30).

5.29

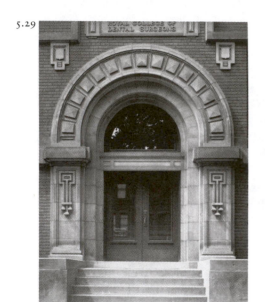

5.28

5.28   Burke, Horwood & White. Royal College of Dental Surgeons (now School of Architecture and Landscape Architecture), Toronto, 1908. Exterior view, no date. Photograph. University of Toronto Archives, Toronto, A65–0004/030, no. 100.61.

5.29   Burke, Horwood & White. Royal College of Dental Surgeons (now School of Architecture and Landscape Architecture), Toronto, 1908. Detail of front door frame, no date. Photograph. University of Toronto Archives, Toronto, A65–0004/030, no. 100.2.

5.30   Burke, Horwood & White. Royal College of Dental Surgeons (now School of Architecture and Landscape Architecture), Toronto, 1908. Interior view, no date. Photograph. University of Toronto Archives, Toronto, A65–0004/030, no. 100.18.

5.30

Indeed the commercial-style building had long been accepted as a suitable format for dental colleges for this very reason: in the 1890s the New York College of Dentistry was housed in such a building on East 23rd Street.[55]

Beginning in the second decade of the twentieth century Burke, Horwood & White returned to more traditional motifs in a series of commissions for the Young Men's Christian Association – the style this time described variously as "colonial" or "Georgian." Used in American residential works by the New York firm of McKim, Mead & White, who reintroduced it on Commonwealth Avenue in Boston in the late 1880s and early 1890s, the red brick and contrasting white-columned porticoes recalled the city's earlier Federalist designs. McKim, Mead & White later adopted the style for a series of New York clubhouses early in the twentieth century.[56]

In Toronto the Young Men's Christian Association began prayer meetings in rented premises in the 1850s, but later erected a building to house its mission work and Bible classes. The Toronto firm of Smith & Gemmell was hired in 1872 to design Shaftesbury Hall at the corner of Queen and James Streets, a project executed in the then fashionable Second Empire mode. Its modest facilities included a reading room, a lecture hall, classrooms, and committee rooms on the upper levels, while a gymnasium – considered the very latest innovation – was located in the basement.[57]

Within fifteen years the structure was considered inadequate, and the Toronto firm of Gordon & Helliwell undertook another mansard-roofed structure, this time with Flemish gables, at the corner of Yonge and McGill Streets. An entire wing was given over to gymnasium facilities, including a running track, bowling alley, and small swimming bath – all to capture the attention of young people who might otherwise be distracted by the more unsavory temptations of city life.[58] While the function of the building was very much in keeping with the commitment to fitness championed by the American Association, its exterior constituted a distinct departure from the Romanesque Revival that had been the first choice for YMCA branches in the United States throughout the 1880s.[59]

Only in 1889 did Gordon & Helliwell adopt the American vogue for their West End Y at the corner of Queen West and Dovercourt. This weighty Richardsonian structure, including a tower, dormers, and corner turret, was executed in red brick and brownstone. Its gymnasium also boasted an unsupported span of forty-six by sixty-two feet carried on iron girders – an indication that American technology was making inroads in Canada.[60]

At the same period the Montreal Association not only built a new Richardsonian building to replace an existing Gothic revival structure but awarded the commission to an American architectural firm into the bargain. Fuller & Wheeler of Albany, New York, were retained at a time when Canadian architects were said to lack familiarity with recent technical advances. A palpable sense of nemesis greeted the news that a collapse had occurred during construction when frost in the brickwork weakened a supporting iron column. Speculation also had it that an error in the placement of the column had contributed to the failure.[61]

The variable quality of American architectural practice was confirmed by Horwood's reports of New York in 1891 citing "the most awful piece of rubble work [he had] ever seen or even heard of" in a prestigious location on Eighth Avenue right against Central Park.[62] Canadian patrons (including the YMCA) continued to employ Americans, however, on the assumption that previous experience would have acquainted them with innovative styles and technology. After two decades the province's architects were still raising questions about the problem. Henry B. Gordon (whose firm had designed two buildings for the YMCA in Toronto) pointed out that American architects also used American materials and apparatus, thereby depriving local suppliers. Possibly referring to the selection of Jackson & Rosencranz of New York as architects for the new YMCA in Ottawa, Gordon noted that all recently erected and proposed Association structures in Canada had been planned by a single American firm. As a former YMCA architect himself, he complained: "It may be true that there are architects in the United States who have more experience than our Canadian architects have, but it would be foolish to say that we have not the architects who are equal to the task of planning buildings that involve intricate problems of infinitely greater magnitude than do YMCA structures." He added that it was poor business and poorer loyalty to pass by those in the community where an institution acquired its wealth and employ outsiders. Such decisions were insulting, he said, to the profession in Ontario, and detrimental to its progress.[63]

Whether or not the complaints had any effect, Burke, Horwood & White were appointed architects for a Toronto-wide YMCA building campaign in 1910.[64] In the United States in the intervening years, YMCA building committees had moved decisively away from the Romanesque, choosing instead the neo-Georgian "*palazzo*" mode.[65] It was this vocabulary to which Burke, Horwood & White fell heir in 1910, much as Gordon & Helliwell had with the Richardsonian Romanesque twenty years earlier.

Two new premises were undertaken almost immediately, one on Broadview Avenue in the east end, and a second at College and Dovercourt replacing the old West End Y. *Contract Record* specifically named Burke as the architect, but at this stage in his career the senior partner was acting as an office manager and had little to do with the design process.

The Broadview scheme was a small, three-storey structure of red brick (fig. 5.31), its plainness relieved by a stone bandcourse above the level of the foundations and a cornice encircling the building below the uppermost parapet. A small porch flanked by Tuscan columns of "cement stone" protected the entrance, while a tympanum bearing a YMCA crest decorated the central window on the second floor. On the interior a lobby lined by administration offices led to a large gymnasium at the rear. A swimming pool, billiard room, and bowling alley

5.31   Burke, Horwood & White. Broadview
YMCA (demolished), Toronto, 1911.
Exterior view, 20 November 1955.
Photograph by J.V. Salmon.
MTRL:SI–3384A.

5.32   Burke, Horwood & White. West End
YMCA, Toronto, 1911. Perspective, 1911.
Watercolour on board. (AO, HC:C 11,
perspectives).

5.31

5.32

5.34

5.33 McKim, Mead & White. Colony Club, New York, 1907–8. Exterior view. Photograph. Museum of the City of New York, New York: 90.44.1.396, McKim, Mead and White Collection.

5.34 Burke, Horwood & White. Women's Christian Temperence Union Building, Toronto, 1911. Exterior view. Photograph. AO, HC:C 11, Additional 5.

5.33

occupied the basement, while the second floor housed an auxiliary gymnasium and classrooms. Residential accommodations were provided on the top floor.

Construction described the result as a typical YMCA, noting the general similarity to such buildings in the United States: "From [Solon S.] Beman [of Chicago] to Burke, Horwood & White, who are among the most successful designers of these structures, there is a marked similarity of design."[66] Yet the journal denied this was imitation, claiming that the plain brick facade, the regularity of the windows, and the practical cornice were an expression of the organization's plain, dignified, and beneficial purposes.

The consulting architects, Shattuck & Hussey of Chicago, supplied a copy of the second floor plan from their YMCA scheme for Hannibal, Missouri, on 28 December 1910 after the Toronto firm had completed the first phase of the Broadview design.[67] It was neither the first nor last time that Burke, Horwood & White would look to American consultants for information. Indeed, it was probably their knowledge of the expertise available and their willingness to establish appropriate contacts in such situations that led to their frequent employment on technically demanding projects.

A month after the tenders were advertised for Broadview, Burke, Horwood & White signed the contract for a new West End YMCA at College and Dovercourt (fig. 5.32). Plans again called for a three-storey red-brick building with an elevated basement and bandcourses of Indiana limestone, but this time the facade was stepped forward at either end to create pavilions. In the presentation drawing the attic is rendered in a lighter shade with a cornice intersecting below the terminal parapet, but no such distinction is evident in the executed structure.[68]

Described as "colonial" in the published reports of the day, the mode adopted for the West End Y produced a work of modest scale and residential proportions. From the Colony Club of 1908 on Madison Avenue by McKim, Mead & White the building borrowed a blind arcade and contrasting keystones (fig. 5.33) while the classical doorframe and stone reveals were a modest parallel to the same firm's Harvard Club of 1900 on West 44th Street. This format was so widely accepted by the Association's architects from Massachusetts to Illinois that by 1910 it was virtually canonical for all YMCA buildings throughout the United States.[69]

The organization sought to appeal to young men by combining the "elements of a social club, an athletic club, a school, a church, and a hotel," and facilities were increasingly consistent between one branch and another – the ubiquitous swimming pool and gymnasium reflecting a growing commitment to physical fitness as the opiate of spiritual equanimity. In the service of this goal the architects Burke, Horwood & White prided themselves on their orderly and efficient planning that eliminated all unnecessary travel within the building.[70]

For the Women's Christian Temperance Union (WCTU), Burke, Horwood & White adopted the same vocabulary. The organization, founded in Fredonia, New York, in 1873 (and established the following year at Owen Sound) to combat the evils of alcohol, had chapters across the continent. Toronto WCTU headquarters were for a time located at 56 Elm Street, but in 1910, at the height of its campaigns for prohibition, women's suffrage, and mother's allowances, the organization decided to build a new and larger premises.[71] Chester Massey and Mrs Massey Treble offered to donate $25 thousand toward a new building if the membership would undertake to match the amount. The old site was sold to finance Willard Hall, named in honour of the first secretary and organizer of the WCTU in the United States. Construction of the red-brick exterior detailed in stone began in September of 1911 (fig. 5.34). Substantially similar to the West End Y, but described this time as "Georgian," the building was narrower and deeper, incorporating two-storey angled bays on either side of a white wooden portico.[72]

The facilities included a gymnasium in the basement, a dining hall and a large assembly hall divisible into a series of smaller lodge rooms on the main floor, as well as residential quarters for one hundred girls on the two floors above. Rooms were finished in oak, ash, and mahoganized birch for durability. The architects were proud to announce that the cost of the completed structure was a mere $0.165 per square foot. The building was so successful that another storey was added in 1921 along with an addition containing a swimming pool.[73]

At this time Burke, Horwood & White were also asked to plan a YMCA for Brantford. Again they erected a red-brick building, this time four storeys high (fig. 5.35). The design drew together features of all the earlier projects including flanking pavilions, horizontal bandcourses, angled bays, and blind arches while windows on the upper floors were accented by stone voussoirs.[74]

5.35

5.36

5.35   Burke, Horwood & White. YMCA
Building, Brantford, 1911–12.
Photograph. AO, HC:C 11, Additional 5.

5.36   Burke, Horwood & White. Central
YMCA Building (demolished), Toronto,
1912. Exterior view. Photograph. AO, HC:C
11, Additional 5.

All this proved to be a dress rehearsal for a far larger undertaking
on behalf of the Toronto Association in August 1911. Parlia-
mentarian W.A. Kemp, chairman of the building committee and long-
time client of Burke's, announced plans for a new Central YMCA to
extend right through the lot between College and Grenville Streets, its
facilities to "rival any on the continent." Construction of the firm's
four-storey, red-brick design began the following April (fig. 5.36).
Again in the "Georgian" mode, wide pavilions emphasized by stone
quoins broke the monotony of the lengthy facade, while contrasting
keystones in the central section also contributed a restless, busy effect
to an otherwise subdued motif. A stone cornice detailed with modillions and dentils encircled the structure below the parapet, providing
additional emphasis.

On the interior the architects strove for a convenient and comfortable "homelike atmosphere," rejecting extravagant or gaudy treatment in favour of a plainness intended to "bespeak the lofty ideals for
which the association stands."[75] Indeed the only evidence of luxury
was the marble-lined entrance and steps. By contrast the main lobby
was fitted with simple wooden pillars of quarter-sawn oak and sturdy
leather furniture modelled on Arts and Crafts designs (fig. 5.37).

In the athletic facilities, too, practicality was paramount with buff-
brick walls assuring minimal maintenance. Separate gymnasia were
provided on the ground floor for men and boys. A palm room with
a skylight added a lavish touch to the pool area in the basement. Also
on the lower floor were five regulation bowling alleys and a billiard
room with seven tables (fig. 5.38). The top two floors, which were
served by an extensive telephone system connected through the main
desk, offered residential accommodation for 187. Within the confines
of the institutional agenda, occupants' comfort was well provided.

Williams & Cole, engineers for the building, were proud to report
that the mechanical equipment was comparable to the best of its kind

5.37

5.38

5.37   Burke, Horwood & White. Central
YMCA Building (demolished), Toronto,
1912. Lobby. Photograph. AO, HC:C 11,
Additional 5.

5.38   Burke, Horwood & White. Central
YMCA Building (demolished), Toronto,
1912. Bowling alleys. Photograph. AO, HC:C
11, Additional 5.

in America. A private power plant generated all the heat, light, and power necessary for the entire building, and ventilation was by forced air filtered from the outside. Water for the showers and swimming pool was steam heated, as was the building itself. In addition centrifugal pumps kept a steady supply of water circulating in the pool.

Construction closed its discussion of the new Central Y with a list of specifications for a modern Association building previously published by Walter Mabie Wood in the American journal *Brickbuilder*.[76] The facilities and activities, he said, must be inviting enough to assure a constituency regardless of other leisure-time events. Costs must be kept to a minimum to appeal to a maximum number of people. Furthermore, buildings should withstand heavy usage and be designed for safe operation by few people. Plans should also provide for future growth by accommodating subsequent remodelling or additions without major disruptions to existing premises. As another American writer on the subject observed, the YMCA system in the past decade had undergone a revolution.[77] It was time for Canadian architects to partake of that change. By adopting the formulaic neo-Georgian motif of their American competitors, Canadians declared themselves the professional equals of their southern neighbours. Along with vocabulary they mastered the demanding technical elements of these designs, assuring credibility through able emulation of their American competitors.

6 Commercial Architecture: The Langley Years and the Simpson Store

> Architecture is not a system of incoherently uttered and illogically occuring fashions ... Architecture is the material expression in stone and iron and brick, of an idea, dominating, consistent, coherent.
>
> "What Architecture is and What it is Not," CAB
> (February 1888)

In January 1894 Toronto architect R.W. Gambier-Bousfield addressed the fifth annual convention of the Ontario Association of Architects (OAA) on "The Construction of Shop Fronts During the Next Decade." He expressed the view that glass and iron or steel would be most appropriate for future commercial structures because "the requirements of trade necessitated in a good many branches the exhibition of wares and stock on every floor." Citing a clothing store on King Street East known as Oak Hall, just built in 1893 (fig. 6.1), and an unidentified building on Bay Street south of Wellington as examples where "the whole front of the building was gradually becoming a front of plate glass," he dismissed traditional load bearing construction as unsuitable because it limited both window area and floor space.[1]

Fellow architect William R. Gregg, commenting upon the presentation, added that "the practice of building thick glass fronts on the ground floor with a heavier building above was so old that it had almost come to be accepted, although architects could never agree that it was pleasing and right." For instance, Robert Walker's well-known dry-goods store of 1867, the Golden Lion, was "a very curious affair" because its lower two floors consisted of plate glass framed in cast iron while the third and fourth storeys were conventional masonry (fig. 6.2).[2] Such designs, as one British commentator had noted in the 1830s, created the expectation "every moment that the huge mass will crush its feeble supports, and crumble to atoms."[3] Gregg judged it better to carry large plate-glass windows to the roofline as architect John James Browne had done in 1890 for Central Chambers, Ottawa (fig. 6.3). Browne's web of bay windows was based on an earlier British precedent of 1864 known as Oriel Chambers by Liverpool architect Peter Ellis. This Gregg considered pleasing in effect despite some reservation that it "might not be architecture."[4]

The question of what was and was not "architecture" also interested Edmund Burke. During the general discussion on suitable forms of expression, he volunteered that "the combining of *proper* architec-

6.1

6.2

6.3

6.4

6.1   Oak Hall (demolished), Toronto, 1893. Exterior view, 1910. Photograph of unknown original. UOFT-RB: *Construction* 3 (September 1910):83.

6.2   William Irving. Golden Lion (demolished), Toronto, 1867. Exterior view, 1868. Photograph by Octavius Thompson. MTRL:TI2616.

6.3   John James Browne. Central Chambers, Ottawa, 1890. Exterior view, 1898. Photograph from W.H. Carré. NA:C7029.

6.4   Gundry & Langley. John Macdonald Warehouse (demolished), Toronto, 1863. Exterior view. Photograph. AO:S 13396.

ture with what was demanded by the modern trades ... seemed ... an almost hopeless task if one desired to follow ancient models." He still expected to fuse "modern requirements with what are considered the best models of ancient architecture," identifying the arch as the only satisfactory treatment for the type of facade Gregg had noted. The chief defect, Burke said, was the obstruction of light on the upper floor caused by the haunches of the arch.[5] Bousfield was more flexible, suggesting that architects should not adopt "any period of architecture as a fixed rule for shop fronts" but modify "the art to suit the requirements of the times."[6]

Among the forms regarded as acceptable for shop fronts, Burke also mentioned the post-and-lintel system, which involved uprights and cross-beams. This type of grid had been adopted by a number of architects in Chicago for retail department stores in the city core. In Burke's view "the Chicago men" had solved the problem of architectural expression "as nearly as it was possible to do, having resolved their supports into simply iron stanchions with sufficient masonry to protect the iron from damage in the case of fire."[7] He confided that any attempted solution of this type filled him with dread. Yet three months later, Burke put aside his apprehensions to design a new retail store for Robert Simpson in precisely this style. The first of its kind in Canada, it marked the beginning of a new era in Canadian commercial architecture.

Burke's years with Langley provided a strong foundation for this new approach to commercial work. Throughout his training and partnership, he had been exposed to a variety of fashionable styles (and presumably to the theoretical considerations they entailed) – from Ruskinian Gothic to Renaissance revival, Second Empire to *néo-*

6.6

6.5

6.5   Langley & Burke. Union Loan and Savings Company (demolished), Toronto, 1878. Exterior view, 1897. Photograph. MTRL: Board of Trade of the City of Toronto, *Toronto 1897/8* (Toronto, 1897), 77.

6.6   Langley, Langley & Burke. Union Loan and Savings Company (demolished), Toronto, 1878. Perspective, c.1878, probably by Frank Burke. Wash on paper. AO, HC:C 11–626–0–1(624)1.

grec. American pre-eminence in the commercial field led a growing number of Canadian architects to adopt American idioms and technologies, but the lithic tradition remained fundamental to Langley's practice until late in the 1880s. Burke's reticence during the OAA discussion of 1894 seems to reflect this background – and is typical of the conservatism that pervaded Canadian architectural practice well into the closing decades of the nineteenth century.

One of the earliest commercial projects by Gundry & Langley had been the John Macdonald dry-goods warehouse of 1863 at 21–23 Wellington Street East (fig. 6.4); a major addition by Langley, Langley & Burke in 1878 likely involved the junior partner.[8] Remarkable for its "great system and gigantic scale," the five-storey structure towered above its neighbours, its facade ornamented in two colours of stone in the Italian Gothic vogue that followed publication of critic John Ruskin's *Stones of Venice* (1851–53).[9] Macdonald's building (considered "an extravagant step, for which he might have to climb the stool of repentence"), with facilities that attracted the lion's share of business in a rapidly expanding economy, soon became the envy of the mercantile community.[10] This visionary dry-goods wholesaler was to

6.7   Richard Morris Hunt. Tribune Building
(demolished), New York, 1873–75.
Exterior view. Photograph. Museum of the
City of New York, New York:
29.100.2292, J. Clarence Davies Collection.

lead the field in marketing techniques, introducing a mail-order system in 1889 and organizing the warehouse by departments in the 1890s.[11] Macdonald's innovations were facilitated by the vast structure containing two acres of floor space – a magnificent "credit to Toronto's mercantile architectural display."[12]

In the late 1870s Langley, Langley & Burke designed two office buildings on Toronto Street in a more thoughtful version of the Gothic revival style, by then a staple of North American commercial design.[13] First came the Union Loan and Savings, of 1878 (fig. 6.5), with three-and-a-half monumental storeys similar in scale and strength of detail to the Macdonald warehouse.[14] Like Macdonald's warehouse, the facade was Ohio stone and New York brownstone, but this time large areas of glass assured a well-lit working environment for twenty offices. The original scheme drawn by Edmund Burke (fig. 2.8) called for long sash windows separated by a pier and flanking colonnettes in the second and third storeys.[15] In the final version, reworked by another draughtsman (probably Burke's brother Frank) (fig. 6.6), these elements were reduced to a single colonnette of New Brunswick granite. This facilitated an increase in the area of glass with additional lighting secured by more attenuated window tracery, wider dormers in the iron-crested mansard, and a narrow mullion instead of a colonnette in the central bay.[16]

Flat arches and stark geometric forms with incised ornaments reduced the facade of the Union Loan to a structural grid reminiscent of Richard Morris Hunt's New York Tribune building of 1873–75 (fig. 6.7). Hunt's unusual fusion of High Victorian Gothic and *néo-grec*, which historian Neil Levine has recently dubbed "crypto-Gothic," united the bold polychromy of Ruskin with the structural rationalism of Henri Labrouste.[17] As early as 1861 Henry Van Brunt had referred to the power of "Greek lines" to purify the "old grotesque Gothic license," *néo-grec* supplying the conceptual framework for an idiosyncratic approach to design that stressed "strong traits of individuality so that every work appears as if its author had something particular to express."[18] In this context the Union Loan displayed a marked sensitivity to issues of space and light – crucial elements of the American commercial aesthetic – implying an incipient appreciation of the mode's theoretical underpinnings. The allusions to American commercial models in what was probably one of the earliest works of this type in which Burke played a significant role appear to portend later developments in his thought and work.

On the east side of the same street the firm also designed the Building & Loan Association offices of 1878 (fig. 6.8). A competition perspective by Joseph Ades Fowler (fig. 6.9) mixed Gothic dormers with a French mansard and interspersed giant order pilasters extending through the second and third storeys.[19] Incised flutes on the pilasters emulated the formal stylizations of American *néo-grec*, but the pilasters themselves were all but eliminated in the built version.[20] The result was pure High Victorian Gothic with multi-layered horizontals of red brick and light stone trimmings. No attempt was made

6.8

6.9

6.8 Langley, Langley & Burke. Building & Loan Association (demolished), Toronto, 1878. Exterior view, 1897. Photograph. MTRL: Board of Trade of the City of Toronto, *Toronto 1897/8* (Toronto, 1897), 70.

6.9 Langley, Langley & Burke. Building & Loan Association (demolished), Toronto, 1878. Perspective, 1874, initialled J.A.F. (probably Joseph Ades Fowler). Pen and wash on paper. AO, HC:C 11–395–0–1(311b).

to maximize window area in the three-and-a-half-storey screen of polychromatic masonry that wrapped the corner and extended 100 feet along Court Street. Yet contemporaries – ambivalent towards issues now thought fundamental – described this conservative, generously scaled structure as possessing "all the latest improvements" in "a modern business building."[21]

Langley's firm handled a prodigious amount of commercial work throughout the 1870s. In one year fully a third of the firm's advertised tenders were of this type.[22] Several commissions, leading up to the Gothic revival works on Toronto Street, reflect a growing awareness of American commercial vocabulary. Diverse stylistic experimentation points to a lively ferment in the Langley draughting room from about 1874 – the period when Burke began supervising his own projects – with new ideas from these years apparently preparing the way for his later design philosophy.

A curious office building on King Street West planned for Canada Life in 1874 is indicative of the changing approach in the Langley office. Its symmetrical three-storey facade – executed in cut stone and possibly including elements of galvanized iron – appears in a perspective by Frank Burke (fig. 2.7).[23] Two wide bays were framed by pilasters that bore the incised flutes of American *néo-grec*. Each was crowned by a triangular Greek-style pediment backed by an attic decorated with antefixes. Banks of sash windows clustered between smaller pilasters created a structural grid that anticipated the Union Loan and Savings on Toronto Street four years later.[24] Despite its ostentatious display of academic conventions, these narrow window mullions leave no doubt that practical considerations directed the organization of the design.[25]

Functional issues were important in another office building executed by the firm in 1874. Imperial Chambers at 32–34 Adelaide Street East was a five-storey Second Empire structure with an excavated "English basement" that provided marketable space in the lower storey (fig. 6.10).[26] Paired sash windows arranged in three bays were flanked by attached columns with a giant reeded order linking the second and third storeys. Narrow mullions separated the windows so that the exterior was little more than a framework of glass and ornamental stone. On the top floor high bonnet dormers consistent with the stylistic mode opened into a mansarded attic.

The adjoining property to the east dictated both scale and vocabulary in Imperial Chambers. Langley's Eighth Post Office, just completed in 1874 (fig. 6.11), corresponded at each level, storey by storey, and cornice by cornice. Stylistically the Post Office (based on a plan

6.10   Langley, Langley & Burke. Imperial Chambers (demolished), Toronto, 1874–75. Perspective signed "F. Burke," December 1875. Pen and wash on paper. AO, HC:C 11–42–0–0–1(49)1.

6.10

6.11

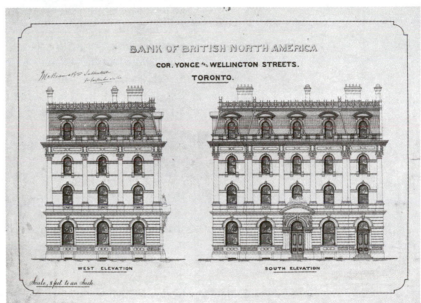

6.12

6.11   Henry Langley. Eighth Post Office at the head of Toronto Street (demolished), Toronto, 1872–74. Exterior view with Building & Loan Association on the right. Photograph by J.V. Salmon. City of Toronto Archives: SC 231–1668.

6.12   Henry Langley. Bank of British North America, Toronto, 1871–72. Elevations. Pen and wash on paper. AO, HC:C 11–505–0–1(463)3.

by Alfred B. Mullett, chief architect of the United States Treasury Department) embodied all the key features of the Parisian archetype. The New Louvre by Visconti and Lefuel, completed in 1857, had established the vogue known as Second Empire style with paired orders in a pedimented frontispiece, a bulbous square dome, and flanking pavilions of channelled ashlar.[27] Of necessity, however, Imperial Chambers incorporated only selected elements: the attached columns, the mansard roof, and the bonnet dormers. Much more significant

6.13   Langley, Langley & Burke.
Horticultural Pavilion (destroyed), Allen
Gardens, Toronto, 1878. Exterior view.
Photograph. MTRL: *Artwork on Toronto*
(Toronto: W.H. Carré, 1898), plate 1.

to the overall scheme was the imperative of large window area. The indices of an office type were in essence beginning to dictate the re-ordering of stylistic veneer.

By contrast financial institutions adhered more closely to conventional precedents. The Bank of British North America of 1871–72, for example, was conceived as a Renaissance *palazzo* (fig. 6.12), a motif associated with banking since the days of the Medici. Updated by a fashionable Second Empire mansard, its attributes recall Roman models of the sixteenth century with continuous giant-order pilasters rising from a base of channelled ashlar.[28] A monumental entrance marked by a segmental pediment was centred in the Wellington Street facade before a later alteration removed the entrance to a side portal on Yonge Street.[29] Apart from discrete round-headed window openings, the lithic mass of the wall is preserved in every respect, conveying an apparent if not actual sense of security and solidity. In this case protection of the contents and the corporate image took precedence over matters of mere convenience.

Stylistic and technical developments in American commercial architecture influenced the work of the Langley partnership from about the mid-1870s on. In 1878 the firm added to its limited experience with large areas of glass when it built the Horticultural Pavilion for Allan Gardens (fig. 6.13). But modern materials infiltrated their architectural vocabulary only infrequently before the end of the 1880s when the design for the Army & Navy Clothing Store at 133–135 King Street East, begun in 1887, marked the beginning of a new phase (fig. 6.14).[30] Like the Golden Lion, this mixed-use structure called for a facade of plate glass and iron components as well as masonry. To overcome the discordant character of such schemes, the architects resorted to a round arch extending from the ground floor to the third storey.

Built in two stages in 1887–88 and 1890–91, the Army & Navy store has twin arches (fig. 6.15). Langley & Burke used cast-iron uprights on the first floor with two iron box-beams bearing the upper storeys of brick and terra cotta.[31] This had the effect of integrating two structural systems (arch and post-and-lintel) as well as combining iron with masonry. Plate glass filled the opening with a main panel of glazing on the second floor tipped forward to catch additional light. In the spandrels, square terra cotta panels replace sections of brick in order to relieve the pressure upon the voussoirs. On the fourth level traditional forms are reasserted in five small round-arched openings and in a cornice of decorative brickwork. A thoroughly cohesive adaptation of an "ancient" model to modern requirements, the store exemplifies the synthesis to which Burke referred at the OAA meeting of 1894.

A slightly later but less sophisticated version by an unknown architect for cabinetmaker Richard Bigley at 92 Queen Street East points up the uniqueness of the Army & Navy design (fig. 6.16). There, the four-storey brick arch frames a cast-iron facade, but instead of being structurally integrated, the ironwork is freestanding and self-sustaining.[32]

6.14 Langley & Burke. Army and Navy Clothing Store on King Street East near St Lawrence Market, Toronto, 1887–89. Exterior view, c.1890. Photograph by Micklethwaite. NA:PA 117978.

6.15 Langley & Burke. Clarkson, Gordon (formerly Army and Navy Clothing Store), Toronto, 1887–89. Exterior view, 1989. Photograph by Angela Carr.

6.16 Richard Bigley Store, Toronto, 1889. Exterior view, 1990. Photograph by Angela Carr.

6.14

6.15

6.16

6.18   William Le Baron Jenney. Home
Insurance Building (demolished), Chicago,
1884–85. Exterior view. Photograph by
J.W. Taylor. Chicago Historical Society,
Chicago: ICHi-00989.

6.19   Richard Waite. Bank of Commerce
(demolished), King and Jordan, Toronto,
1888–89. Exterior view, 1890s. Photograph.
NA:RD 531.

6.18

6.19

TRANSITIONAL YEARS: THE NEW AESTHETIC

The round arch was especially associated with Romanesque revival,
which rapidly became the dominant fashion in the United States
and Canada at the end of the 1880s.[33] Few examples of Toronto's
commercial architecture were as forward-looking Langley & Burke's
Army & Navy store, however. At a meeting of the OAA in 1893 Frank
Darling had questionned the use of iron in the facade of Canada Life's
new seven-storey, Romanesque-style office building on King Street
West because its massive sandstone and red-brick walls were entirely
capable of carrying the weight of the building unassisted. Burke noted
the same was true of the Freehold Loan on Adelaide Street by
E.J. Lennox and the Bank of Commerce "near the market." He went
on to describe the practice as a waste of material.[34]

The new Canada Life building (fig. 6.17), designed in 1887 by architect Richard Waite of Buffalo replaced Langley's *néo-grec* scheme after only a dozen years.[35] An indication of how corporations were planning for future growth, the new building was the first to break Toronto's five-storey height convention. Centred around its elevator, office space far exceeded existing corporate needs.[36] A massive brick-and-sandstone exterior, derived from the work of the late American architect Henry Hobson Richardson, was meant to inspire public confidence. From the architectural point of view, however, the structural system failed to generate any significant reduction in the thickness of the outer walls, like the freestanding metal frame of the landmark Home Insurance building completed two years earlier in Chicago (fig. 6.18). The design neglected to take advantage of modern technology in another way, too, as brick and terra-cotta partitions used to fireproof the interior encroached upon usable floor space.[37]

Across the street (on the south-west corner of King and Jordan) Waite constructed a similar building for the Bank of Commerce (fig. 6.19). Small technical advances – such as the use of metal trusswork in the ceiling of the banking hall instead of supporting piers – made the structure marginally more progressive than its neighbour. But Waite's designs brought only the most conservative American commercial technology to Canada.[38]

Similarly Toronto architect E.J. Lennox, known for his Richardsonian motifs, used iron uprights to reinforce the brick-and-brownstone exterior of his Freehold Loan and Savings designed in 1887 (fig. 6.20).[39] Inside, an iron frame protected with fireproof brick was said to be constructed "in a new and novel manner" so that partitions could be removed without affecting other floors. In practice,

6.17

6.20

6.17 Richard Waite. Canada Life Assurance Building (demolished), Toronto, 1887. Perspective, no date. Courtesy of Canada Life, Toronto.

6.20 Edward James Lennox. Freehold Savings and Loan Building (demolished), Toronto, 1889–90. Exterior view. Photograph. AO: *Artwork on Toronto* (Toronto, W.H. Carré, 1898), 89.

however, these were like the ones Waite had built in Canada Life – so bulky as to be immovable. Conceptually Lennox understood the potentials of the metal frame, but as Burke observed did not make the most of its possibilities.[40] In fact the engineer's aesthetic perfected by the "Chicago men" was singularly absent from Canada until Burke experimented with it in the mid-1890s.

The delay in accepting new ideas can be explained perhaps by Canadian criticisms of the "craze for cheapness and inordinate haste" to the south.[41] In return Americans regarded their northern neighbours as chronically behind the times.

Even staid old Canada has of late years erected some tall office buildings ... Most of them, however, are the work of American architects. Such, for instance, is the New York Life Building in Montreal, by Babb, Cook & Willard of New York. It is the most pretentious affair there ... Canadians are rather slow in adopting novelties ... Their elevators are few and far between, and are looked at askance by many yet who would as soon attempt to walk upon the waters, as Peter did of old, as to trust their precious lives in one of those "bird-cages."[42]

Montreal's New York Life building of 1888 on Place des Armes (fig. 6.21) was a weighty tower of Scottish sandstone, its floors and roof born on steel beams carried at every level by the load-bearing outer wall – a method just as *retardataire* by Chicago standards as those employed in Toronto by Richard Waite and E.J. Lennox.[43]

Canadian high-rise office buildings followed American models whether they were executed by Canadian or American architects because commercial precedents had been perfected almost exclusively in the United States.[44] Yet Canadians were slow to risk new construction techniques – often with justification. For example, the Toronto Board of Trade held a competition for its new building at the corner of Yonge and Front Streets in 1888, and the adjudicator, Professor William R. Ware of Columbia College in New York City awarded first place to James & James of New York for their seven-storey Romanesque design (fig. 6.22).[45] Construction began in May 1889, but was halted the following February after a major collapse. The Board of Trade responded by dismissing the local contractor, but later found that the architects had failed to properly calculate the loads for steel floor beams supported on brick piers (fig. 6.23).[46] Edward A. Kent of Buffalo took over and added iron columns to the piers, securing the interior at a generous cost of $35,000 to $40,000.[47]

The irony was that the Board of Trade, at the instance of the adjudicator, had ascertained the names of the contestants before awarding the commission – on the pretext that this would give "further evidence as to the professional resources at the command of the author of [the] design." Professor Ware's choice of James & James was confirmed over two of Toronto's finer firms, Gordon & Helliwell and Darling & Curry.[48] Following the dismissal of James & James, one Canadian commentator pointed out that "Competency and incompetency are

6.21

6.21   Babb, Cook & Willard. New York Life
Insurance Building, Place des Armes,
Montreal, 1888. Exterior view. Photograph.
NA:PA 45937.

found in any country ... The man who insinuates ... that Canadian architects are all incompetent, while all American architects are competent, may be written down either as a fool or a knave."[49]

Controversies about American methodologies were usually clouded
by the assumption that Canadian architects were not only less willing
but less able to manage these innovations than their American
counterparts. Canadian professionals responded with educational
initiatives and protectionism. As early as 1880 Richard Waite's
appointment as architect for the offices of Western Life Assurance on
Wellington Street had occasioned a complaint from one local practitioner about the need for a "National Policy" to favour "native indus-
tries" over "foreign products"[50] and accusations that Waite had been
permitted to spend "twice if not three times as much as any Canadian

6.24

6.22

6.22   James & James. Board of Trade (demolished), Toronto, 1889–90. Exterior view. Photograph. Toronto Transit Commission Collection: 17122, Metropolitan Toronto Archives, Toronto.

6.23   James & James. Board of Trade (demolished), Toronto, 1889–90. Interior view showing structural system in lobby, 1929. Photograph. Toronto Transit Commission Collection: 6867, Metropolitan Toronto Archives, Toronto.

6.24   Broadside of "New Parliament Buildings" showing Darling & Pearson scheme (above) and Richard Waite design (below). Broadside, 1892. MTRL-BR: Broadside Collection, 1892, copy only.

6.23

architect would have been allowed."[51] His appointment to the Canada Life project was also condemned on the basis that a purely Canadian company "making its revenues out of Canadians, its chiefs Canadians," ought to have chosen a Canadian architect.[52] As a direct result demands grew for a Canadian school of architecture so that a diploma might offer the profession "as high a standing before all the world as … our doctors and lawyers."[53]

Resentment was all the more intense because of Waite's involvement with the notorious competition for the new Ontario legislative buildings in Queen's Park. Appointed by the government in 1880 as one of three judges, together with the Hon. Alexander Mackenzie and Toronto architect William G. Storm, he confirmed the worst fears of the competitors six years later when he successfully wheedled the prestigious commission for himself, having torpedoed winning entries by local firms.[54]

From the outset there was dissatisfaction with the entries in the Queen's Park competition, the architects having been hamstrung by the limited budget of $600,000.[55] The judges' joint report of 1880 stated: "In architectural character these designs are inferior to some others, but they nonetheless comply more closely with the conditions of the competition especially that of cost." It went on to say that "each is in plan and elevation unworthy of the site." Nevertheless the premiums were awarded with an eye to cost – "a governing principle to which general Architectural excellence must give way."[56]

When Waite took over the project in January 1886 Toronto architects were indignant. Marshall B. Aylesworth lobbied his fellows to form a professional organization capable of representing Canadian practitioners on a national level, citing the "unlimited 'gall' [of a foreign competitor], posing, after years of intrigue, as a disinterested expert."[57] Even the *American Architect and Building News* published its Canadian correspondent's report describing the proceedings of the competition committee as "reprehensible."[58]

Waite's allegations about defects in the competitors' plans appear to have been accepted at face value because of the negative tone of the original report. One anonymous government defender even went so far as to write that "if Toronto architects would do better work, we should not need to go elsewhere."[59] Yet Waite's scheme, described by the *Globe* as "Nero Greek," was criticized in turn as "so wretchedly bad in composition that no possible beauty of detail or profuseness of carving can redeem it" (fig. 6.24).[60] The *Canadian Architect & Builder* was incredulous:

That a foreign architect should be appointed to design this most important building in preference to a Canadian, is bad enough, but that a good design by Canadians should be cast aside, and a building erected according to such an inferior one by a foreigner, is worthy of the strongest condemnation. Until Canadians believe in themselves, there will never be any national life worth speaking of, nor will the ablest among our young men remain in their native land.[61]

Later, during the course of construction the front elevation was altered, a decision that appears to confirm the allegations of its inadequacy.[62]

Crossman has described Waite's "ability and willingness to introduce American innovations ... to Canada" as a reason for his success.[63] Yet high-rise construction and metal-frame technology were not the issue in the legislative buildings so much as stylistic and planning differences between British-influenced neo-Gothic and Waite's American Romanesque. By adhering to unreasonable budget restrictions and accepting stylistic models stipulated in the terms of the competition, two of the leading firms in the city had opened themselves to charges of incompetence at the hands of the same government that had established the parameters in the first place.[64] It is against such a background that Burke's efforts to improve his knowledge of American technology and to establish a professional organization for architects in the province must be considered.

EDMUND BURKE: SOLE PRACTITIONER

By the early 1890s information on metal-frame technology was readily available in Canada.[65] Burke was sufficiently well-versed in the field by March of 1892 to deliver a lecture to the Toronto Architectural Sketch Club on "Structural Iron Work."[66] His discussion discloses a detailed knowledge of tension and compression strengths in cast and wrought iron beams as well as the problems of uneven castings in iron columns. In addition the relative strengths of different materials during exposure to extreme heat were noted.

A second lecture Burke delivered before the same group emphasized the practical aspects of the builder's art in the following terms:

Building consists in putting the materials we have at [our] command in certain positions, and giving them certain forms. The size and shape of these forms depend on certain statical considerations. Arithmetic, mathematics and geometry can alone enable us to solve the necessary statical problems; so these elements must first be mastered to enable us to solve the statical problems that present themselves. Next comes the knowledge of the strengths and capabilities of the materials we have to use.

He went on to observe that calculations could now be made with far greater accuracy than in the past, but that the limitations of this data always required the architect to make allowances for a "factor of safety," including a margin of error to cover the "factor of ignorance."[67]

The following year, before the third annual meeting of the OAA in March 1893, Burke read a letter from Horwood in New York. It referred to a city by-law which required all buildings to be fireproofed if the roof beams rose more than eighty-five feet above the pavement. Noting that most tall structures of this type (i.e., twelve or thirteen storeys) were built with cast-iron supports, the writer indicated that internal framing always took a consistent form, variations being limited to how "the external wall was treated in relation to the adjoining floor." Three alternative methods represented the available options: (1) masonry walls and piers could be of sufficient strength to carry their own weight plus that of the floors, roof, and contents of the building; (2) walls and piers might carry their own weight while the floors were carried on a frame of iron supports extending from foundation to roof, with columns if necessary being recessed in the walls; or (3) a frame of columns and girders could carry the outer walls as well as adjoining floor construction.[68]

Burke, who read the account into the record, expressed surprise that an iron cantilever could support a column, and noted that walls could be made lighter if iron framing carried the load.

Evercautious, president S.G. Curry closed the session by expressing doubts that American building techniques could "well be compared with work done in Canada or the old country." He is reported to have said that

The architectural appearance of a building, of course, was another question, but that, as a rule was not considered in this [commercial] class of buildings to any great extent; they were required for a certain purpose, and it was incumbent upon the architect to do the best he could under the limitations. After all, the buildings were to all intents and purposes, in a sense, the works of engineers rather than architects.[69]

Such reservations lingered in the minds of most participants, only to resurface the following year during Bousfield's discussion of shopfronts.

This was the problem confronting Burke in May of 1894 when (less than two years after establishing his own practice) Robert Simpson asked him to design a new department store at the corner of Yonge and Queen. By January 1895 the scheme was published in the *Canadian Architect and Builder* (fig. 6.25).[70] With a sparse grid of posts and lintels, Simpsons was the first building in Canada to assimilate the momentous contemporary developments of the American Midwest. Just six months and four days in completion, the six-storey structure opened in time for the retailer's Christmas rush, its construction hastened by the introduction of a steel frame that allowed the contractor to "carry up the walls with utmost speed."[71]

Erected to a height of thirty-two feet above the sidewalk, the steel frame allowed the contractor to commence bricking at the third floor level while cut-stone cladding was installed below. On the interior, rolled steel columns and beams were used to carry southern pine joists and flooring was plastered with Acme cement (fig. 6.26).[72] Time constraints imposed by the patron's retail season and budgetary limitations meant the building was not otherwise fireproofed, an economy that proved to be its undoing. The open warehouse plan was vulner-

6.25   Edmund Burke. Robert Simpson Store
(destroyed), Toronto, 1894. Perspective,
1894. Pen on paper. UofT-RB: *CAB* 8 (January
1895): after 18.

6.26   Edmund Burke. Robert Simpson Store
(destroyed), Toronto, 1894. Section detail,
1894. Pencil and wash on paper. AO, HC:C
11–24–0–1(26)8.

6.25

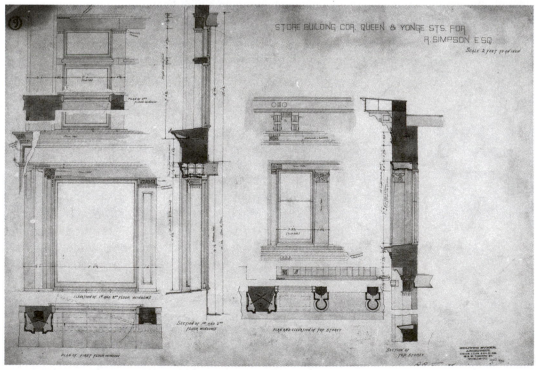

6.26

able to fire, and just a few weeks later, in the early hours of 4 March 1895, the store burned to the ground – the target of an arsonist's torch (fig. 6.27).[73]

The profession quickly lept to Burke's defence. Marshall Aylesworth eulogized the structure in the following terms:

The Simpson building was the best representative of its class in the city, a style of temple expressly designed to meet the demands of the modern mammon worshipper – the greatest display in the slenderest building. The architect deserves credit for the triumph obtained for his employer – a strong building with the minimum of space occupied by the supports, and faultless in exterior detail.[74]

Lack of fireproofing was the fault of lax municipal regulations that failed to govern "commercial barons [who] do not readily submit to such wholesome restriction."[75] Robert Simpson took the point, and declared safety the foremost consideration in rebuilding his showpiece.[76]

Edmund Burke, now joined by his compatriot John Horwood, undertook the reconstruction.[77] The exterior of the second store was a virtual copy of the first, but facades on both streets were extended by several bays because fire had destroyed neighbouring properties (fig. 6.28). On the interior, however, the structure was completely redesigned – this time with a free-standing, rivetted iron skeleton – a sight which impressed visitors to the Industrial Exhibition. Specifications required that the frame be fully fireproofed with poured concrete around the columns and concrete block infill between the beams. By October the *Canadian Architect and Builder* was able to report that Simpson's was once again "towering up at the corner of Yonge and Queen streets," its final cost $100,000 more than the original.[78] Robert Simpson could fairly boast that the building was indestructible by fire.

Once described as "the best unit of construction for department stores [which has been] widely adopted all over America [and] little improved upon over the years," the Robert Simpson store was indeed a Canadian first.[79] But the design was derived from American models, not vice versa. The main centre for such commercial structures was Chicago,[80] and Burke's awareness of the "Chicago men," as he called them, is clear from his discussion at the OAA meeting of 1894.[81] He evidently attended the World's Columbian Exposition in that city in 1893, and was acquainted with writings on the subject by the noted American critic Montgomery Schuyler.[82] His expertise even extended to a knowledge of raft foundations developed by John Root for the Montauk Block in 1881.[83] Burke's former associate and future partner Murray Alexander White, who worked in Chicago from 1892 until 1907, may also have been a source of information.[84]

The first Simpson's store erected by Burke in 1894 was an exploration of what had been termed the work "of engineers rather than of architects." Its grid of horizontals and verticals discarded the masonry

6.28

6.27   Robert Simpson Store (destroyed), Toronto, 4 March 1895. View of the remains after the fire. Photograph. MTRL:T-13288.

6.28   Burke & Horwood. Robert Simpson Store, Toronto, 1895. Exterior view after addition at the corner of Yonge and Richmond Streets, 1898–99. Photograph. AO, HC:C 11, Additional 5.

6.29   Edmund Burke. Robert Simpson store (destroyed), Toronto, 1894. Exterior view from the north-east, 1895. Photograph. AO, HC:C 11, Additional 5.

6.27

aesthetic of Waite and Lennox and began a tentative investigation of warehouse construction (fig. 6.29). Continuous piers of stone and brick, all of equal dimensions, surrounded the structure. The ground floor was of generous proportions with large panels of plate glass facing the two main thoroughfares, Queen and Yonge. Passers-by were afforded a view into the basement through smaller, angled windows at pavement level (fig. 6.30). Above was an equally liberal mezzanine storey, each bay of which was subdivided by a single brick mullion. This was surmounted in turn by three floors of triple windows with transoms, forming a lattice of mullions within the larger grid of piers and spandrels. In the attic storey a dense repetition of rectangular openings – this time four per bay articulated by a colonnade of attached columns – brought the block to a rational termination. A configuration that anticipated by several years the program laid out by Chicago architect Louis Sullivan in his classic essay "The Tall Building Artistically Considered," the motif was probably drawn from direct observation of existing Chicago-style precedents.[85]

Despite its appearance, the exterior of the first Simpson's store of 1894 did not express a complete metal skeleton. The steelwork only

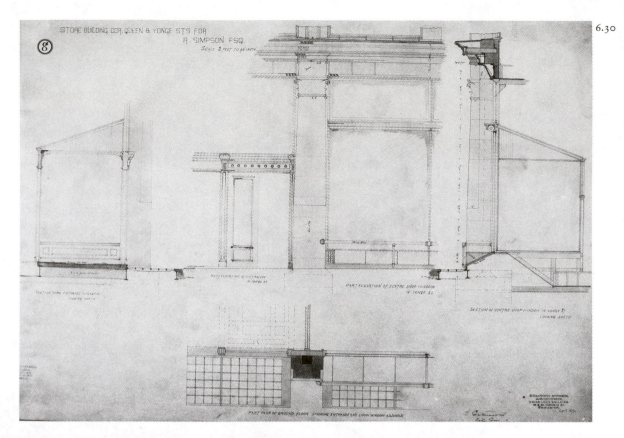

6.30

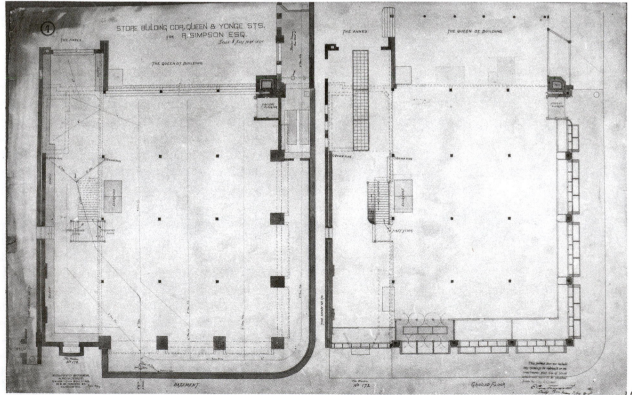

6.31

went as high as the second floor, and the wall above that point carried its own weight. Resting on three horizontal I-beams at the mezzanine, the brick piers rose in line with the bays formed by interior metal columns (fig. 6.31). Only after the rebuilding in 1895 did the iron skeleton sustain the brick cladding at every level of the facade.

Historically, the external expression of a structure was often unrelated to systems of structural support.[86] Iron founders James Bogardus and Daniel Badger perfected prefabricated iron buildings with narrow window mullions in New York at mid-century.[87] Badger applied pre-cast segments to building facades while Bogardus sought to integrate metal facades with cast-iron framing.[88] The Bogardus factory of 1848–49 at Centre and Duane Streets and the Harper & Brothers building of 1854, both in New York, went some distance toward this goal.[89] Yet another New York building, John Kellum's A.T. Stewart store of 1861–63, cast by Peter Cooper, is more widely accepted as the earliest of this type.[90] Other European and North American commercial buildings faced with slender stone piers or iron mullions sometimes had no corresponding relationship with the internal framing.[91]

In North America the import trade required vast wholesale warehouses in which natural lighting and the largest possible storage area could be combined. Practicality necessitated that internal and external structures coalesce, and as retail establishments discovered the merits of this system, the requirements were translated into architecture.[92] Architect James McLaughlin's scheme for Shillito's Cincinnati department store of 1877–78 is an early example in which narrow brick piers and extensive plate glass ensured as much light as possible while an internal iron frame supporting wooden joists facilitated uninterrupted display space. A rendering and ground-floor plan published in the *American Architect and Building News* discloses a tripartite exterior with two monumental lower storeys forming a base for three upper floors grouped beneath an attic and cornice (fig. 6.32). Each pier was aligned with and bolted to the metal frame, bearing its own weight and that of the flooring in the outer bay (fig. 6.33).[93]

Engineer William Le Baron Jenney of Chicago emulated Shillito's in his first Leiter store of 1878–79 (fig. 6.34).[94] But his training as at the Ecole Centrale des Arts et Manufactures in Paris prepared him to carry the synthesis a step further. The five-storey Leiter store was similar in concept to the Cincinnati example, but iron columns were placed immediately behind the brick piers so that piers carried only their own weight and that of the metal I-beams extending across each bay – in other words, the outermost inches of the facade instead of the entire width of the perimeter bay.[95]

As an expression of structure the first Leiter building was perhaps more "honest" but less "architectural" than the Cincinnati example. Each member was separately clad, and a stylized capital covered the intersection of pier and spandrel. The result was an evenly balanced grid of verticals and horizontals without continuous piers or the layering of base, shaft and capital. The non-hierarchical grid spoke more to structure than to art.

6.30 Edmund Burke. Robert Simpson Store (destroyed), Toronto, 1894. Section of basement windows, 1894. Pencil and wash on paper. AO, HC:C 11–24–0–1(26)9.

6.31 Edmund Burke. Robert Simpson Store (destroyed), Toronto, 1894. Plan of Basement and Ground Floor, 1894. Pen and wash on paper. AO, HC:C 11–24–0–1(26)1.

6.32

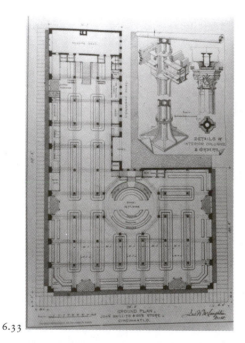

6.33

6.32   James MacLaughlin. John Shillito Store (altered), Cincinnati, 1877–78. Exterior view. UofT-RL: *AABN* 2 (13 October 1877):no. 94.

6.33   James MacLaughlin. John Shillito Store (altered), Cincinnati, 1877–78. Plan and detail. UofT-RL: *AABN* 2 (13 October 1877):no. 94.

It would be a mistake, however, to emphasize the progressive aspects of Jenney's skeletal economies without observing the more conventional aspects of his *oeuvre*. His celebrated Home Insurance building of 1883–85, noted above, was the first American structure to carry the outer wall on a self-sustaining metal frame, an achievement concealed beneath a mass of Romanesque masonry.[96] As in Toronto, Chicago's unwritten laws of institutional symbolism took precedence over new structural vocabularies.

Jenney's next opportunity to explore the warehouse type came in 1889 when he undertook the second Leiter store (fig. 6.35).[97] This time metal framing was integrated with the facade so the cladding is carried floor by floor. Two monumental lower floors form a base for continuous piers of white Maine granite that extend through the upper six storeys. At the corners their breadth is doubled to reinforce the mass of the block – an artistic conceit that ignores the configuration of the underlying frame. A deep fascia and dentils articulate the structure's relationship to classical Greek models, while an infinitely complex arrangement of mullions and colonnettes demonstrates a level of artistic synthesis far beyond the requirements of mere engineering.

A second commission from the same period, also by Jenney, was less successful.[98] The Fair store was likewise constructed on a steel frame, this time covered by salmon-coloured terra cotta (fig. 6.36). But a band of rustication carelessly applied at the sixth-floor level had the effect of slicing the eleven-storey structure in half. Heavy ornament also negated the simplicity of the underlying grid. The failure to successfully deal with the issue of artistic expression in this instance suggests that strict theoretical analysis applied by modern writers to the Chicago development is something of a gloss. In the circumstances

6.34

6.35

6.34   William Le Baron Jenney. Leiter Store (demolished), Chicago, 1878–79. Exterior view. Photograph by J.W. Taylor. A1ofC:C45491.

6.35   William Le Baron Jenney. Leiter Store II (now One Congress Centre), Chicago, 1889. Exterior view. Photograph by J.W. Taylor. A1ofC.

it is all the more surprising that Burke should have achieved such a coherent synthesis in his first attempt at interpretation.

Others who, like Chicago architect Louis Sullivan, sought to perfect the warehouse precedent, undoubtedly influenced Burke. In 1892, for example, the *Inland Architect & News Record* published a project by Adler & Sullivan involving a wholesale store for the estate of M.A. Meyer.[99] The proposal consisted of a seven-storey block, six bays by eight (fig. 6.37). On the ground floor the piers were rusticated and carried a strong entablature, then plain piers in every bay rose uninterrupted through five storeys to the level of the attic: here a band of rectangular windows was strung together beneath a heavily ornamented cornice. In the body of the structure – between the ground floor and the attic storey – the windows were enclosed within a single rectangular frame outlined in terra cotta.

Both of Burke's designs for Simpson's resemble the Meyer project strongly in the treatment of the window bays and the configuration of the attic storey. But unlike the Chicago examples Burke resisted the temptation to reinforce the building's corners, preferring structural honesty to artistic fiction. The result indicates a high degree of theoretical synthesis – far beyond what one might have expected in light of the conservative attitudes of the Canadian profession at the time. In the words of the *Canadian Architect and Builder*,

The problem, a packing box full of windows, is an exceedingly difficult one, and Mr. Burke had succeeded in giving a dignified solution without in the least entrenching upon the first requisite of such a building – abundance of light. Indeed the very determination to fulfill the conditions perfectly saved

6.36   William Le Baron Jenney. Fair Store
(demolished), Chicago, 1889. Exterior
view. Photograph by J.W. Taylor.
AIofC:C45503.

6.37   Adler & Sullivan. Project for a
Wholesale Store for the Estate of
M.A. Meyer, Chicago, not executed.
Perspective, c.1892. Photograph from mi-
crofilm copy. ICHi: *IANR* 19 (April 1892):
after 42.

6.36

6.37

the design. Being full of light from top to bottom, the usual abrupt transition from solidity to plate glass is avoided, and though the show windows are unusually wide, the effect is unusually solid.[100]

A turning point in the career of the architect and a milestone for Canadian architecture, the Robert Simpson store was the foundation upon which the partnership's future reputation was built.

7 New York and Chicago: Manifest Destiny and the Later Commercial Works

> [The early twentieth century] gave birth to higher aspirations, due probably in large measure to the great architectural development of the United States, which, in itself, was due to the European training which led to the handling of problems in a freer and broader spirit, and also led to a more penetrating study of the old work.
>
> Alfred Chapman, "Development of Architectural Design in Canada," *Construction* (1917)

In the autumn of 1894, after an extensive European tour, John Horwood returned to Toronto where he joined Edmund Burke's firm, formally entering into partnership on 1 January 1895.[1] Their artistic personalities were distinct, as were the sources from which they drew inspiration. Burke's affinity for simple and economical design was reflected in the sparsely ornamented post-and-lintel system he chose for the Robert Simpson store, whereas Horwood was strongly influenced by the historicist traditions of New York and the observations of his recent European sojourn.[2] His influence can be discerned in the firm's more ornate designs.

THE NEW YORK CONNECTION

On 6 January 1895 the offices of Toronto's *Globe* newspaper burned to the ground just five years after a substantial renovation by Knox & Elliot (fig. 7.1).[3] Because that firm had moved to the United States in the meantime, Burke & Horwood were asked to undertake the rebuilding.[4] The new design was to occupy the same narrow twenty-eight-foot lot bounded on three sides by Yonge, Melinda, and Jordan streets, and take account of the fact that a corner tower had been prominent in the earlier scheme.

The cramped site was similar to one Horwood had specifically noted in one of his letters from New York – at 29 Broadway the thirteen-storey Columbia building of 1890–91 (fig. 7.2) occupied a lot less than thirty feet wide.[5] So narrow was the building that construction was practicable only because steel-skeleton construction liberated additional floorspace.[6] On the exterior a lengthy side-street facade was decorated by Romanesque arches extending through several storeys, while a massive circular tower accented the narrow elevation on Broadway.

Burke & Horwood took their lead for the Globe building from the foundations of the old structure, then introduced several motifs that

7.1

7.1 Knox & Elliot. Globe Building (destroyed), Toronto, 1890–95. Perspective, 1890. MTRL-BR: *Saturday Globe* (13 September 1890).

7.2 Youngs & Cable. Columbia Building (demolished), New York, 1890–91. Exterior view, 1890s. Photograph by Robarts Library. UOFT-RL: M. King, *King's Handbook of New York* (Boston, 1892), 632.

7.2

are remarkably reminscent of the New York example. Two heavy cornices partitioned the facade top and bottom encircling the corner tower on Yonge, while a series of multi-storey arches articulated the Melinda Street facade (fig. 7.3).[7] For the print shop Horwood's knowledge of metal construction must have guided the design of the iron columns and I-beams that supported the fireproofed interior (fig. 7.4). *Canadian Architect and Builder* referred to this as "skeleton construction, similar to the new Simpson building further up the street [except that] all the columns are built into the brick walls and the floor beams encased in concrete."[8] There is no indication in the drawings, however, that the frame was actually free-standing, although the structure was undoubtedly one of the firm's early attempts at fireproofing.[9]

At about the same time, before fire devastated Burke's Robert Simpson store, the partners prepared an important project for the Independent Order of Foresters (IOF), who planned to build an office block at the north-west corner of Bay and Richmond. In response to the organization's invitation, the submission provided for a six-or

7.3   Burke & Horwood. Globe Building (demolished), Toronto, 1895. Perspective, 1912. Halftone. AO: *Toronto: Canada's Queen City* (Toronto, 1912).

7.4   Burke & Horwood. Globe Building (demolished), Toronto, 1895. Section, 1895. Pen and wash on paper. AO, HC:C 11–815–0–1(774)3.

7.3

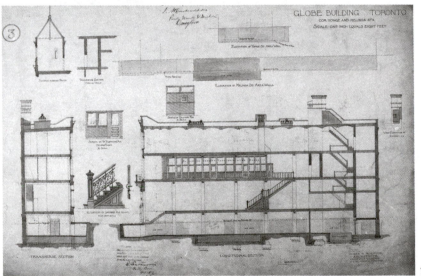

7.4

eight-storey, fireproof structure on a steel frame "according to the Chicago method" (fig. 7.5).[10] The exterior was pure Beaux-Arts – a tripartite Renaissance *palazzo* – consisting of a two-storey base, a shaft with three storeys grouped beneath continuous flat arches, and an attic decorated by an overhanging cornice. This was New York's latest vogue, and it anticipated by over a decade Canadian tastes of the early twentieth century. The patron (perhaps disturbed by the ensuing Simpsons fire or unprepared for such novel vocabulary) chose instead George Gouinlock's weighty Romanesque design in the style of American architect Henry Hobson Richardson, its metal frame hidden beneath a vast cloak of masonry (fig. 7.6).[11]

7.5

7.5 Burke & Horwood. Project for the Independent Order of Foresters Building, Toronto, not executed. Elevation and sections, 1895. Pen on paper. AO, HC:C 11(968)11.

7.6 George Gouinlock. Temple Building for the Independent Order of Foresters (demolished), Toronto, 1895. Exterior view. Photograph. MTRL-BR: *Artwork on Toronto* (Toronto: W.H. Carré, 1898), plate 88.

Within weeks of the IOF submission, the partners were otherwise occupied with the reconstruction of the Robert Simpson store following the fire of March 1895.[12] Horwood must have contributed significantly to planning the new building's free-standing iron frame, but the architectural expression was true to Burke's original post-and-lintel concept. Later, the same grid was used in the store's first annex of 1898 erected at the corner of Yonge and Richmond Street. Only in 1908, when seven additional bays were erected along Queen Street, were a series of continuous round arches framed in floral terra cotta introduced at each of the new entrances (fig. 7.7). Later, when Horwood had assumed full responsibility for design, these elegant if inapposite modifications were applied to the original portion.[13] The junior partner's longstanding affinity for ornamented architecture superseded Burke's carefully controlled austerity.[14]

Commercial *palazzi* with Romanesque arches encompassing several storeys were the latest American vogue, the best-known but by no means the earliest example being Chicago's Marshall Field Wholesale store of 1885–87 by Henry Hobson Richardson. The so-called arcaded building, studied in detail by art historian Sarah Bradford Landau, is believed to date back to New York's Bank of the Republic, of 1851–52, by Hurry & Rogers. Its precedents in turn come from such diverse sources as Labrouste's Bibliothèque Sainte-Geneviève of 1843–50 and British warehouse designs of the early nineteenth century. Refined in the 1870s and 1880s by architects like George B. Post,

7·7

7.7 Burke & Horwood and Burke,
Horwood & White. Robert Simpson
Company Store, Toronto, 1895 and 1908.
North facade during addition, 1908.
Photograph. AO, HC:C 11, Additional 5.

the arcaded building soon became a common feature of New York's commercial scene.[15]

Horwood was knowledgeable about New York's arcaded buildings and even recorded his own part in the design of one fine example – St Bartholomew's Parish House at 205 East 42nd Street, which was endowed in 1891 by Mrs W.K. Vanderbilt (fig. 7.8).[16] Twenty years later Burke & Horwood reconsidered the motif in a rather less ambitious version for the Ryrie building (owned by the prominent jewellery retailers who were related by marriage to Edmund Burke) of 1913 at the corner of Yonge and Shuter Streets (fig. 7.9). The northerly four bays were part of an existing structure. A further three bays were added to the south, and both parts were refaced.[17] Two lower floors (since altered) were almost entirely glass and framed by piers of channelled ashlar, with angled bays in the upper storey to assure maximum natural light. Above is a giant brick arcade uniting the third and fourth storeys, while on the fifth level a band of sash windows clustered in threes lights the attic.[18] A clear contrast to the rectilinear forms Burke chose for Simpson's, the arcade was yet another distinctive addition to the repertoire of commercial designs for which the firm was well known in its practice.

STEEL FRAME AND FIREPROOF CONSTRUCTION

In 1891, while still in partnership with Langley, Burke had bemoaned the fact that

[Old] methods are retained with a tenacity which indicates a very conservative habit of mind and an unreasoning adherence to traditions of methods of building which are unworthy of this scientific and progressive age.[19]

Horwood's correspondence from New York had obviously inspired Burke with the possibilities of new methods and technology. The following year, as he entered practice on his own, he ventured to undertake a public lecture on the subject of tension and compression strengths in cast and wrought iron.[20]

At the age of forty-two, with all the constraints of an established career, Burke was precluded from studying in the United States as both his future partners John Horwood and Murray White were doing. Yet his interest in technical issues, regarded by many as the province of the builder or engineer rather than that of the architect, marked him as a man of the future.[21] Apprenticeship had not prepared him for the complexities of curtain-wall construction, but by 1892 Burke assimilated the fundamentals of Chicago foundations and the metal frame. Then, in 1893, a visit to the Chicago World's Fair supplemented his knowledge, as may his contact with former associate and future partner Murray White, who was then working in Chicago for Holabird & Roche. Although the available information was often fragmentary, this stimulus, combined with Horwood's letters from New York, prompted a dramatic shift in Burke's thinking and methodology.[22]

In the spring of 1894 Burke planned the Robert Simpson department store, but lacked the experience to insist upon more expensive fireproofing for the interior in the face of his client's preference for cheaper wooden joists and floors. The dire implications of this decision did not become clear until after Horwood returned to Toronto later the same year. Even before fire had destroyed his venturesome new project, Burke was conscious of the need for new building by-laws.[23] After the store's destruction the *Canadian Architect and Builder* concluded: "It does not appear, in these larger cities [such as New York and Chicago] where this plan of building [warehouse construction] is so much followed, that very much better methods of fire protection and construction are adopted than in Toronto, where the experience has not been so great." A "well-known local architect" who had at one time "practised in New York" supported this contention by citing a similar warehouse fire that had recently taken place in the United States.[24] Burke's legislative review, supplemented by Horwood's first-hand knowledge of American examples, brought the firm's expertise to a level comparable with any in the United States.

There was a lapse of four years before the senior partner published any further lectures, but in 1898 the OAA invited Burke to discuss two more aspects of steel construction – rustproofing and fireproofing. He

7.8

7.8 Renwick, Aspinwall & Renwick. St Bartholomew's Parish House (demolished), New York, 1890–91. Exterior view, 1890s. Photograph by Robarts Library. UofT-RL: M. King, *King's Handbook of New York* (Boston, 1892), 324.

7.9

RYRIE BUILDING
CORNER OF
YONGE AND SHUTER STREETS
TORONTO

elaborated various techniques for preventing corrosion, and went on to detail laboratory tests reported in *Engineering Record* as well as recent findings from fires in Pittsburgh and Detroit.[25] Terra cotta was considered the best protection against fire, followed by hard burned clay, and finally by concrete.[26] After his experience with the Robert Simpson fire, Burke was probably the most fully informed Canadian practitioner, and he kept abreast of the literature on how to protect metal framing from excessive heat.

Nor did Burke's interest in fire safety end as he turned his attention to issues such as urban planning after the turn of the century. In 1901 he wrote yet another article on how to reduce fire losses in buildings, suggesting that insurance companies should make a scientific study of the risks in order to adjust their classifications and premiums accordingly. This market approach could then be used to discourage the building of cheap fire-traps. Metal-wrapped shutters, woven wire glass, enclosed elevators, and automatic sprinkler systems could also supplement existing fireproof construction. And in the case of commercial buildings still employing wood, the construction should always be of the slow-burning variety with beams and joists of heavy timber, and floors of thick planks.[27] His recommendations parallel those of an American writer a decade earlier.[28] During the intervening years the growing sophistication of American methods had had an important impact on Canadian architectural practice.

Canadian corporations who persisted in the belief that American firms had more experience in large commercial ventures often overlooked the accomplishments of native-born architects like Burke and his partner Horwood. In 1905, for example, Traders Bank of Canada invited the leading New York firm of Carrère & Hastings to prepare plans for a fifteen-storey office building on Yonge south of King Street (fig. 7.10). Complying with the OAA's requirements, the firm sent its Canadian-born associate Eustace G. Bird to set up an office in Toronto and supervise the construction. Canadian contractors were employed on the project, and upon its completion in 1907 an admiring article appeared in the *Canadian Architect and Builder*. The New York firm then added both the Royal Bank of Canada and the Bank of Toronto to its list of clients.[29]

Underlying attitudes, both American and Canadian, were revealed when Eustace Bird granted an interview to the Toronto *Star* newspaper in which he described Canada as a "new country" where architecture was necessarily "undeveloped." He suggested that Canadian architects ought "to rely on established principles ... perfected in New York or Europe." He admitted, however, that he, not the American office, had prepared the new plans for the Bank of Toronto for approval by the New York office – despite his relative lack of experience compared with that of the Canadian contenders Sproatt & Rolph, George Gouinlock, and John Lyle.[30]

Construction magazine responded by printing a scathing attack upon Bird and his New York principals. In reply Carrère & Hastings claimed that their agent had been misquoted, and pleaded that no ar-

7.9 Burke & Horwood. Ryrie Building, Yonge and Shuter, Toronto, 1899–1904. Exterior view, 1904. Photograph. AO, HC:C 11(1173)149.

7.10   Carrère & Hastings. Traders Bank of Canada (now Premier Trust), Toronto, 1905. Exterior view. Photograph. AO: Acc. 4952, s7427.

7.11   Burke, Horwood & White. Competition Entry for the Dominion Express Building, Montreal, not executed. Perspective, c.1910. Watercolour on board. AO, HC:C 11, perspectives.

7.11

7.10

chitect of any standing and good repute could possibly sympathize with the editor's motives. The rebuttal from *Construction* was ascerbic:

So remember! Canadian architects, that if you resent the inference that you are untrained because you live in a country where architecture is undeveloped, if you do not agree that it is only reasonable that large Canadian corporations should go to New York for architects to design their buildings – if you agree with the resentful spirit of an article that undertakes to protect the profession against the insidious attacks of a foreign architectural firm, then, mark you! because of these things you are not an architect of "standing and repute."[31]

Carrère & Hastings completed their work in Toronto and withdrew.

None of this was lost on Canadian architects. In 1910 when a competition was held for the Dominion Express building in Montreal, Burke, Horwood & White modelled their eleven-storey proposal after Traders Bank – the tripartite French Renaissance *palazzo* recapitulating the Beaux-Arts eclecticism of the American design right to its cantilevered balcony two floors below the cornice (fig. 7.11).[32] The motif was a feature of George B. Post's Havemeyer building in New York of 1891–92, which Horwood admired during his time in that city (fig. 7.12).[33] The firm's second unsuccessful attempt at an office highrise after its IOF submission, the Dominion Express project went instead to the Maxwell brothers of Montreal, whose Beaux-Arts training in the ateliers of Boston and Paris perhaps offered the "enlightenment" Eustace Bird had found lacking in Canada (fig. 7.13).[34] No longer secure in the ways of the past, Canadian professionals were forced to measure their performance against the most qualified of their American competitors, resorting to favoured American styles in order to achieve crediblity in the eyes of their Canadian clients.

7.12 George B. Post. Havemeyer Building (demolished), New York, 1891–92. Exterior view. Photograph. New York Historical Society, New York:48520.

7.13 E. & W.S. Maxwell, Dominion Express Building, Montreal, 1910–12. Exterior view. Photograph. NA:PA-45945.

7.12

7.13

BEAUX-ARTS: THE NEW CHICAGO STYLE

When it came to retail sales design, Burke & Horwood were on more secure ground: the new Simpson's department store had made their reputation. In February 1911 the Hudson's Bay Company was preparing to embark on a major rebuilding program in the Canadian West with flagship locations in Calgary, Vancouver, and Victoria. On the recommendation of H.H. Fudger, then one of the owners of the Robert Simpson Company store, Burke, Horwood & White were chosen in preference to Daniel H. Burnham & Co. of Chicago.[35] Hudson's Bay Stores Commissioner Herbert E. Burbidge later informed his London head office: "I have engaged Mr. J.C.B. Horwood of the firm Burke, Horwood & White, Toronto, as architect. He has had considerable experience in the erection of large stores and was the architect for Messrs. Simpson's new store in Toronto, and has also made a study of the large departmental establishments in New York and other large cities in the United States."[36] The partners thereby gained their most illustrious corporate patron and a lucrative series of commissions extending over two decades.

The imminent expansion of competitors from Eastern Canada forced the Hudson's Bay Company to discard its image as a trader in blankets and furs.[37] Calgary was the first location to be developed because its dynamic economic growth promised a rosy future. A site was purchased at the corner of Seventh Avenue and First Street early in 1911, and Stores Commissioner Burbidge pressed ahead with excavations at once, intending to complete the project before Christmas. Horwood's plans contemplated a six-storey, steel-framed structure with stone-clad piers on the two lower levels and brick facing on the upper floors (fig. 7.14). At an estimated cost of $1.5 million, the store was intended to assure the company's premier position by outstripping its competitors.[38]

When informed of the projected cost of the Calgary scheme London was incredulous, and suggested there had been some mistake.[39] The cabled response from Burbidge was succinct: "Excavation commenced two weeks ago; iron arranged, plans published. Disastrous [to] stop now in view of new developments and would mean eighteen months delay seriously detrimental to the company's prestige if building not proceeded with."[40] In a follow-up letter he urged his principals to consider the expectations of "such a pretentious city as Calgary," suggesting that the window of opportunity might be lost.[41] London failed to appreciate the magnitude of recent growth in ranching where only three decades before the market had been adequately served by a trading post.[42] With Dominion Bridge waiting to set a record for the delivery of structural steel, London insisted that the project be postponed for a year.[43]

By March of 1912 the company had studied the situation more thoroughly, and authorization was forthcoming not only for the Calgary store but for a similar premises in Vancouver as well. Following a visit by Horwood to London, the head office advised Burbidge that:

7.14

7.14   Burke, Horwood & White. Proposal
for Hudson's Bay Company Store,
Calgary, not executed. Perspective, c.1911.
Photograph by Robarts Library. UOfT-RB:
Contract Record 27 (1913):44.

7.15   Burke, Horwood & White. Hudson's
Bay Company Store, Calgary, 1912–13.
Exterior view of first section, 1917.
Photograph by W.J. Oliver, Calgary.
Glenbow Archives, Calgary:ND-8-280.

7.15

The [Calgary] building is to be erected to the design of the exterior of the sketch for the Vancouver store building, *which has been adopted as a model for all future buildings that may be erected for store purposes*, although to enable the steelwork already purchased to be utilized, the pillars will be flat fluted instead of round fluted as in the Vancouver plan. The pilasters are to be kept sufficiently small, compatible with perfect safety, so as to permit of the utmost possible window space, and with regard to the first story which is to be used as a showroom, the small pillars to the windows should be reduced to the greatest possible extent.[44]

The revised plan (fig. 7.15) was stylistically far removed from Horwood's original concept. The new scheme was based on the magnificent Beaux-Arts department design Daniel H. Burnham & Co. had conceived for American retailer Harry Selfridge in London (fig. 7.16).[45] Described as a "decorated warehouse" by Chicago scholar Neil Harris, Selfridge's peripteral Ionic colonnade of stone conceals a modern steel frame that assures an open interior suitable for American-style retail selling.[46]

Colonnades had first appeared in commercial buildings early in the nineteenth century, as Burke, Horwood & White well knew. Both the Petersburg Bourse of 1804, by French architect Thomas de Thomon, and A.T. Brongniart's Paris Bourse of 1808, evoked the grandeur of ancient Rome with files of unfluted freestanding columns.[47] Arranged on an elevated stylobate with shafts supporting an architrave and cornice, neoclassical rationalism articulated the fictional logic of the rustic hut proposed by French theorist Abbé Laugier.

A century later when Selfridge commissioned his "noble building along Greek lines," the vocabulary was more permissive.[48] The colonnade of the Oxford Street store is elevated on a one-storey base lined with large display windows while its Ionic order, reeded and decorated in the style of A.-J. Gabriel's Opéra de Versailles of 1760, ascends through three monumental storeys.[49] An attic and balustrade of French derivation cap the design. The result unites the classical and

7.16   D.H. Burnham & Co., Francis Swales, Frank Atkinson, J.J. Burnet and others. Selfridge's Department Store, London, 1907–9. Exterior view, 1909. Photograph. AO, HC:C 11, Additional 5, for illustration from *Builder* (1909).

7.17   Carrère & Hastings with Eustace Bird. Bank of Toronto (demolished), Toronto, 1911–13. Exterior view, no date. Photograph. NA:PA 60396.

7.16

7.17

7.19

7.19 Elzner & Anderson. Ingalls (Transit) Building, Cincinnati, 1903. Exterior view, 1909. Photograph. UofT-RB: *Construction* 2 (March 1909):47.

the Renaissance with Mannerism and Baroque in an American reprise of the bold eclecticism propounded by the French Ecole.[50]

Beaux-Arts forms similar to those developed by Burham had already entered Canada directly from the United States. The Bank of Toronto at the corner of Bay and King, already mentioned in connection with the Carrère & Hastings fiasco, was one such example (fig. 7.17). Its attached Corinthian order in grey Tennessee marble concealed five levels of offices.[51] Such classical temple precedents could be made to serve almost any commercial purpose with associations that lent a sacrosanct air to the most worldly and mundane of life's proceedings.

The Hudson's Bay Company chose the peripteral format to impress the most critical and demanding of Calgary's *nouveau riche*. Burnham's palatial motif was the last word in department store design in the early years of the century, and there could be little doubt that this emblem of American modernism would satisfy Canadian tastes. Backed by Murray White's years of experience with the Beaux-Arts in Chicago, the firm was poised for its most challenging and opulent undertaking to date.

As in many western cities, Calgary's thriving economy had propelled it from frontier town to modern metropolis virtually overnight.[52] Early in the boom years American technology flooded across the Prairies, beginning in Winnipeg at the turn of the century, and extending to Calgary by 1908.[53] Where previously two storeys had been the rule, the boom spawned a generation of high-rise office buildings. Calgary's first modern block was the six-storey Grain Exchange completed in 1909 (fig. 7.18) by local architects Hodgson & Bates. While its sandstone facade was in the tradition of the city's low-rise commercial buildings, its Kahn system of reinforced concrete framing was in keeping with the latest technological developments in the United States.[54]

Concrete reinforcement had only just achieved a level of predictable performance despite a half-century's knowledge of the underlying principles.[55] Before Julius Kahn, brother of the well-known Detroit architect Albert Kahn invented the Kahn system in 1903, empirical testing had been the only way to ascertain structural safety of the product. The new system, devised according to scientific principles, was marketed through the Trussed Concrete Steel Company of Youngstown, Ohio.[56] At the same time Kahn's competitor, Ferro-Concrete Construction, designed and built a reinforced concrete frame for the Ingalls Transit building in Cincinnati, of 1902–3, by Elzner & Anderson (fig. 7.19). At sixteen-storeys, it was the first concrete skyscraper ever erected.[57] Then in 1905 a treatise detailing forty-four known systems of reinforcement was published, and in 1908 major cities in the eastern United States and Canada began enacting by-laws to govern its use in commercial structures.[58]

Because of the expense of shipping steel overland, reinforced concrete was an immediate success in Calgary. By 1912 Hodgson, Bates & Co. had followed their earlier triumph with another Kahn-system building, this time for ranching tycoon Patrick Burns. First planned as two-storey project, it expanded to six in response to favourable economic conditions (fig. 7.20).[59] This time, however, the narrow rectilinear block was faced with cream-glazed terra cotta, an economical and easily maintained substitute for cut stone that enjoyed a limited vogue in the wake of Chicago's White City of 1893.[60]

Architects from the East adopted similar materials when they worked in Calgary. Brown & Vallance of Montreal, in a project undertaken for Canada Life, chose reinforced concrete and glazed terra cotta to create a six-storey commercial *palazzo* with a curved porcelainic exterior for the corner of Eighth Avenue and Second Street West (fig. 7.21).[61] On occasion, however, structural steel was preferred for its durability or because reinforced concrete was considered too recent an innovation. Edmonton's McLeod building of 1909 and Calgary's Lancaster building of 1913, both by American architects, and the Palliser Hotel in Calgary, by the Maxwell brothers of Montreal, were unusual for their use of steel framing.[62]

From his vantage point in Toronto, Horwood could not have appreciated the cost of shipping large quantities of steel to the West. Only in subsequent undertakings did the London head office consider

7.18   Hodgson & Bates. Grain Exchange, Calgary, 1908–9. Exterior view, 1910. Photograph by Progress Photo Co. NA:PA 29703.

7.20   Hodgson, Bates & Beattie. Burns Building, Calgary, 1912–13. Exterior view, 1913. Photograph. Glenbow Archives, Calgary:NA-2159–11.

7.18

7.20

taking advantage of this economy.[63] Savings were possible, however, in the choice of Doulton terra cotta in preference to the cut stone originally considered for the store's exterior.[64] Flat pilasters were substituted for attached columns when it was discovered that the dimensions of the structural steel (already purchased before the new elevation was approved) would not be suitable for the giant order then being planned.[65] The project began, at last, in the spring of 1912, and the store finally opened in August of the following year.[66]

Apart from the delay occasioned by London's hesitation, the Calgary store took longer than the Robert Simpson project because it was so much more elaborate. Instead of curtain-wall construction, the terra cotta had to be pieced together to give the appearance of load-bearing construction. Contemporary theorists justified the application of this decorative veneer to the underlying frame on the basis of the clear relationship between the two.[67] In a 1908 article reprinted in the *Canadian Architect and Builder*, one American writer noted that "steel and concrete structure can ... be well expressed [by partly engaged columns and pilasters], the engaged column often following literally the support within it, and the entablature indicating the deep girders."[68]

Like Simpson's, the Hudson's Bay store in Calgary articulated all its vertical members consistently, the corner piers sharing the same width as the pilasters.[69] This was in sharp contrast to the Midwest practice of doubling or tripling the breadth at the corners out of all proportion to the dimensions of the structure beneath.[70] It suggests, too, that the Canadian firm understood the necessity for structural "truth" and avoided verbatim copying of American precedents. Yet the Hudson's Bay Beaux-Arts motif mirrored the pattern of retrenchment in American architectural theory that followed the World's Fair of 1893. Such evident convergence in stylistic interpretation therefore makes the firm's truthful approach to expression all the more significant.

The United States was unmatched as a source for architectural precedents in the field of commercial architecture. As one commentator remarked, "The office building is to modern America what the church was to medieval Europe, the typical building from which architecture must be shaped."[71] Yet Western Canadians were no more amenable to American competitors than their Eastern counterparts. When the Pittsburgh millionaire Andrew Carnegie funded Calgary's first library in 1908, Alberta's architects were outraged when McLean & Wright of Boston, Massachusetts, secured the commission without even entering the competition.[72] Similarly many railroad projects went to Americans, either as designers or contractors, provoking intense reaction from their Canadian counterparts.[73]

As far as the Hudson's Bay Company was concerned, its future reputation and competitive position were in the hands of its Canadian architects, and the company's corporate prestige depended upon their awareness of world-wide developments. Nor did this expectation diminish over the years. When Horwood & White were retained in 1928 to double the size of the Calgary store, the chairman of the

7.21   Brown & Vallance. Canada Life
Building, Calgary, 1913. Exterior view, no
date. Photograph donated by Albert Marche,
Flesher Marble and Tile, Calgary.
Glenbow Archives, Calgary:NA-1469-3.

7.22   Burke, Horwood & White, and
Horwood & White. Hudson's Bay
Company Store, Calgary, 1912–13, and
1928. Arcade, 1928. Photograph by
W.J. Oliver. Glenbow Archives,
Calgary:NA-2037-22.

7.22

7.21

Canadian committee suggested the addition of an arcade – like one he
had seen in Brussels – to extend the full length of the First Avenue
frontage (fig. 7.22).[74] Not only did it protect shoppers from the
weather, but the company was pleased draw comparisons with similar examples in all the finest European cities.[75] Officials also toured
stores in Minneapolis, Chicago, Newark, and New York to acquaint
themselves with the latest designs. Taussig & Flesch of Chicago were
commissioned to plan the fixtures for the extension, and company
governor Charles Sale stated, "We are all anxious that [the new build-
ing] should represent the best and most up-to-date practice!"[76] Such
aspirations ended with the Depression, but, for a time, Burke,
Horwood & White and their client were at the forefront of competitive retailing.

When the western building campaign was initiated in 1911, the
Hudson's Bay Company also decided to proceed with a new store for

Vancouver. Horwood's proposal called for six storeys (fig. 7.23) with provision for four additional floors (fig. 7.24). Its frame was of ferro-concrete covered with attached columns of terra cotta.[77] Excavations began in September of 1913, and by January 1914 the installation of the terra cotta was underway. Two years later the store opened, its completion delayed by the outbreak of World War I.[78]

The elegance of the new Vancouver facility was in striking contrast to the town's first Hudson's Bay Company outlet – a shingled warehouse erected in 1887 on Cordova Street to serve a tiny settlement at the end of the transcontinental railway. As the population grew through access provided by the railway, the company found it necessary to move to a four-storey red brick building at the corner of Granville and Georgia Streets. Soon the demands of the Klondike Gold Rush pushed this facility to its limit, and after several additions and annexes it seemed time to build anew.[79]

Reinforced concrete technology had been introduced in Vancouver in 1908 by the local architectural firm of Parr & Fee in their design for the Hotel Europe on Powell Street (fig. 7.25). The building's distinctive flat-iron design with its dramatic Italianate cornice was carried on a concrete frame built by Ferro-Concrete Construction Company, whose 1902–3 scheme for the Ingalls Transit building in Cincinnati has already been mentioned. Parr & Fee, like their Calgary counterparts were well versed in the latest American innovations, Parr having trained in Winnipeg, and Fee in Minneapolis.[80]

Other Vancouver architects were not so quick to adopt new ideas. Woodward's, the Bay's chief retail competitor, for example, built a modern store at the corner of Hastings and Abbott in 1908, but settled for traditional wooden posts and beams. Of the high-rise buildings erected in the city that year, most were framed in tried-and-true structural steel instead of the more innovative ferro-concrete. But by 1910 another local architect, W.R. Somervell, had experimented with reinforced concrete for his eight-storey Bauer (now Pemberton) building on West Hastings.[81] By the time the Hudson's Bay Company began its own premises in 1913, poured reinforced concrete was a well-established local material.

The Vancouver architectural profession also accepted white-glazed terra cotta. In 1910 Parr & Fee had used it to cloak the steel-framed Vancouver Block on Granville Street just behind the Hudson's Bay site (fig. 7.26). A year later Seattle architects Gould & Champney followed suit with the Rogers building several blocks further north along Granville. And on the corner opposite the site of the new store, Somervell & Putnam had added a third example to the city's inventory with their Birks building of 1912–13.[82] With the growth of the White City out of a cluster of clapboard warehouses at the end of the western rail line, Vancouver became one of the country's major cities and its most important port of entry on the Pacific rim.

The Hudson's Bay Company seemed to have been aware of the growth potential of Vancouver from the outset and conceived a major location there. The first five bays on Georgia Street were only a begin-

7.23

7.25

7.24

ning (fig. 7.27). Eventually Horwood & White were authorized to undertake a $2.5 million expansion in 1925, which coincided with plans the company had had in mind since 1913. So great had been the growth in the previous two decades that the company had planned a block-long street frontage on Georgia when the project began. Provision was also made to add a four more storeys should this be required at a later time. Redraughting in 1925 provided for a six-storey section on a lot diagonally adjoining the 1913 store (fig. 7.28). The 1893 store, which still occupied the corner lot, was then torn down to accommodate the expansion on Georgia Street as originally proposed (fig. 7.29). Instead of adding to the height, the store spread over most of a city block, so that by November its facades were contiguous.[83] The new scheme recognized a consensus among retailers that high-rise structures were not economic because of the costs involved in powering elevators for thousands of shoppers.[84]

More elaborate than the original, the enlarged store included a small shopping concourse similar to the more ambitious Calgary colonnade erected three years later. Still concerned with running a tight ship, the company criticized Horwood's store-window designs for "excessive ornamentation," and pressured the architect to see "eye-to-eye" over desired economies.[85] Even after budget trimming, the facility included a lending library, writing room, and contract bridge shop, as well as a lecture hall that became a locus for talks by Arctic explorers and South Sea adventurers, and the home of a children's theatre, girls' choir, and local little theatre association. In short, the store was a cultural centre for the community, its events designed to attract customers and inspire the loyalty of a new generation.[86]

For its Victoria store the Hudson's Bay Company purchased a site at the corner of Douglas and Fisgard streets from St John's Anglican Church. Plans began in 1913 for a four-storey structure of the type previously approved for Calgary and Vancouver (fig. 7.30). Provision was made for ten storeys as business warranted. The *Daily Colonist* touted the $450,000 appropriation as an indication of the high-class character of the building, while the manager assured his customers that the facility would include "a modern café and all other features which now are considered indispensible parts of the modern *American* institution of the kind in question."[87]

How different this was from the small wooden fort the company had first occupied on the island in 1843 after abandonning the Oregon territory to the westward march of American settlers. Sixteen years later the company had moved to a red-brick warehouse on Wharf Street that accommodated the needs of two generations of prospectors in the Caribou and the Klondike. By 1913 local boosterism almost demanded that Victoria have a facility that would compete with its sister project on the mainland.[88] Pundits considered that the injection of funds "would react upon the capital now held in abeyance by other corporations, and so inaugurate a general movement."[89]

In July, a few months before the Vancouver project began, Horwood wrote to his office in Toronto with instructions about the

7.26

7.23   Burke, Horwood & White. Proposal for Hudson's Bay Company Store, Vancouver, 1913. Perspective, c.1913. Watercolour on board. AO, HC:C 11, perspectives.

7.24   Burke, Horwood & White. Proposal for Hudson's Bay Company Store, Vancouver, 1913. Perspective with proposed four-storey addition, c.1913. Photograph. AO, HC:C 11, Additional 5.

7.25   Parr & Fee. Hotel Europe, Vancouver, 1908. Exterior view, no date. Photograph. CVA 229–12.

7.26   Parr & Fee. Vancouver Block, Vancouver, 1910. Exterior view, no date. Photograph from Samuel J. Zacks. NA:PA 117959.

7.27

7.27   Burke, Horwood & White. Hudson's Bay Company Store, Vancouver, 1913. Exterior view, June 1922. Photograph by Leonard Frank. Vancouver Public Library, Vancouver (VPL):11258.

drawings for Victoria. He advised that, "as Van Raalte is familiar with all this on Vancouver, he had better work this out for the Victoria Building also." Clearly all the work had been executed in the Toronto office, and draughtsman Solomon S. Van Raalte – whose bold hand is unmistakable in many of the firm's projects – had been entrusted with many of the awkward technical details. In Victoria, meanwhile, Horwood continued his negotiations with the city's building department, initiating a change in local by-laws to facilitate construction of the building's reinforced concrete frame.[90]

At the time the city's most modern commercial structure was the Belmont building of 1912 on Humbolt Street (fig. 7.31). Planned as a hotel but built as offices by architects Norton & Phipps, the eight-storey structure was one of the first in the city to utilize reinforced concrete.[91] In September 1913 the Hudson's Bay Company sought to follow this lead. Work progressed well through the reinforced concrete framing and terra-cotta cladding until war was declared the following year. In the circumstances it was decided to moth-ball the project, and only those items necessary to render the premises safe were finished. It was 1920 before Horwood was called upon to complete the interior, and the autumn of 1921 before all departments were operational.[92] In the meantime the architects had experienced a number of setbacks with their corporate patron, which eventually brought their long association to an end.

The rift began as Horwood was retained to plan a fourth major location in Winnipeg. The company purchased a site on Portage Avenue, but the city's proposal to turn the stretch of land into a processional mall leading to the new legislative buildings jeopardized the project. Arrangements were made to adjust the location of the lot, but ensuing economic declines put the scheme in abeyance. Then in 1916 the company reexamined the situation and decided to explore the possibility of a temporary structure. Horwood recommended that the work be undertaken as the first stage of a permanent project because the soil was too unstable to build without caissons and fireproof materials were necessary in any event.[93]

7.28   Burke, Horwood & White, and Horwood & White. Hudson's Bay Company Store, 1913, and 1925–26. First phase of addition, 1925–26. Photograph, 26 March 1926. (CVA 64–1).

7.28

7.29   Burke, Horwood & White, and
Horwood & White. Hudson's Bay
Company Store, Vancouver, 1913, and
1925–26. Second phase of the addition
showing poured concrete framing, 1 June
1926. Photograph by Stuart Thomson.
(VPL:11260).

7.30   Burke, Horwood & White. Hudson's
Bay Company Store, Victoria, 1913–21.
Perspective, c.1913. Watercolour on board.
AO, HC:C 11, perspectives.

7.30

7.31   Norton & Phipps. Belmont Building, Victoria, 1912. Exterior view, no date. Perspective from *The Week* (Victoria) 1 June 1912. Provincial Archives of British Columbia, Victoria:70148, D-6422.

7.31

London gave instructions that the new Winnipeg store should be such as to command "world-wide attention," so in 1917 when Horwood was asked to proceed he proposed a twelve-storey building arranged around three courtyards with the centremost topped by a dome that would have rivalled St Paul's (figs. 7.32 and 7.33). The first stage was to be six storeys, occupying one third of the site. Pilasters located between the display windows and a "flat wall" design would have permitted extensions without disrupting the exterior. In November 1918, however, the governor and committee dismissed the design as disappointing: "The facade is an entire departure from the style of architecture employed for the buildings at Calgary, Vancouver, and Victoria, which you will remember was adopted by the Board as the style of architecture to be employed in the chain of Stores to be built by the Company throughout the West, so that travellers who had seen one store would be able to recognize the others at a glance."

They also criticized the internal arrangement of the pillars, and proposed to submit the project to public competition.[94]

In his reply to the committee, Stores Commissioner Burbidge tried to be upbeat: "I am sure there are no other Architects in Canada possessing greater knowledge than their Mr. Horwood in connection with the designing and construction of departmental stores." He went

7.32 Burke, Horwood & White. Proposed
Hudson's Bay Company Store, Winnipeg,
not executed. Elevation, 1917. Pen on
linen. Hudson's Bay Company Archives,
Provincial Archives of Manitoba,
Winnipeg:A.12/s 543/2, folio 181.

7.33 Burke, Horwood & White. Proposed
Hudson's Bay Company Store, Winnipeg,
not executed. Plan of Ground Floor, 1917.
Pen on linen. Hudson's Bay Company
Archives, Provincial Archives of Manitoba,
Winnipeg:A.12/s 543/2, folio 174.

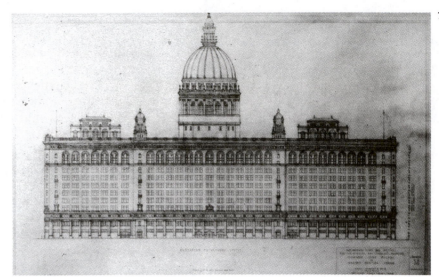

7.32

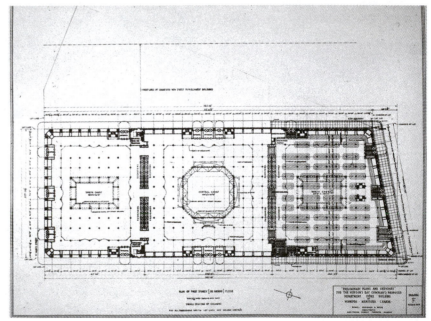

7.33

on to observe the long standing association saying, "The Architect
only draws up plans of the structure to meet the wishes of the owner."
Horwood was then authorized to proceed, and at the request the deputy chair of the Canadian committee even introduced a shopping arcade into the design of 1920. The company did not reveal the full
extent of its reservations until April 1922. By this time, it was so preoccupied with extricating itself from any future commitment to the architects, it refused to discuss anything further until the outstanding
fees were settled.[95]

Horwood was forced to point out that his charges for all the previous projects had been based on the assumption that he would be undertaking all four of the company's major buildings. If the arrangement was to be changed, fees would have to be assessed at the full rate. A lengthy correspondence ensued, at the end of which Horwood & White settled for one fifth of what they claimed together with a commitment that they would be employed as the architects for the Vancouver store additions.[96] Barrott & Blackader of Montreal were asked to take over the Winnipeg project, and delivered a rather modest design with flat pilasters instead of the round columns the company had been so insistent Horwood use (fig. 7.34).

An internal memorandum written one year before Horwood's death when the Hudson's Bay Company was contemplating further additions to its buildings weighed the relative merits of the two firms. Barrott & Blackader were termed "too casual" and inclined to "let George do it." On the other hand, Horwood & White were considered "very thorough" if overly cautious and inclined "to double up on everything to provide for use during Leap Years." In the end the new projects went to a Winnipeg firm, Moody & Moore, because Horwood & White were by this time perceived to be "too slow" and "not up-to-date."[97] Yet the effort Horwood lavished upon his works has stood the test of time – all his Hudson's Bay structures are now recognized as historically significant monuments. His three Beaux-Arts masterpieces are emblematic of the self-confident expansionist mood of the Canadian West in the boom years between 1908 and the First World War when, like Athena, the metropolitan centres sprang "fully-formed" from the prairie and the Pacific coast.

7.34 Barott & Blackader. Hudson's Bay Company Store, Winnipeg, 1925 on. Exterior view, September 1928. Photograph. (NA:C-033696).

7.34

7.35   Burke, Horwood & White. Methodist
Book and Publishing Company Building
(now City TV), Toronto, 1913–16.
Perspective, 1913. Photograph. AO, HC:C
11, Additional 5.

7.35

While the firm's western Beaux-Arts works may be his most striking
accomplishment of this period, two other commercial examples in
Toronto are equally evocative of the later commercial designs of
Burke, Horwood & White in this time and of the requirements of individual clients: the Methodist Book and Publishing Company of
1913–16 which was decorated in terra cotta with a Gothic motif that
some thought suitable to the religious affiliations of the enterprise
(fig. 7.35), and Thomas Ogilvie & Sons warehouse of 1907 in red
pressed brick trimmed with grey stone, a kind of commercial hybrid
of Richard Norman Shaw and George B. Post (fig. 7.36).[98] In the variety of their stylistic approaches Burke, Horwood & White exemplify
the values of their era. More concerned with high standards of execution than issues of "national" significance, their firm traverses the
great divide between British conventions and American innovation,
leaving the question of cultural identity to the younger generation.

7.36   Burke, Horwood & White. Thomas
Ogilvie & Sons Warehouse, Toronto,
1907. Perspective, c.1907. Watercolour on
board. AO, HC:C 11, perspectives.

8 Professional Organization: Education and the Public Interest

> The man of science is a professional man, perfectly clear as to professional etiquette, professional ethics and professional fees; decidedly in favour of compulsory registration.
> MacKay Fripp, "Architecture – A Profession or an Art?"
> *Construction* (February 1915)

In the last two decades of his life Edmund Burke turned his attention to what might best be described as community service. His involvement with the Ontario Association of Architects, which began at its inception in 1889, became a major commitment in the early years of the new century. Having served one term as president of the provincial organization in 1894, he was elected again in 1905–7, at the same time acting as chairman of the Toronto chapter. In 1906, during his tenure as provincial president, he chaired the federal government's board of assessors in a public competition for the design of the Departmental and Justice buildings in Ottawa. He also joined Toronto's Civic Guild, and became involved in a number of town planning projects, including a radial road system for the city, the widening of certain arterial routes, a site plan for the grounds of the Canadian National Exhibition, and the architectural design of the Bloor Viaduct. Indeed Burke seems to have involved himself in so many projects at this point in his career that his activities traverse most of the important public issues of his day.

In 1887 both Burke and Langley were among the founding members of the Architectural Guild of Toronto. Eleven years earlier they had participated in the short-lived Institute of Architects, but this time the effort was more successful. Widespread concern over Richard Waite's appointment as architect of the province's legislative buildings the year before and a strike in the building trades brought matters to a head. A group of well-known practitioners met at the offices of William G. Storm, and that October the Architectural Guild was formally established.[1]

The idea of a society to represent architects was not new. As early as 1834 (the same year the Institute of British Architects was founded) William Warren Baldwin, a Toronto medical practitioner, sometime lawyer, and amateur architect, suggested such an organization to improve Toronto's building standards. Nothing came of this until 1849 when the Canadian Institute was founded for engineers, architects, and surveyors. Over the next decade the Institute's activities were largely confined to scientific endeavours. A second group known as the Association of Architects, Civil Engineers and Public Land Surveyors was set up in 1859 under the presidency of architect

William Thomas, but after his death a year later surveyors dominated the organization.[2]

When the Architectural Guild was eventually established it functionned as a social club for practising architects. Its objects included the promotion of good fellowship, discussion of subjects of general professional interest, criticism of members' works with the intention of producing the best architectural results, recognition of the profession by the public, and improvement in standards of professional ethics.[3] Burke attended the meetings regularly, and in January of 1888 was elected to the executive. In the following years he served not only as a member of the Guild but also played a significant role in founding the Ontario Association of Architects, which developed from it.

As the architectural profession in the province strove to establish its credibility, a monthly professional journal *Canadian Architect and Builder* began publication in January 1888. Its first issue noted "the rapid improvement in methods and materials of construction, in decorative art, and in sanitary appliances, which has marked the history of the last ten years in Canada, and the field of usefulness which seems to lie open to a printed medium of information and communication between thousands of persons interested in such subjects."[4] The editor voiced support for the idea of an architectural department at the School of Practical Science in Toronto, asking the government's assistance in funding such an undertaking. By July the Honourable George W. Ross, minister of education, had responded by requesting the Guild's recommendations for a chair in architecture at the School of Practical Science in Toronto.[5]

A committee appointed by the Guild met with the minister of education the following November. Not only was a professor of architecture to be appointed "at an early date" and a technical school opened, but the province's architects were asked to incorporate a professional body with power to examine candidates for admission to practice. At a time when architecture was only beginning to gain recognition as a profession and no statutory registration of any kind existed in any jurisdiction, the proposal must have seemed momentous.[6] Indeed Henry Langley, who delivered the report of the meeting, declared the committee to have been unprepared for such an effective and elaborate scheme.[7]

Within six months the Guild had issued invitations to architects throughout the province, calling a meeting for 21 March 1889 at the Queen's Hotel in Toronto. Edmund Burke, as one of the organizers, had the honour of putting the motion that "the Architects here present form themselves into an Association." Sixty-two founding members then adopted a constitution with the object of uniting in fellowship the architects of the province, combining their efforts to promote the artistic, scientific and practical efficiency of the profession, cultivating and encouraging the study of kindred arts, and endeavouring to obtain legislation by which standards of professional knowledge and experience would be required by all persons practising the profession. William G. Storm was elected president, and Burke was among the first directors. Within the year the Association had applied for incorporation.[8]

The initial intention was to elevate the standard of practice by creating what was known as a "closed corporation" to license all architects carrying on business within the province. This would have excluded foreigners unless they secured standing with the Association. Legislation passed in 1890 fell short of this goal by failing to prohibit the use of the title "architect" by non-members. Instead those qualified under the act were authorized to call themselves "Registered Architects."[9] As a result, the OAA began its existence as a voluntary organization with an optional system of examinations.

The lack of provision for mandatory registration weakened the organization's position, particularly with respect to its control over standards. Responsible members found themselves hamstrung in rooting out abuses – amidst widespread ethical inefficacy at other levels, most notably in urban politics.[10] At the first organizational meeting of the OAA, Burke put forward a motion to prohibit kickbacks from contractors and material suppliers:

[That] no member shall accept direct or indirect compensation for services rendered in the practice of his profession other than that received from his clients.

He articulated a norm respected by reputable practitioners, and in keeping with professional standards, but the problem must have been serious enough to require a further motion three months later:

That all members of this Association be asked to inform the Secretary of any attempt on the part of any person or persons, supplying material who have offered them directly or indirectly a commission that such action may be taken as will reduce this evil to the greatest extent.[11]

Burke was also invited to prepare a paper on ethics for the next convention.

On 20 November 1889 Burke addressed his fellows on the subject of professional conduct, stating that architects must show strict and unswerving loyalty to the interests of the client, insist upon direct supervision of all aspects of the work, and refuse to make the contractor a scapegoat for deficiencies. As "expert and umpire" (Burke's terminology) the architect had an obligation to steer a judicious and temperate course, placing himself under financial obligation to no one but his client.[12] Work was not to be taken away from other architects, nor should there be unfair fee competition, disparaging remarks about fellow professionals, or unprofessional advertising – principles already endorsed by the medical fraternity. Such standards would maintain the dignity and integrity of the profession while putting an end to the petty jealousies, which association president William George Storm viewed as a major cause of past organizational failures. At the close of these remarks Burke's former mentor Henry Langley rose to protest blatant advertising on new building projects, and a resolution to ban this in future carried.[13]

Among the unethical practices that were brought to the attention of the profession at the time were commissions offered to third parties for business referrals and reductions in client fees brought about by extorting the difference from contractors and suppliers. The Architectural Guild had already been admonished by one of its members for harbouring in its ranks a "disreputable individual" known to engage in such practices. A mechanism for investigating such accusations was suggested, but the name of the offending party was never recorded.[14]

Many years later Burke & Horwood received a letter from a Wisconsin company offering 5 percent of the contract price if they would recommend the installation of certain equipment in their projects. They were asked to name clients so that buyers could be directly approached and then referred to the architects' firm as a "disinterested" party. Burke & Horwood promptly published the letter and the firm's response, which stated that no reputable practitioner would partake in such a scheme. Further solicitations of this type, the partners wrote, should be avoided if the company wanted to retain the good will of right-minded architects.[15]

Along with his commitment to ethical practice, Burke also gave a great deal of his time to the education of the younger members of the profession. His responsible approach was, no doubt, a legacy of the Langley draughting room, which placed a premium on student training. But the OAA's inability to insist upon compliance with its rules must have made Burke's task a frustrating one. Those who were already in practice registered without sitting exams, while new applicants had to prove their competence. Graduates of a university arts program were exempt from the first of a three-tiered examination process, and those with qualifications from the School of Practical Science were also forgiven two years of the mandatory five-year articling term.[16] As a minimum, candidates were required to finish the second form of high school or its equivalent in order to qualify for the first exam.

Burke served on the first board of examiners with C.H.C. Wright, of the School of Practical Science, and S.H. Townsend, who had articled with W.G. Storm. He set the finals for practical knowledge of the building trades and the nature and properties of materials, as well as the intermediate level exams for both structural ironwork and elements of building construction.[17] As one of the city's busiest practitioners, his involvement testifies to a serious personal commitment in the matter of training and professional standards.

The testing process was a rigourous one: drawings of the orders were required at the intermediate level, and written topics included elements of construction, history of architecture, mathematics, and applied mechanics. A second examination called for detail drawings, together with a knowledge of style characteristics, strength of materials, graphic statics, structural ironwork, and electricity. Finally the student had to prepare a full set of drawings and demonstrate an appreciation of the nature and properties of materials, a practical knowledge of the building trades and heating and ventilation, as well as of applied mathematics, sanitary science, and architectural jurisprudence.[18] Yet there was little inducement to undertake such an onerous program of study, because students could still article without sitting the exams.

Because of the problems associated with its ambiguous status, the OAA began to lobby for a "closed corporation" of the type the minister of education had originally proposed. Following the 1895 convention there was a concerted but unsuccessful effort to have the law amended. Later, beleaguered by declining revenues and an underutilized examination program, members sought to have the government assume responsibility for testing.[19] This demand became all the more pressing in the closing year of the century following a protest by a group of young architects, including John Horwood, over the accreditation of junior members. It was discovered that a young applicant had been passed over in favour of an older individual with lower examination marks. To register their disapproval, a number of supporters banded together to form the Toronto Architectural Eighteen Club.[20] The group decided to emphasize the artistic aspects of the profession instead of lobbying for legislation and examinations on technical subjects.[21] Strongly influenced by the Arts and Crafts movement in Britain, the group adopted the views of Richard Norman Shaw and T.G. Jackson in opposing compulsory registration, and sought to raise the standing of the profession in the community through voluntary educational programs and participation in annual exhibitions. The Eighteen also affiliated itself with the Architectural League of America for a time, and later established a studio system for students which adopted the atelier methods of the Beaux-Arts.[22]

Challenged at its 1899 convention by the dissidents, the OAA decided to shift its priorities to education.[23] A liaison committee was set up, and by 1901 the ideas of the Eighteen's president Eden Smith were translated into a new curriculum ordered around science, business, and studio subjects. Arrangements were made with the School of Practical Science to have students receive scientific training while completing their articles, and patrons were appointed to oversee studio work. Within a year it was apparent that students were too poorly qualified to deal with the system, so the OAA and the Eighteen jointly established a new program of classes. True to their artistic interests the Eighteen handled the instruction in design, while the OAA assumed responsibility for mathematics.[24]

Meanwhile the Association continued its efforts to reconcile with the Eighteen. President Edmund Burke was chief among the conciliators for the OAA – his partner Horwood was an equally vocal exponent for the Eighteen. In 1905 the latter group petitioned the University of Toronto to include artistic training in its architecture program, and Burke sponsored a motion to amend the OAA charter so as to facilitate the unification of the two organizations, but the complexity of amendments demanded by the Eighteen confounded the move.[25]

In 1908 the OAA decided to take another run at the registration problem, and the university was asked to conduct qualifying examinations for the profession. It was left to the government to decide whether the Association should have any status as a registering body. But public opposition caused withdrawal of the bill. Then a 1909 *Construction* editorial favouring government licensing brought vehement objections from Horwood, who claimed that registration would not protect the public and that education was the only method by which standards could be raised. A.H. Gregg, an OAA member, agreed with Horwood's assertions but insisted that a minimum standard had to be required. The battle of the pens continued, but in June the Eighteen agreed not to oppose statutory registration as long as it was based on education ascertained by examinations under direct government control. In October the university agreed to expand its facilities, and the program became a mandatory condition precedent to student articles. The immediate necessity for registration was thereby eliminated, and the Eighteen eventually merged with the OAA in 1912.[26]

In addition to the educational initiatives of the OAA, the ministry of education proposed to establish a technical school. The government wanted an institution to teach "such subjects as may promote a knowledge of mechanical and manufacturing arts." In January 1892 the Toronto Technical School opened its doors with a program that concentrated on mathematics, and included mechanics, chemistry, physics, and draughting. Classes were held five nights a week between eight and ten o'clock, and were offered free to all city residents.[27] Edmund Burke and Samuel George Curry joined the board as representatives of the Architectural Guild in 1891, and Burke continued in the post for four consecutive years. As the *Canadian Architect and Builder* pointed out, "Everything in the success of such an institution must depend upon the zeal of the board of management, and the ability of the instructors."[28] By 1894 the staff had grown to nine instructors and the aggregate attendance reached 631, a testimonial to the success of the five municipal councillors, five Trades and Labour Council representatives, two stationary engineers, two professional educators, one manufacturer, and two members of the Architectural Guild who handled its management.[29]

Enthusiasm engendered by the new professionalism paid dividends in terms of community involvement in other areas. In January 1895 when the OAA held its annual convention, Burke was finishing his first term as president. Earlier that month two serious fires had destroyed the Globe and Osgoodby buildings. Burke's opening address responded to recent events by suggesting amendments to existing by-laws, such as thicker party walls to act as fire breaks, metal shutters to protect window openings, corbels to support timber framing without piercing brickwork, and fireproofing for steel-framed buildings over seventy feet in height.[30] It was a grim irony that his speech preceded by less than two months the destruction of his own Robert Simpson store, apparently at the hands of an arsonist.

The 1895 speech marked Burke's first involvement with urban regulation, an issue that was to preoccupy him throughout the closing years of his life. In response to his plea for more comprehensive by-law controls, fellow architect Kivas Tully recollected past attempts when fire destroyed the eastern district of Toronto including St James Church in 1849. He noted that the proposals were later watered down for the benefit of speculative builders.[31] A requirement that warehouses covering more than thirty "squares of building" be divided was said to be "more honoured in the breach than in the observance."[32] Tully, Burke, and a former Langley student, Henry B. Gordon, undertook to review the matter. Within days the OAA registrar advised City Council that a submission was being prepared, and requested that any new legislation be deferred until the OAA report could be presented. Over the next two months a series of meetings took place during which building ordinances from other major cities were studied. By 18 March 1895, just twelve days after the Robert Simpson store fire, proposals were ready for the city's consideration.[33]

Council was asked to implement some of the changes right away, notably fireproofing for public buildings and buildings exceeding seventy feet in height, enclosure of elevator shafts, dividing walls for any structure exceeding four thousand square feet of floor area, and noncombustible fireproofing for structural iron work. After two months a restriction on undivided floor space was enacted together with a requirement that "proper" fire escapes be provided in public buildings over two storeys in height. Within a year exemptions were allowed for fireproof structures and those equipped with an automatic sprinkler system.[34] Then, further action was deferred.[35]

Civic planning, as such, only came to the fore after the turn of the century, but the annual meeting of the OAA in 1895 is noteworthy as the first occasion on which the issue came before the Association's delegates. Again Burke introduced the subject, referring to a proposal by the Province of Quebec Association of Architects for a civic committee to supervise the design of public monuments and parks in Montreal. Similar initiatives were already underway in the United States – mainly in Chicago, New York, and Boston. In Chicago the Court of Honour at the World's Columbian Exhibition provided the impetus for urban beautification, whereas in the other two cities there were park systems designed by the American landscape architect Frederick Law Olmsted. Burke thought municipalities across Canada might profit from similar ideas.[36]

Association members expressed approval believing that Toronto needed wider streets and open spaces "such as were found in Detroit and other American cities" Only Kivas Tully felt that OAA interests should be limited to the issue of building regulations. Over his objections a committee of six architects was struck to study the ornamentation and layout of the city.[37] For the next three years the Committee on Municipal Adornment continued its work, only to disband in 1898 after the foundation of an independent organization dedicated to similar goals.[38]

The Guild of Civic Art was established in 1897 to "promote and encourage civic art, including mural paintings and decorative sculptures, fountains and other structures or works of art of an artistic character."[39] At first activities were limited to mural projects for city hall and the legislature. Then in April of 1901, with its membership at a low ebb, the Toronto Architectural Eighteen Club suggested a meeting to discuss a general plan for Toronto, and sponsored a lecture by Philadelphia architect Albert E. Kelsey on "The Architectural Adornment of Cities." With the support of a number of other groups, the Guild called together a large committee to persuade City Council to employ an expert to prepare plans for the improvement of the city.[40]

When the Guild failed to gain City Council support, it took up a public subscription to provide $5,000 for a committee of the OAA to proceed with the project. Under the chairmanship of Toronto architect William A. Langton, work on a comprehensive plan of civic improvement was undertaken and completed in 1905. Burke, then in his second term as OAA president, was among the members of the committee. During the course of the year, the group settled on a series of recommendations, including the development of radial roads to provide direct access to the city core from outlying districts, a "circumambient" system of parks around the city, and a scheme to beautify the entrance to the city at the foot of York Street. In January of 1906 the committee handed over of its report to the Guild.

At the OAA convention in 1906 Burke encouraged delegates to educate the public and city authorities about the benefits of civic planning. Then William Langton gave a comprehensive address on the state of urban planning in the United States and its application to the city of Toronto. He described the three-phase scheme the plan committee had developed to accent the natural beauty of the city and assure its efficient functioning in the future (fig. 8.1). These projects would, Langton said, create a town of "some character," capable of generating civic pride among its inhabitants. The subtext, as historian John Weaver has pointed out, was that "the silk-stocking members of the Civic Guild ... stood four-square behind endeavours to purge parks and planning of graft and inefficiency."[41]

After Langton's talk, Byron E. Walker, manager of the Canadian Bank of Commerce, discussed the practical implementation of the committee's ideas. Recalling the establishment of New York's Central Park, he recommended immediate purchase of undeveloped land before population expansion took over prime sites and costs skyrocketed. Selective expropriation was also suggested as a means of assuring the success of the radial road proposal. Even the Americans – a people he described as "so impetuous and so ambitious that one [could] hardly imagine them projecting anything that [would] take

8.1

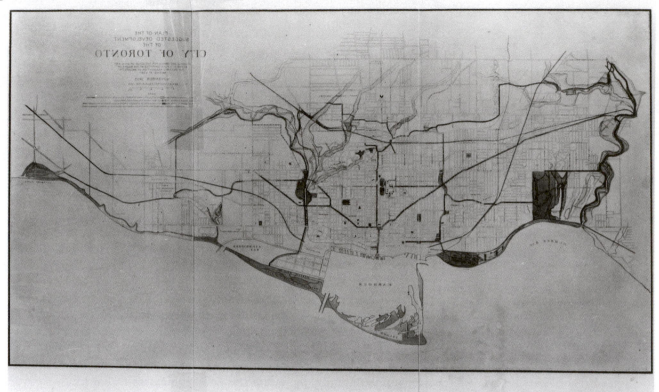

8.1   Ontario Association of Architects
and Toronto Civic Guild. Proposed
Improvements for the City of Toronto, 1905.
Photograph by Robarts Library. UofT-RL:
Ontario Association of Architects,
Proceedings (Toronto, 1906), after 90.

more than one year to accomplish" – had plans that would take a century to execute. Concrete legislation and fully funded governmental agencies were the only means by which such a scheme could be entrenched for future generations. The question the audience had to consider was "whether Toronto has reached the point where it should consider its surroundings and its future, and whether it has the courage and intelligence to do those things which every one of us know ought to be done."[42]

In the ensuing months the plan committee sought the Civic Guild's authorization to employ an outside expert to help them develop their ideas more fully. British architect Sir Aston Webb, known for his work on the mall approach to Buckingham Palace in London, was retained.[43] The Guild's partial subscription of his fee of $2500, with an additional $1000 for a draughtsman, was assisted by a small grant from the city.[44] In 1907 the draughtsman travelled from England to survey the situation for himself. In the closing months of 1908 a revised report was prepared and printing arranged.[45]

Several members of the plan committee, including Burke, were asked to collect photographs of civic improvements elsewhere. After a hasty tour of three American cities, Burke reported his observations in the *Canadian Architect and Builder*.[46] The impressive scale and

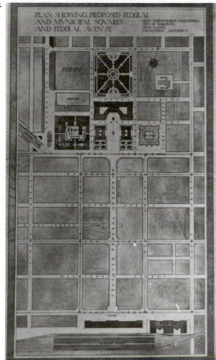

8.2   John Lyle. Proposal for Federal Avenue, Toronto, 1911. UofT-RB: *Construction 2* (July 1911):51.

broad radial avenues of Washington he contrasted with Philadelphia's congested grid-iron street pattern. And Baltimore, recently ravaged by fire, planned to widen streets and build new ones in the burned-out area, "an opportunity which Toronto should have seized after last year's fire." In the final version of its report the plan committee noted the impetus provided by the Beaux-Arts planning of the World's Fair at Chicago. It also referred to and illustrated urban planning schemes in major cities throughout the world, including Paris, Vienna, London, and Frankfurt-am-Main, as well as Washington, Cleveland, Baltimore, and New York.[47] Both plan and report were later exhibited at an international conference on planning at Philadelphia in the spring of 1911.[48]

Two traditions were combined in the recommendations of the plan committee. The radial boulevards had their roots in the scenographic grandeur of Pierre L'Enfant's late Baroque plan for Washington and the imposed geometric order of Baron Haussmann's 1853 scheme for Paris (which earned him fame as "Attila of the straight line").[49] This rigorous methodology was also adopted by Daniel Burnham for the Court of Honour at the World's Columbian Exhibition.[50] Yet the radial road proposal was less closely related to Beaux-Arts precedents than the text implied. The meandering access corridors were laid out with more attention to the practicality of traffic flow than geometric effect.[51] The goal, it appears, was to overcome the inefficiencies of the 1792 survey grid rather than to impose a strict geometric order of the type propounded by Burnham and the Beaux-Arts. The park systems, by contrast, were derived from the British picturesque tradition, preserved and amplified in the work of Frederick Law Olmsted.[52]

Once the Civic Guild presented its report, City Council decided to set up its own civic improvement committee to report on parks, boulevards, and driveways with a view to preparing a comprehensive city plan. Between February 1909 and December 1911 the civic improvement committee met jointly with the Civic Guild committee, and established several subcommittees to report on various topics, including planning and legislation. Edmund Burke headed the plan subcommittee, which concentrated on the transportation problems facing the city. Modifications to existing routes were proposed, and the problem of inadequate street width was examined. The legislation subcommittee even managed to obtain a provincial enactment granting excess expropriation power to the municipality for road widening,[53] powers they never exercised to bring the project to completion.[54]

When the civic improvement committee finished its deliberations, it too produced a report, which included many of the same features as earlier schemes.[55] One significant addition, however, was a new proposal for a civic centre linking the future Union Station with Queen Street. Architect John Lyle, who had trained in the United States, prepared the scheme for Federal Avenue with the axial regularity of the Beaux-Arts, lending "an air of dignity and spaciousness to the heart of the City" (fig. 8.2).[56] This proposal went the way of its predeces-

8.3

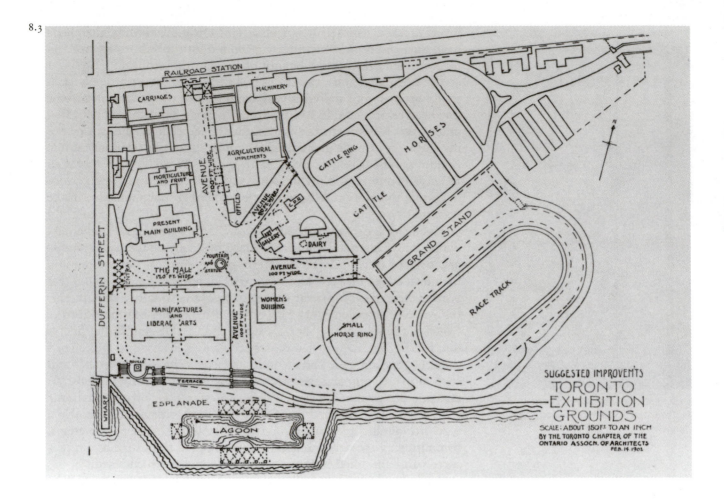

8.3   Canadian National Exhibition, Toronto, 1902. Grounds Plan. Photograph by Robarts Library. UofT-RB: *CAB* 15 (February, 1902):29.

sors amidst a growing emphasis on more practical aspects of city planning, but the remnants of the concept survive in the broad boulevard now known as University Avenue.

Other projects in which Burke participated during this period included a new site plan for the grounds of the Toronto Industrial Exhibition. In 1901 the Exhibition Association proposed to add three new buildings to its grounds, and asked the OAA to judge its competition entries. Instead the Association sent a delegation of architects including president Frank Wickson, Edmund Burke, and Eden Smith to propose a formal grounds plan, citing the "pains the Pan-American Exhibition people have gone to in the grouping of buildings, [and] landscape architecture." After consultation a committee was established under Burke's chairmanship.[57]

In February 1902 the committee put forward a proposal (fig. 8.3).[58] A grand avenue 120 feet wide was to lead from the Dufferin street entrance to a large plaza, where a series of lesser branches would radiate like the spokes of a wheel. At the centre a large fountain was to provide a focal point, while each vista terminated in a suitable architectural accent. On the lakefront, then little more than a "disgraceful dumping ground for rubbish," a terrace and lagoon would restore the beauty of the natural setting.[59]

The city parks and exhibitions committee adopted the report with modifications, and within a year many roadways, walks, and lawns had been rearranged. In addition the Women's building was relocated and a new Manufactures building constructed.[60] By the end of the decade a promenade graced the lakeshore, and a fifteen-foot marble fountain, billed as an "exact reproduction" of the type found in St Peter's Square, was donated by George H. Gooderham.[61]

During the course of his tenure on the plan subcommittee, Burke was also involved with the design of the Bloor-Danforth viaduct. In January 1911, because suburban expansion was restricted on the east by the dual geographic obstacles of the Rosedale ravine and Don valley,[62] City Council placed before the electorate a proposal to build a high-level steel bridge. The Civic Guild opposed the plan on the grounds that it would destroy the natural beauty of the area, impair the value of many existing properties, and be an inefficient link between the two localities. As a result of the Guild's campaign, the by-law was defeated.[63]

The City Engineer's office went back to the drawing board and came up with four options, which it submitted to the Civic Guild. In addition there was a scheme by Eustace G. Bird, who proposed a low-level structure connected by a steep grade on either side. Finally, a plan by John Lyle, consulting architect for the civic improvement committee, proposed to terrace the west side of the ravine as a traffic corridor to the south where the most heavily travelled routes in the city were located. These in turn were to be connected with the eastern road system with minimal damage to existing property. Of the many proposals, Lyle's plan was universally agreed to be the best, and electoral approval was sought and received in 1913.[64]

At first the Engineer's department wanted to execute the viaduct entirely in steel. But the Guild thought concrete would be more interesting architecturally and have a lower structural maintenance cost, despite the expense of the initial outlay. A series of articles in the professional magazine *Construction* touted the decision as a test of Toronto's civic intelligence. After inviting firms to submit designs for a concrete structure, the City Engineer's office opted for concrete pylons and hinged steel arches, pleading lack of experience with reinforced concrete as grounds for the decision. Later, it transpired there were sound structural reasons for using the lighter design. Work began in January 1915 and was schedule for completion at the end of 1917.

As consultant for the architectural portion of the viaduct, Burke worked with the City Engineer's office on the $2.5 million scheme (fig. 8.4). In the main section were five steel spans supported between concrete pylons, and a concrete-slab roadbed carried on steel eliminated objections about the noise and instability of a metal structure. The result was a platform eighty-six feet wide, accommodating two

8.4

8.4   Edmund Burke and the City Engineer's Department for the City of Toronto. Bloor Viaduct, Toronto, 1915–17. Photograph. City of Toronto Archives, Toronto: RG8–10–853.

lanes of twenty-two feet each, as well as two eleven-foot sidewalks. Provision was also made for a rail line on the lower deck in anticipation of the city's future transportation needs. Its profile crowned by a formal balustrade, the structure had the substance and permanence of its Beaux-Arts models – models which provided the forms for the urban planning movement itself.[65]

In the end the Bloor viaduct was one of only a few proposals that came to fruition out of all the plans prepared by the Civic Guild and civic improvement committee. There were, however, some adjustments to the city's roads that succeeded in facilitating the circulation of traffic, and Burke was instrumental in preparing the plans for these. In 1909 the Guild successfully promoted the widening of St Clair and Danforth Avenues, and in 1913 an attempt was made to improve the intersection at Bay and Queen by rounding the corners, a plan that foundered because of an inadequate allotment of land. Such victories were small and rare. Of the many projects planned and hours expended in their preparation, satisfaction could only have come from the knowledge that a new set of priorities would lay the foundation for the future.[66]

Apart from his work with the Civic Guild, which consumed many hours of his time, Burke was also involved with another major undertaking in his capacity as president of the OAA. Competitions had been a long-standing source of controversy for the architectural community in Ontario and elsewhere. The problem often centred around the unwelcome intrusion of foreign interlopers,[67] but just as frequently there were questions about who should select the winning design, how invitees should be remunerated, and what constituted precise compliance with the terms of competition. In 1892 the OAA established a list of standard conditions: that there be three judges, all of whom had architectural expertise, that entrants should adhere to instructions in every particular, furnishing line drawings in black ink only, and that while explanatory memoranda might be included, no writing or any form of identification except by motto was allowed. Once chosen the winner of the competition was to be entrusted with the work unless the selection committee considered that the individual required the assistance of a consultant.[68]

At the 1901 convention William Langton suggested that architects in private practice lobby for the right to compete on public works commissions, a right granted to American practitioners under the Tarsney Act in 1893. It seemed that Canada's Parliament had responded when in 1906 the Department of Works set up a competition for the Departmental and Justice buildings in the capital. Burke in his capacity as president of the OAA was asked to chair the Board of Assessors, which included Alcide Chaussé, president of the Province of Quebec Association of Architects (PQAA), and David Ewart, Chief Architect for the Department of Public Works. The requirements followed the criteria the OAA had established fourteen years earlier.[69]

Conditions were sent to every known architect in Canada, and only resident Canadians were permitted to enter. Competitors were required to lay out a site plan for the proposed location at Major's Hill Park and include a monumental foot bridge linking the new buildings to Parliament Hill. The style of architecture was optional, but some phase of Gothic was preferred because of the existing structures. Four premiums were offered ranging from $8000 for the best design to $1000 for fourth place. The closing date was set for 15 April 1907, but later extended to 1 July.[70]

While the terms made clear that winning designs were the property of the Government of Canada, the minister declined to give any assurance that the winning architect would be employed. The press reported the government's intention to have a public works architect execute the project along the lines of the winning competitive schemes. The OAA convention, in Ottawa for the first time, was visited by a delegation from the PQAA. Both associations passed resolutions urging that the requisite assurance be given, and on 16 January 1907 three representatives met with the minister. Satisfied, the associations decided to proceed.

It passed unnoticed that the same minister on 22 February 1907 advised the House of Commons:

In the first place this is a departmental work, and the department has officers who are responsible to the government for the erection of all government buildings everywhere. There would be manifest difficulty if an outside architect, not amenable to departmental control, was given charge of a building of this character. In the second place, it is possible and even likely that the plans that come in may have to be modified.[71]

There were just twenty-nine entries, in part because of the uncertainty about the government's intentions. First prize went to the Maxwell brothers of Montreal whose plans were judged to be of a quality that the government could "safely entrust [to the Maxwells] the preparation of the working drawings and the supervision of the work."[72] In the end, however, the project was turned over to the Department of Public Works, and by February 1909 revisions were underway.

The penny finally dropped on 26 November 1909 when the Minister declared that the Departmental buildings "are not being constructed upon any plan from the outside. The plans on which it is proposed to proceed with construction are prepared by the chief architect of the department."[73]

A flurry of petitions ensued. The newly established Royal Architectural Institute of Canada, PQAA, OAA, Manitoba Association of Architects, and Alberta Association of Architects all protested the government's action. The Institute even quoted a portion of the House of Commons debates from 22 February 1907, omitting the passage cited above and claiming that "so far as we are aware [the] statement of November 26, 1909 is the first information given the public that the preparation of plans for the Departmental Buildings had been entrusted to the employees of the Department of Public Works."[74]

Uproar followed and the decision was deferred. Then in 1911 a government committee decided that the Sussex Street site was "inadequate" for Departmental requirements (a portion had been alienated for the Château Laurier Hotel). Shortly thereafter the Laurier government was defeated, and the incoming Conservative minister tried to sort out the problem as the Maxwells attempted to press their claim to the commission.[75] In 1913–14 the government proceeded with the Connaught Building on the site purchased for the Major's Hill project, and planning began all over again for the Departmental complex.[76] A new competition was instituted, but the First World War ultimately supervened.

The same year the Departmental competition was instituted, participants at the Ottawa convention broached the subject of a Dominion-wide organization of architects. This had been suggested on many occasions, but an abortive attempt to pass a registration bill in the British Parliament inspired renewed efforts. By 1907 the wheels were in motion for what would become the Canadian Institute of Architects (later the Royal Canadian Institute of Architects) as Alcide

Chaussé wrote an editorial in support of compulsory registration at the national level to protect the public. The first objection, however, came from his own PQAA on the grounds that such a system would jeopardize the provincial licensing system in place since 1898.[77]

Among the many critics of the registration proposal was John Horwood, who opposed the measure as an attempt to establish an exclusive clique. He rejected any comparison with the licensing system in Illinois because the Institute was not a government body. Eden Smith noted the recent decision of the American Institute of Architects to avoid any involvement in lobbying for legislation affecting the profession, and the *Globe* also condemned the proposed Institute for not offering educational programs. The newspaper also noted that the registration provisions would trench on the province's exclusive constitutional powers over property and civil rights.[78]

With Chaussé and J.W.H. Watts of Ottawa, Edmund Burke went before the miscellaneous bills committee of the House of Commons to discuss the format of the proposed act. As a result the closed corporation clause was eliminated, and the Institute was incorporated as an umbrella organization affiliated with the provincial associations. Burke served as vice-president on the first executive, alongside Eden Smith, who was also appointed to the council.[79] This brought together the advocates on both sides of the registration controversy – Burke, the proponent of formal training and licensing, whose first interest lay in the technical aspects of his calling, and Smith, long-time member of the Eighteen, who believed that creative skill could not be tested by examination. Divided for a decade, both sides now aligned themselves to claim the recognition that had eluded the profession for so long.

Conclusion

In 1856 Owen Jones described architecture as "the material expression of the wants, the faculties, and the sentiments of the age in which it is created."[1] Current scholarship often characterizes the nineteenth century as a period of conflict between the historicizing influences of style and the rationalism of structure, but both are in fact equally "logical" legacies of the Enlightenment. This opposition is implicit in the OAA discussion of "Shop Fronts in the Next Decade" and in Burke's defence of the adaptation of traditional forms to modern uses. His design for the Robert Simpson store, begun a few weeks later, went far beyond these parameters to test the "engineer's aesthetic" of Chicago. As a later commentator noted: "The distinctive American idea is that art should keep closer to science than it has ever been before. The beauty of buildings should grow upon their utility."[2] Burke fully appreciated that the United States was the font of a new commercial type soon to be copied around the world.

Many nations in Europe and South America imported American ideas and technology. But Canadian federation followed that of the United States by nine decades. Canadian institutions were barely established before these new cultural pressures began. Canada remained longer in the British fold than its neighbour and fed on Imperial styles and educational methods. The first American school of architecture had been established in 1866, Canadian initiatives followed two decades later and then only in response to the perceived threat of American competition. In the interim architectural education consisted of apprenticeship with highly variable standards and a predisposition to perpetuate conservative methods. As Canadians contemplated an independent destiny for the first time, it seemed that the precedents formerly supplied by Britain were scarcely adequate for the task.

While the first architectural schools were being established in the United States, many prominent American practitioners of the late nineteenth century studied in Paris either at the Ecole des Beaux-Arts (as in the cases of Richard Morris Hunt, Henry Hobson Richardson, and Louis Sullivan) or at the Ecole Centrale des Arts et Manufactures (in the case of William le Baron Jenney). By contrast, in the total absence of schools in Canada, Canadians (like former Langley student, Frank Darling) went to Britain or (in the case of Burke's future partners, J.C.B. Horwood and Murray A. White) to the United States. Darling was among the best-known and most-respected of his generation not only in Toronto but across Canada; yet two important competition entries by his firm – one for the Ontario legislative buildings in 1880, the other for the Board of Trade a decade later – were edged out by American schemes considered better by the American adjudicators who selected them. It appeared that anyone who wished to succeed must emulate the trends in the United States or risk being considered out of date.

In the United States the 1876 Centennial celebrations cued nationalist aspirations for indigenous forms of architectural expression. Richardson's unique Romanesque synthesis was succeeded by experiments with Shingle style, colonial revivals, and the remarkable commercial developments of Chicago and New York. Canadians like Burke considered themselves akin to their American neighbours in some respects, particularly in the shared problems of climate and convenience in planning. Nationalist sentiments seemed to be reserved for those occasions when Canadian patrons employed American architects, or when individuals like Percy Nobbs sought to promote Arts-and-Crafts methods in preference to those of the Beaux-Arts.

No such preconceptions hindered Burke in his approach to the architectural "problem." He adopted the best methods regardless of their source, seeking a middle ground between the labour-intensive style of the British and the hastily assembled American work. For him the United States was the nearest available reference to supplement the precedents of his apprenticeship and a brief tour of Europe in his youth. His interest in American ideas began with his first independent commission in 1874, and continued to provide a reference point for his ecclesiastical and institutional works throughout the 1880s. American technological advances were also of particular interest to him as a devotee of the "scientific" and "professional" aspects of his calling. Horwood's letters from New York and Burke's own experience of the Chicago World's Fair further peaked his interest and inspired him to re-examine his approach at the age of forty-four.

Having launched his own firm in 1892, Burke embarked two years later on the biggest challenge of his career attempting a partial curtain-wall construction in the Robert Simpson store – a direct influence from the American Midwest and the first of its type in Canada. After rebuilding following a fire, the design became a model for similar undertakings across the country. Fifteen years later, the firm undertook three similar projects, this time, for the Hudson's Bay Company. They used the same unit of construction, but the exterior was cloaked in an extravagant Beaux-Arts array that charted the latest stylistic turn of Chicago's Burnham & Co.

The vocabulary of Burke, Horwood & White increasingly reflected stylistic fashions and technical advances from south of the border. Other Toronto firms adopted the same approach to deal with American competitors whose expertise on large projects Canadian patrons took for granted. Americans argued that their presence in the Canadian market "would elevate the standard of design," but local practitioners asserted there was nothing wrong with Canadian standards, pointing to instances in which buildings designed by Americans had collapsed in the course of construction. Canadian architects responded by establishing a professional organization to provide a framework for licensing within the province. Their aspirations for a "closed corporation" were frustrated, but the Ontario Association of Architects (in which Burke was an active participant) provided a forum for the exchange of information and undertook a series of educational initiatives.

A chair in architecture established at the School of Practical Science increased the availability of technical information, usually the weakest aspect of a practitioner's training in a time of rapid transition. At the turn of the century the Toronto Architectural Eighteen Club objected to the emphasis being placed upon technical matters, preferring instead to focus upon the artistic aspects of their calling. Burke's interests aligned him with the OAA and its endorsement of the programs at the School of Practical Science, while Horwood found his *métier* with the Eighteen. It is a tribute to both men that their methodological differences had no effect upon their partnership, and that the firm's work encompassed the technical and the artistic, the Arts and Crafts and the Beaux-Arts, British ideas and American without any preference other than for the highest quality of execution.[3]

Burke's architecture in many ways reflects the man. A Liberal, he supported the Conservatives' national policy of protectionist tariffs. He believed that Canada should be a united nation free from sectarian or class distinctions, and justified his opposition to dual languages and separate schools on this basis. As a member of the National and Canadian Clubs he favoured Imperial unity, but was equally at home with ownership of public franchises and compulsory arbitration of disputes affecting the general public.[4] In his will he left his library to his partners Horwood and White "in recognition of their loyal and faithful help from the days of their studentship onwards," an indication that the partnership had grown out of long-standing mutual regard and consideration among its members. To Jarvis Street Baptist Church, where he served as deacon, he left a generous endowment, noting it to be of "paramount importance," and then concluded with the words: "I leave this world in a sure and certain hope of a glorious immortality not through any merit of my own but led by the Holy Spirit to believe in the testimony of the sacred word of God to accept the Lord Jesus Christ as my only savior and commend the truth of His gospel to all."[5]

It is somehow characteristic of his devout and sober nature, the careful and prudent methodologies, the untiring devotion to his professional duties, and his desire to leave something of consequence behind him that such a text should have survived among fragmentary biographic details. Burke was a dedicated practitioner who strove to place architecture in Canada on a professional footing – his adoption of a multiplicity methods and precedents constituted one means to that goal.

Notes

ACKNOWLEDGMENTS

1 See also Angela Carr, "'On the Highest Plane of his Possibilities': The Career of Toronto Architect Edmund Burke (1850–1919)." PH.D. dissertation, Department of the History of Art, University of Toronto, 1990.

CHAPTER ONE

1 Jameson, *Winter Studies*, 1:99–100.
2 Ibid.

CHAPTER TWO

1 Stokes, "On Observation," 212–13.
2 Eden Smith, "Architectural Education–1900," 109.
3 "Ontario Architects' Convention," *Construction* 2 (February 1909):40, reports that the number of students registered in the School of Practical Science was negligible.
4 Following Capper, "University Training in Architecture," 15.
5 Students were usually under age so parents signed articles of indenture, see HC: Indentures of Agreement 1871–1909, MU 3985, AO.
6 Shillaber, *Massachusetts Institute of Technology*; and "Architectural Education in the United States, Part I," 46–7. For the influence of the Ecole, see Kostof, *Architect*, chapter 8.
7 Architectural Guild of Toronto Minutes, 8 November 1888. Ontario Association of Architects Papers, MU 2734, AO
8 Capper, "Architecture in the University," 179–82, refers to the "recently established Chair of Architecture." Toronto merely extended its engineering studies whereas McGill aimed at a fully rounded architectural program.
9 "Annual Banquet," 43.
10 This is a generalization. Traditions in Quebec, the West, and Maritime Canada involve significant regional variations, but in the 1860s much of the economic wealth was in the hands of those who looked chiefly to Britain for ideas.
11 A.D.F. Hamlin, "Influence of the Ecole des Beaux-Arts on Our Architectural Education," 5, refers to "the beginning of the great art revival which dates from 1876."
12 Crossman, *Architecture in Transition*, 109–21.
13 Architectural Guild of Toronto Minutes, 8 November 1888, Ontario Association of Architects Papers, MU 2734, AO.
14 Ibid., 17 May 1888. The Board of Trade's decision to invite two Americans and only one Canadian to compete for its new building was considered a slight to city architects. By October 1888 the ministry of education was exploring ways to establish an educational program for Canadian architects. Also "Ontario Association of Architects," CAB 8 (February 1895):21.
15 Constans Fides, "An Appeal for Organization," 3; Arthur, *Toronto*, 237–41; Tausky and DiStephano, *Victorian Architecture*, 61–4; Crossman, *Architecture in Transition*, 28–35; Simmins, *Ontario Association of Architects*, 20–49, for the Canadian Institute of Architects (1876), Architectural Guild of Toronto (1887), Ontario Association of Architects (1889), Province of Quebec Association of Architects (1890), and Toronto Architectural Eighteen Club (1899). See also "An Educational Standard for Architects," 173–4. For British organizations, see Jenkins, *Architect and Patron*, 113–15, regarding the Architect's Club (1791), the London Architectural Society (1806), the Architectural Society (1831), the Institute of British Architects (1835), and the Architectural Association (1846); also Kaye, *Development of the Architectural Profession*.
16 *Might's Toronto Directory* (1867), for William Burke; Arthur, *Toronto*, 254, 269, for Henry Langley and William Burke of Smith, Burke & Co.; J.E. Middleton, *Municipality of Toronto*, 2:41, for summary of Edmund Burke's career.
17 Horwood Collection drawings indicate that the partnership began in 1872, despite the fact it was not formally recorded until the following year. See

Partnership Register, York County, 27 June 1873, RG 55, 694 CP, AO.

18 Brosseau, *Gothic Revival*, plate 31, for St John the Baptist Anglican Cathedral by George Gilbert Scott. Bond, "Notes from St John's, NF," 9, records the building's destruction by fire.

19 Gifford, *Edinburgh*, for John Henderson and his son George who later became Hay's partner. For William Hay, see Armstrong, *City in the Making*, 212–26; Beszedits, *Eminent Toronto Architects*, 33–8; Arthur, *Toronto*, 250.

20 Arthur, *Toronto*, 250 and chapter 4, refer to St Basil's Church of 1855, Oaklands of 1860, and an unexecuted design for the chapel of Trinity College from 1858. Other examples like the Toronto General Hospital on Gerrard Street of 1855–56 and the House of Providence of 1855–58 (both demolished), combined Gothic revival details with a mansard roof. For the Yorkville Town Hall of 1859–60 (destroyed by fire in this century), see LC:178–88, MTRL. Scadding, *Toronto of Old*, 299, thought the latter motif had "strayed from Ghent," but did not mention the obvious Ruskinian influence. "The Late Mr Wm Hay, Architect," 11, credits Hay with the introduction of medieval revival in Toronto, but Henry Bowyer Lane had already built a number of Gothic revival churches, and William Thomas had executed St Michael's Cathedral by 1845.

21 Arthur, *Toronto*, 260–2. William Thomas and Fred Cumberland trained in Britain, Kivas Tully in Ireland, but W.G. Storm and William T. Thomas – though born in England – were educated in Canada with William Thomas the elder.

22 Toronto Board of Trade, *A Souvenir*, 241, says Langley was seventeen when he joined Hay. Beszedits, *Eminent Toronto Architects*, 65, relying upon the same source, calculates Langley's age as nineteen. See also *Rowsell's City of Toronto ... Directory* (1850), 1:lxi, for Toronto Academy (1846–52), which offered English, classics, and commercial education combined with thorough scriptural instruction. E.C. Bull was the drawing master. The academy shared space with Knox College, but was nonsectarian after 1849, see Toronto Academy, "Prospectus of the Toronto Academy," File 110/00007, Presbyterian Church of Canada Archives, Knox College, Toronto.

23 "The Late Mr Henry Langley," 14.

24 Arthur, *Toronto*, 249, for Thomas Gundry.

25 Gilbert Scott, *Personal and Professional Recollections*, 56. See also Jenkins, *Architect and Patron*, chapter 8, including quotations from Dicken's *Martin Chuzzlewit*.

26 Saint, *Richard Norman Shaw*, 17, 187.

27 Langton, "On the Architect's Part in His Work," 28–9; and O'Gorman, *H.H. Richardson and his Office*, 16–30.

28 Roth, *McKim, Mead & White*, 59.

29 "Architectural Offices," 123, for the layout of the Langley & Burke office.

30 "A Question of Privilege," 157. In reply to an inquiry about drawings made by a draughtsman for his employer and under his direction, the editor states that "the draughtsman has no right to put anything whatever upon [the drawing] except by [the employer's] authority or permission."

31 "The Late Mr Henry Langley," 14, lists Edmund Burke, Frank Darling, H.B. Gordon, A.A. Post, R.J. Edwards, Wesley Peters, Charles E. Langley, Fred Langley, C.H. Acton Bond, J.C.B. Horwood, J.H. Marling, Fred Kelley, Murray White, Ernest Wilby, and W.F. Howland as former Langley students.

32 Gambier-Bousfield, "Architectural Education in Canada," 46.

33 Saint, *Richard Norman Shaw*, 188, describes Shaw's practice of teaching his students "to measure up buildings, and to draw plans acceptably and in the 'office' style." Office style was unquestionably part of the Langley method, and carried over to Burke's firm. In 1918 Burke, Horwood & White still had difficulty distinguishing the hands of their own draughtsmen; see HC: 1101, AO, for a drawing dated 1912, which bears the notation, "I think this drawing was made by Makepeace – after a scheme of Blackstone in Chicago," and the reply (initialled JCBH, 11 June 1918) "Looks like Shepard's printing." *Toronto City Directory* (1913), for Stanley Makepeace of McConnell & Makepeace, architects, and Ralph K. Shepard, architect (information on Makepeace courtesy of H. Russell, Parks Canada).

34 [Ure], *Hand-Book of Toronto*, 258, states this Early English style church of white brick with freestone dressings (demolished) opened in January 1857 at a cost of £3754. Contract drawings executed in pen and wash on Whatman paper were common at this period whereas later techniques included linen tracings and blueprints. For Whatman paper, see Balston, *William Balston*, and *James Whatman*.

35 Langley began his articles about 1854 or 1855, so the sophisticated technique suggests the authorship of William Hay. Contract drawings followed conventions of colour coding throughout the century, which were later recorded by Spiers, *Architectural Drawing*. Also Spiers, "Architectural Drawing" (24 April 1874):443, (1 May 1874):470.

36 Goodhart-Rendel, "Architectural Draughtsmanship of the Past," 127–37, warns "against employing the system of shadows, otherwise you may find some intelligent workman executing them." See also Lever and Richardson, *Architect as Artist*, 11, 18, for coloured and shaded sections introduced by Sir William Chambers in 1759.

37 For the Metropolitan Methodist Church on McGill Square (now Metropolitan United Church), see Arthur, *Toronto*, 221. Drawing style is discussed by Blomfield, *Architectural Drawings*, 5–8.

38 Burges defended his stylistic preferences in "Architectural Drawing," 15–28.

39 Blomfield, *Architectural Drawings*, 5–8.

40 For Yorkville Town Hall, see Arthur, *Toronto*, 148. The sheet is watermarked 1856, and the verso is stamped Langley & Howland, which identifies it as part of the Langley corpus. The latter firm was founded in 1907 by Henry's son Charles in partnership with William Ford Howland (a former Langley student).

41 Langley's style was either established at the time he joined Hay's staff (he was about eighteen and considerably older than most students) or he developed independent skills in evening classes like those offered by the Mechanics Institute. See Toronto Board of Trade, *Souvenir*, 241, for brief biography.

42 Occasionally a bright wash is found in an elevation, but this is unusual: vivid washes are most characteristic of sections – upon which the builder relied to determine the relevant materials.

43 Spiers, "Architectural Drawing" (24 April 1874): 443, advised that colours be applied "unmixed, because it is difficult to obtain the same gradation of tone in subsequent mixtures."

44 LC:56, MTRL.

45 Goodhart-Rendel, "Architectural Draughtsmanship," 132.

46 Beszedits, *Eminent Toronto Architects*, 77–83; Arthur, *Toronto*, 244; Percy Nobbs, "The Late Frank Darling," and F.S. Baker, "An Appreciation," 205–7.

47 It seems extraordinary that a diploma work should be wholly or partially executed by another, but the building was Langley's work, and the perspective carried out under his supervision and control. "Our Office Table," 301, reported the council of the Royal Academy had decided "to give preference to those drawings evidently the actual productions of the architects who exhibit them." According to "Architectural Association," 643, one of the annual examinees was disqualified "from the fact that his drawings, though executed by himself, are signed by his father as joint executor of the buildings thereon delineated." See also "Designers and Draughtsmen," 428–9, for disapproval of the practice of employing specialists to execute presentation drawings. On the other side, "A Question of Privilege," 157, suggested that a draughtsman is not entitled to initial a work without the consent of his principal.

48 Beszedits, *Eminent Toronto Architects*, 77; Arthur, *Toronto*, 244, for Darling's studies with Blomfield and Street.

49 For Shaw's reaction, see Burges, "Architectural Drawing," 15, 26. Also Saint, *Richard Norman Shaw*, 188, records Shaw's description of a strident red wash applied by a student as "hideous" and "vulgar."

50 A perspective by Darling dated 1888 is reproduced by Weir, *Lost Craft of Ornamented Architecture*, no. 59.

51 HC:451, AO, now Our Lady of Mount Carmel, St Patrick's Street. See also HC:451a, AO, for an unsigned perspective of *St Patrick's, Carlton Street* dated July 1869, in which the style is virtually identical but the execution is more cursory.

52 Burke's perspective implies some knowledge of watercolour. Richard Baigent, drawing master at Upper Canada College and sometime tutor in ornamental painting at the Mechanics Institute, is one possible source. Baigent was an active member of the Ontario Society of Artists from its foundation in 1872, and regularly participated in their annual exhibitions. His landscapes were described on at least one occasion as "libels on nature," but his modest renderings display a competent painterly technique. See *Mail* (Toronto) 20 June 1874, 2; Toronto Mechanics Institute, *Thirty-Fifth Annual Report* (1866), 6; Ontario Society of Artists Minutes, 1872–1890, Ontario Society of Artists Papers, MU 2254, AO; Harper, "Ontario Painters, 1846–1867,"

16–32. Another possiblity is the architect James Avon Smith of Smith & Gemmell who also taught at the Mechanics Institute. His work is recorded in Murray, *Ontario Society of Artists*, plate 110. For a list of the city's first art classes, see "A History of the Progress of Art in Ontario," Ontario Society of Artists Papers, MU 2252, AO.

53 Toronto Mechanic's Institute, *Thirty-Fifth Annual Report* (1866), 6. Henry Langley was one of the directors. The courses offered included architectural and mechanical drawing taught by the architect James Smith and a landscape, figure, and ornamental class by Richard Baigent. In 1863–64 there were twenty students in the former, none in the latter, the following year seven in each, and by 1865 enrolment had rebounded to sixteen in architecture and fifteen in the landscape section.

54 Toronto Mechanics Institute, *Thirty-Sixth Annual Report* (1867).

55 Register of Pupils 1838–70, UCC Files, A74-0018/96, UofTA, indicates that Burke usually placed second in his class; Dickson and Adam, *History of Upper Canada College*, 113–26.

56 Gilbert Scott, *Personal and Professional Recollections*, 56, on the necessity for supplementary work – particularly in drawing.

57 See Ontario Society of Artists Minutes, 13 January and 23 December 1873, 7 April 1874, Ontario Society of Artists Papers, MU 2254, AO, for the election of Frank Darling, Henry Langley, and Edmund Burke respectively. Architects and artists had been associated in similar organizations since the establishment of the Society of Artists and Amateurs in 1834, and later with the Toronto Society of Arts in 1847 and 1848. Both organizations held exhibitions which included architectural renderings, see Lowrey, "Society of Artists and Amateurs," 99–118; and Lowrey, "Toronto Society of Arts," 3–44. The Upper Canada Agricultural Society also staged annual art exhibitions from 1846 on. In such exhibitions architectural pieces were often mixed with other types of drawings; but a separate award was made after 1856. Hay and Langley were frequently among the judges of the fine arts section, see *Canadian Agriculturalist* (Toronto, 1849–52); *Journal and Transactions of the Board of Agriculture of Upper Canada* (Toronto, 1855–71); and Harper, "Ontario Painters 1846–1867," 16–32, for further discussion.

58 Ontario Society of Artists, *Second Annual Exhibition* (1874), nos. 189–98 (Burke's drawing was no. 193). Drawings for this project are in HC:465 and 1065, AO. Among the other participants were Smith & Gemmell, James & Connolly, and R.C. Windeyer.

59 Langley is not listed among the prize winners in the fine arts section of the annual Upper Canada Agricultural Exhibitions, perhaps because he served as a judge. Reports do not list participants apart from winners.

60 HC: Indenture of Agreement, 3 July 1871, MU 3985, AO, with an unusual provision that Frank be paid for his work after the second year. F. Burke is last recorded in *Toronto Directory* (1878), 243. Marianna Richardson, *Ontario Association of Architects*, 21, lists a copy of Bannister Fletcher's *Quantities* (1877) bearing Frank's signature and the note "London, Dec. 1878." (Edmund Burke's only son – born in 1882 – was also to be named Frank, suggesting that the brother may have died in the meantime.)

61 See Weir, *Lost Craft of Ornamented Architecture*, nos. 26–7 (wrongly identified as Edmund Burke). The buildings are discussed among the early commercial works in chapter 5 above.

62 Ontario Society of Artists Minutes, 1 April 1876, Ontario Society of Artists Papers, MU 2254, AO.

63 *Report of the Canadian Commission*, 2, in App. 4.

64 See Ontario Society of Artists Minutes, 4 April and 3 October 1876, Ontario Society of Artists Papers, MU 2254, AO, regarding the committee to organize the art school. See also Art Gallery of Ontario, *100 Years*, 11. Margaret Richardson, *Architects of the Arts and Crafts*, 8, records the British situation: "An architect trained at that time in an office where the pupil's parent paid for his son to be articled for a set period. Articled pupils could also attend lessons in the evening, usually from 6 to 9 p.m., three evenings a week; at the South Kensington Schools, Royal Academy Schools or at the Architectural Association."

65 Ontario Society of Artists, *Seventh Annual Exhibition* (1879), no. 196. Two other entries by the firm, one of them possibly HC:311b, AO, depicted the offices of the Building and Loan Association, see Douglas Richardson, "Glory of Toronto," no. 23. Other drawings of this subject (HC:311a, AO) bear the pseudonym "Bona Fides," and are attributed to D.B. Dick.

66 HC:623 (1), AO, is undated but for the countermark of 1874. The design was actually built as the Union Savings and Loan on the west side of Toronto Street facing Court House Lane: see Douglas Richardson, "Glory of Toronto," no. 24, who observes that the elevation was originally designed for 18–20 King Street West.

67 It is difficult to believe that Burke would have picked up these ideas in art classes because he is unlikely to have taken instruction at this stage in his career. It seems more probable that he was influenced by someone like Frank Darling, who returned from England in 1873.

68 The pencilled inscription identifies the project (possibly a house for W.S. Thompson) as one Burke took with him when he departed Langley's practice in 1892.

69 Margaret Richardson, *Architects of the Arts and Crafts*, 17, 32, 60, observes that Philip Webb's working drawings combined "different details drawn to different scales ... on the same sheet, often recto and verso, showing his complete knowledge of craftwork." She also notes the sepia pen-and-wash technique of Sir Ernest George and Sir Edwin Lutyens' dislike of outlines, which he mocked on one occasion by drawing a quizzical figure peering around a border with the caption, "What does the builder do with this?"

70 "Architectural Offices," *CAB* 3 (November 1890): 123. The office was in the 1889 Canada Life building (demolished), by R.A. Waite, whose works are discussed in greater detail in chapter 5.

71 A series of articles about architectural offices has been assembled by Robert Hill. For Burnham & Root and Adler & Sullivan, both of Chicago; Shepley, Rutan & Coolidge, Boston; Wilson Brothers and Theophilus P. Chandler, both of Philadelphia; Samuel Hannaford & Son, Cincinnati; George B. Post and McKim, Mead & White, both of New York City, see "The Organization of an Architect's Office. Nos. 1–8," *Engineering Record* 21 (1890):83, 165, 181, 195; 22 (1890):5, 180; 24 (1891):362–3; 25 (1892):4–5, where between a dozen and sixty draughtsmen were employed. See also Saint, *Image of the Architect*, 86.

72 HC:1269a, AO.

73 Beszedits, *Eminent Toronto Architects*, 74–6.

74 "Architectural Drawing in Pen and Ink," 71, by contrast, disapproves the watercolour sketch technique adopted by Horwood and favours traditional pencil or ink rendering.

75 Ontario Society of Artists, *Catalogue of Winter Exhibition* (1885), nos. 63 and 64. For *House on Bloor Street* of 1883, see HC:617, AO.

76 Ontario Society of Artists, *Catalogue of Annual Exhibition* (1886), no. 208, is a *Design for a Suburban Residence* under the name Langley & Burke. This title is on the verso of HC:543(4), AO, while the name of Horwood appears at the lower right recto.

77 See "The Academy's Unwritten Laws as to Architectural Drawings," 479, regarding the Academy's refusal to display coloured perspectives. Michels, "Late Nineteenth-Century Published American Perspective Drawing," 291–308, traces the development of drawing styles in American publications. For "dazzle" technique, its origins, and its relationship to photolithography, see Goodhart-Rendel, "Architectural Draughtsmanship," 133.

78 Architectural Draughtsman's Association of Toronto Minutes, 7 February 1887, Ontario Association of Architects Papers, MU 2734, AO; "The Architectural Draughtsman's Association," *CAB* 1 (January 1888):4; (February 1888):3; (March 1888):4; (April 1888):8; (November 1888):5.

79 See Architectural Guild of Toronto Minutes, 8 November 1888, Ontario Association of Architects Papers, MU 2734, AO, dealing with the appointment to the School of Practical Science of a professor of architecture and the organization of the Ontario Association of Architects, both concerned primarily with engineering and scientific education.

80 The Sketch Club's activities were reported regularly, see "Toronto Architectural Sketch Club," *CAB* 3 (January 1890):6; (February 1890):17; (March 1890):26–8, 45; (May 1890):53; (September 1890):102; (October 1890):110; (November 1890): 125–6; (December 1890):136, 140; 4 (January 1891):4–5; (February 1891):24; (March 1891):31; (April 1891):52; (June 1891):61, 64; (July 1891): 71; (September 1891):89; (November 1891):95, 100; (December 1891):106; 5 (February 1892):ill.; (April 1892):41; (May 1892):46–8; 8 (December 1895):139, 145; 9 (June 1896):xi; (February 1896):supp. ill.; (March 1896):45; 19 (March 1906):34–5. See also *Globe* (Toronto) 30 January 1890, 8; and *AABN* 27 (March 1890):142. The Burke & Horwood office was later the site of a meet-

ing of the Architectural Students' Club, see *CAB* 14 (May 1900):96.

81 For Renwick & Aspinwall, see Withey, *Biographical Dictionary of American Architects*, 23, 126, 501, 523. "Renwick, James" (Placzek, *Macmillan Encyclopedia of Architects*, 4:541–9) by Selma Rattner has no information about Horwood's employment with the Renwick firm. Horwood is sometimes said to have worked for Clinton & Russell as well, but the entry on Russell (who was related to Renwick) indicates he entered partnership with Clinton in 1894 when Horwood was in Europe.

82 *Catalogue of the Third Annual Exhibition* lists J.C. Horwood among the department members (according to Deborah Wythe, Archivist of the Brooklyn Museum Archives). Classes in architectural drawing had been established since 1891: Minutes of Brooklyn Institute of Arts and Science, 6 November 1891, 329, Brooklyn Archives, Brooklyn.

83 Otto, "Press Kit."

84 HC: Sketchbooks, MU 3980, AO.

85 Horwood, "American Architectural Methods," 8–9. Two other articles by Horwood entitled "Architecture in New York," 6–7, and "Some Observations on Fireproof Building in New York," 36–8, are discussed in chapter 5.

86 HC: Indenture of Agreement, 26 October 1901, between Charles Philip Sparling, guardian of William Frederick Sparling, and Burke & Horwood, MU 3985, AO; and "Ontario," 108, for Sparling obituary.

87 Toronto Architectural Eighteen Club, *Fourth Annual Exhibition* (1905), no. 31.

88 Kaplan, *"The Art That is Life,"* 374–5, plate 195, quoting the work of M.H. Baillie Scott, "Decoration and Furniture for the New Palace, Darmstadt," *Studio* (March 1899):107–15.

89 Toronto Society of Architects (formerly Toronto Architectural Eighteen Club), *Fifth Exhibition Catalogue* (1909), 8–12, for history of Club. See also "The Architects' Eighteen Club," September 1899, 181; "Exhibition of Architectural Drawings," November 1900, 219; "Toronto Architectural Eighteen Club Competition in Rendering from Photograph for Students," 232; "The Toronto Architectural Eighteen Club Exhibition," February 1901, 29; "The Architectural Students Club," 96; "Toronto Architectural Eighteen Club," 166; "Architectural Exhibition," 64; "The Second Annual Exhibition

of the Toronto Architectural Eighteen Club," June 1902, 71–2; "Toronto Architectural Eighteen Club," 188; "Eighteen Club Exhibition," 2; "Drawing at the Eighteen Club Exhibition, Toronto," 19; "Architectural Eighteen Club," ix; "The Toronto Architectural Club," 11; Crossman, *Architecture in Transition*, 85–105; Simmins, *Ontario Association of Architects*.

90 Shaw and Jackson, *Architecture, A Profession or an Art?*

91 Toronto Architectural Eighteen Club (later Toronto Society of Architects), *First Annual Exhibition* (1901); *Second Annual Exhibition* (1902); *Fourth Annual Exhibition* (1905); *Fifth Annual Exhibition Catalogue* (1909); *Sixth Exhibition Catalogue* (1912), MTRL. There appears to have been no catalogue for the third annual exhibition.

92 Toronto Society of Architects, *Fifth Annual Exhibition* (1909), includes the report Burke prepared.

93 The Toronto Beaux-Arts Club was established in 1905, see *CAB* 18 (January 1905):7.

94 *Construction* 3 (September 1910):57, for captioned illustration; Douglas Richardson, "Glory of Toronto," no. 41.

95 Egbert, *Beaux-Arts Tradition*, 12, indicates that *concours* drawings were almost always plan, section, and elevation.

96 Harbeson, *Study of Architectural Design*, 157, 281–7.

97 A photograph of a rendering entitled *Hudson's Bay Store, Victoria* was exhibited at the Canadian National Exhibition (CNE) in 1915 (HC: Add., AO). See also Ontario Association of Architects, *Catalogue of the Exhibition* (1927), no. 1309a, for a perspective of the planned expansion to the Hudson's Bay Store, Vancouver (now HC, VCA, Vancouver). The latter is the work of S.H. Maw, associate architect of the Toronto Stock Exchange of 1937, and better known as a skilled renderer, see obituary, *Royal Architectural Institute of Canada Journal* 29 (November 1952):343.

98 For Selfridge's department store of 1907–9 by Francis Swales, Daniel Burnham, Frank Atkinson, and J.J. Burnet, see Service, *Edwardian Architecture*, 168.

99 "L.R." signed many perspectives for various participants in the Toronto Architectural Eighteen Club exhibitions cited above. The full signature (which is

unreadable beyond the initials "L.B.R.") appears on a rendering of the *Proposed New Building for the Central Canada Loan and Savings Company, Toronto,* by Sproatt & Rolph published in *CAB* 17 (July 1904):supp. ill. Howard Shubert of the Canadian Centre for Architecture has also pointed out the initials "L.R." on a perspective of the *Proposed Bank of Commerce, Winnipeg,* by Darling & Pearson published in *Construction* 5 (April 1911):64.

100 Maxwell, "Architectural Education," 21–5.

101 Otto, "Press Kit."

CHAPTER THREE

1 Seventy Ontario churches are attributed to Langley, see Mallory, "Three Henry Langley Churches," 1:107–14.

2 Westfall, *Two Worlds,* 126–58, notes the transition from Georgian neoclassicism to Gothic revival in the 1840s.

3 Pugin, *Contrasts; True Principles; Apology.* Also Geoffrey Scott, *Architecture of Humanism,* on "Ethical Fallacy."

4 The Cambridge Camden Society was the founded by a group of Anglo-Catholics at Cambridge University: White, *Cambridge Movement,* 25–47.

5 Douglas Richardson, "Wills, Frank," in *Dictionary of Canadian Biography*; Brosseau, *Gothic Revival,* 68–9, 72–3; Stanton, *Gothic Revival & American Church Architecture,* 129–30. For St Mary's, Snettisham, see "Fredericton Cathedral," 81.

6 Douglas Richardson, "The Spirit of the Place," 22; Gilbert Scott, *Personal and Professional Recollections,* 203, regarding the impact of ecclesiology: "So imperious was their law, that any one who dared to deviate from or to build in other than the sacred 'Middle Pointed,' well knew what he must suffer."

7 Brosseau, *Gothic Revival,* 70–1; Arthur, *Toronto,* 250; Armstrong, *City in the Making,* 212–26.

8 Hay, "The Late Mr Pugin," 70–3.

9 White, *Cambridge Movement,* 48–79.

10 White, *Protestant Worship,* 95–8, on the auditory church. Until the twentieth century, evangelical meeting houses in Britain and the United States were often either vernacular or classical in derivation: Betjeman, "Nonconformist Architecture," 161–74; Drummond, *Church Architecture of Protestantism.*

11 This also applies to the works of Fred Cumberland, see Morriss, "Nine-Year Odyssey of a High Victorian Goth," 42–53.

12 White, *Cambridge Movement,* 5–6, 69, 87, notes that the ecclesiologists favoured fourteenth-century Decorated motifs, but Early English was later accepted for parish churches: "On Simplicity of Composition, Especially in Churches of the Early English," 118–22.

13 The scheme was completed over a period of years. The asymmetry and absence of transepts identify this as a parish church. See "On Some of the Differences Between Cathedral and Parish Churches," 181–3; Morriss, "The Nine-Year Odyssey," 42–53. Brick was deemed a most suitable material for town churches: White, *Cambridge Movement,* 97–8, 186; Pugin, *Apology,* 25.

14 Other Gothic-style churches built between 1843 and 1846 include three Anglican churches in Toronto by British *emigré* Henry Bowyer Lane. These were followed by St Michael's Roman Catholic Cathedral of 1845–48 and Knox Presbyterian Church of 1847–48, both by William Thomas, and St James Anglican Cathedral of 1850–52, by Cumberland & Ridout: Arthur, *Toronto,* 86–97, 128–37. For St Basil's roof as it originally appeared, see Robertson, *Landmarks,* 5:455. In terms of this feature, Hay's work was one of the more advanced examples of ecclesiology in the city at the time. MacRae and Adamson, *Hallowed Walls,* 171–2, also describe Hay's St George's, Newcastle, outside Toronto. Pugin, *Apology,* 37, notes "Every building that is treated naturally, without disguise or concealment, cannot fail to look well." Likewise White, *Cambridge Movement,* 98, quotes *A Few Words to Church Builders:* "The first great canon to be observed in Church-building is this: let every material employed be real."

15 LC:125–9, MTRL; [Ure], *Hand-book of Toronto,* 258; Robertson, *Landmarks,* 4:544–50, 5:456; MacRae and Adamson, *Hallowed Walls,* 171. Owned by the Catholic Apostolic Church after 1887, the building was later demolished.

16 For example the Alexander Street Baptist Church, of 1866, by Gundry & Langley: LC:1–4, MTRL; Robertson, *Landmarks,* 4:490.

17 The cost of Langley's design also exceeded original estimates. See St John, *Firm Foundations,* 41–4.

18 Ibid.; LC:55–82, MTRL; HC:621, 1240, AO. The church was destroyed by fire in 1928, and rebuilt

by J. Gibb Morton on a basilical plan. See also *Daily Globe*, 25 August 1870, 4; "The Wesleyan Methodist Church," 241–3; Westfall, *Two Worlds*, 126–58.

19 St John, *Firm Foundations*, 44, says the design was modelled on St George's Parish Church, Doncaster, 1854–58, by Gilbert Scott, illustrated in Cole, *Work of Sir Gilbert Scott*, 63–4, plates 57 and 58 (reference from Mallory). See also Champion, *Methodist Churches*, 122; Dendy, *Lost Toronto*, 114–17.

20 Minutes of the Toronto Conference of the Methodist Church of Canada (1880), 334, VicUA.

21 For early Sunday schools, see White, *Protestant Worship*, 118–30; Drummond, *Church Architecture*, 93–101.

22 Simpson, *Cyclopedia of Methodism*, 18–19, for a description of the Akron scheme and illustration of the First Methodist Church, as well as earlier examples of adjoining schoolrooms in American Methodist churches dating from 1861. See also Regional Church Planning Office, *Church in Akron*, 115–17, for a history of the Akron plan. Harmon, *Encyclopedia of World Methodism*, 73, indicates the Akron Church burned down in 1911. For more information on this type of plan, see Kidder, *Churches and Chapels*, 32–5, 45–52 (reference courtesy of Douglas Richardson).

23 Grant, *Profusion of Spires*, 174.

24 Westfall, *Two Worlds*, 10–11.

25 Drummond, *Church Architecture*, lists many examples.

26 "The Royal Academy Exhibition," 65, on a project by architect J.F. Brown.

27 HC:451, AO. Robertson, *Landmarks*, 4:335–7; Douglas Richardson, "Glory of Toronto," no. 17, for what is now Our Lady of Mount Carmel; McHugh, *Toronto Architecture*, 185.

28 White, *Cambridge Movement*, 97.

29 HC:452a, AO, for a perspective of the 1864–66 building dated July 1869. See also Robertson, *Landmarks*, 4:36–40; White, *Cambridge Movement*, 97–8. After a fire in 1973, the interior was painted. Compare Thomas Fuller's St Stephen-in-the-Fields Anglican Church of 1858, which Gundry & Langley restored in 1865: Arthur, *Toronto*, 135.

30 Hay's Anglican Church, Brampton, 1854, is illustrated in "Ecclesiastical Architecture: Village Churches," 21–2. Morriss, "Nine-Year Odyssey of a High Victorian Goth," 51, citing George Truefitt, *Designs for Country Churches* (1850), Design XVI, as a prototype; Mallory, "Three Henry Langley Churches," 2:12, also refers to this example. For later additions to the Necropolis chapel, see Ontario Association of Architects, *Catalogue of the Fifth Biennial Exhibition* (1935).

31 "Ecclesiastical Architecture: Village Churches," 20–2.

32 For cemetery chapels, see "Cemeteries and Cemetery Chapels," 9–13, which states, "Chancel, nave, tower, and porch, may be pronounced the only indispensible parts of our building, but the pious wishes of private munificence may be indulged in the erection of aisles to hold monuments, or mortuary chapels." The Necropolis, being non-sectarian, is without a chancel.

33 Westfall, *Two Worlds*, 10–11.

34 White, *Protestant Worship*, 85–133, on the elevated central pulpit and other modifications introduced in the Protestant churches of Europe and adopted by the Church of England when Wren designed what he described as "auditories" – churches for preaching as well as communing purposes. See also Betjeman, "Non-Conformist Architecture," 161–74.

35 HC:12a, 599, 891, Ledger, and Certificate Ledger, AO; Collection des plans d'architecture, Nos. 372–4, ANQM; and *Daily Globe*, 27 April 1874, 3, for tenders.

36 Fire destroyed the original interior in 1938, but the building was restored by Horwood & White. The new interior includes a dramatic rosewheel skylight. For the practical appeal of the amphitheatre plan, see J.A.F., "Modern Church Building, Part 2," 66–7. For examples of this type in Britain, see Drummond, *Church Architecture*, 82–4.

37 Jarvis Street was tendered in April 1874, whereas Zion's cornerstone was laid in June of the same year, by which time the building's construction must have been well advanced.

38 *Canadian Methodist Magazine* 1 (1875):93–4, 189–90, 382, for two schemes by Langley, Langley & Burke, and Zion Tabernacle by Joseph Savage. All these schemes were published in response to a request from the committee on church architecture that a depository be created for acceptable plans of Methodist churches, see Minutes of the Committee on Church Architecture (1873), 94; (1874), 236, VicUA. For additional information on Zion

Tabernacle and Savage, see *Daily Spectator* (Hamilton) 9 April 1875, 3; 21 May 1875, 3.

39 Cathcart, *Baptist Encyclopaedia*, 1159–60.

40 Fox, *Letters of William Davies*, 135; Johnston, *McMaster University*, 1:21.

41 Johnston, *McMaster University*, 1:21, 91–112, on the controversy in 1910 between Harris and the trustees of the Toronto Baptist College over the teachings of its staff members; see that chapter also regarding Walmer Road Baptist Church of 1892 (which Burke built for Harris) and Tecumseh Street Baptist of 1896–97 (for William Davies).

42 "Theatre Services in London," 567–8; Morrison, *Early American Architecture*, 117.

43 Silver, *Lost New York*, 46, for Broadway Tabernacle (demolished 1857); Cathcart, *Baptist Encyclopaedia*, 1162–3, for Tremont Tabernacle; Drummond, *Church Architecture*, 58–9.

44 Meeks, "Romanesque Before Richardson," 19.

45 Petit, *Remarks on Church Architecture*, 1:89–90, asked, "Might not a style be matured upon the suggestions thrown out to us by these old [Romanesque] buildings of Italy, France and Germany?" For the controversy provoked, see "Mr Petit's *Remarks on Church Architecture*," 81–3; "Romanesque and Catholick Architecture," 5–16.

46 Hitchcock, *Architecture*, 117–18; Dixon and Muthesius, *Victorian Architecture*, 197, for Wyatt & Brandon, Wild, and Gibson; Stell, *Non-Conformist Chapels and Meeting-houses*.

47 Dixon and Muthesius, *Victorian Architecture*, 224–8.

48 "A Victorian Style," 372.

49 Adams, "Free Church Architecture," 473, objects to the use of a sanctus bell-turret to conceal a ventilator on a Congregational chapel where the bell could have no religious significance.

50 Meeks, "Romanesque Before Richardson," 23–4; Pierson, "Richard Upjohn and the American *Rundbogenstil*," 223–42; Steege, "*Book of Plans* and Early Romanesque Revival in the United States," 215–27; Curran, "German *Rundbogenstil* and Reflections on the American Round-Arch Style," 351–73. Curran states that American motifs did not incorporate the Greek-Gothic synthesis fundamental to the German theory of *Rundbogenstil*. Also Whiffen, *American Architecture*, 61–7, lists Romanesque revival churches from the 1840s and 1850s; and Hitchcock, "Ruskin and American

Architecture," 193, regarding Jacob Wray Mould's Byzantine-style All Souls Church of 1854–55 in New York.

51 "The Decoration of Trinity Church, Boston," 164–5; O'Gorman, *H.H. Richardson and His Office*, 42–51; Ochsner, *H.H. Richardson*, no. 45; White, *Protestant Worship*, 137.

52 Tallmadge, *Story of Architecture*, 175, 192–4; Drummond, *Church Architecture*, 93–5.

53 Tallmadge, *Story of Architecture*, 193. Later commentators were not enamoured of the Akron plan and its successors, see Conover, *Building the House of God*, 65: "We are hoping that the dark ages in American religious architecture have passed but we cannot be too sanguine. The corner pulpit, theatrically bowled floor, curved pews, moveable partitions and pseudo-Gothic are still with us."

54 *Globe*, 13 December 1856, 2, for illustration of the Adelaide Street Church. Cumberland & Storm's Queen Street Wesleyan Chapel of 1856 was similar, see HC:101, AO. For tradition of round-headed windows in Methodist architecture, see Dolby, *Architectural Expression*. For similar American designs, Steege, "The *Book of Plans* and the Early Romanesque Revival in the United States," 216.

55 HC:663, AO; Robertson, *Landmarks*, 4:357–61, 5:473, for Carlton Street Methodist (demolished); HC:670, AO; Arthur, *Toronto*, 167, regarding St Andrew's at King and Simcoe.

56 Westfall, *Two Worlds*, 132, for the division of the Old St Andrew's congregation between Storm's St Andrew's Presbyterian of 1875 and Langley, Langley & Burke's new Old St Andrew's of 1878.

57 Robertson, *Landmarks*, 4:225–33.

58 *Saturday Globe*, 30 May 1891, 2; Robertson, *Landmarks*, 4:480–8, 5:458. Lennox is listed as a Congregationalist in the 1881 Census Return, NA.

59 HC:489, AO, for plans of Beverley Baptist dated 31 May 1886. Beverley Street Baptist Church Minutes, 1881–1911, CBA, Hamilton, indicate that Langley, Langley & Burke were also architects for an earlier structure erected in 1881. Robertson, *Landmarks*, 4:440–4, 5:493; McHugh, *Toronto Architecture*, 190, for what is now the Chinese Baptist Church.

60 Whiffen, *American Architecture*, 137, quoting Schuyler: "While [H.H. Richardson] was living and practising architecture, architects who regarded themselves as in any degree his rivals were naturally

loath to introduce in a design dispositions or features or details, of which the suggestion plainly came from him. Since his death has 'extinguished envy' and ended rivalry, the admiration his work excited has been free to express itself either in direct imitation or in the adoption and elaboration of the suggestions his work furnished."

61 The final cost appears to have been closer to the $60,000 Storm originally estimated, and a threatened lawsuit over the extras was only settled in 1891. Sherbourne Street Methodist Church Trustees Minutes, 1871–94, 168–225, 243–4, 261, 316, 323–30, 344, VicUA.

62 Edmondson, *History of Sherbourne Wesleyan Methodist Church*, 38, 47, 57–8, 67–8; Robertson, *Landmarks*, 4:363–4, 5:465; Champion, *Methodist Churches*, 189–91; McHugh, *Toronto Architecture*, 157, under the current name of St. Luke's United Church. The interior has been altered from an amphitheatral plan to a longitudinal one.

63 Champion, *Methodist Churches*, 177–88, for description of interior; Dendy, *Lost Toronto*, 132–3, regarding demolition.

64 The project was so closely controlled by certain members of the congregation, others objected that the land was held in private hands rather than in trust for the church; Western Trinity Church Trustees' Minutes, 4 March 1888, VicUA.

65 HC:547, 555, AO. Western Trinity Methodist Church Trustees Minutes, September/October 1887, VicUA, state that Burke was the consultant on the plans. See also Robertson, *Landmarks*, 4:402–3; Champion, *Methodist Churches*, 219–22.

66 HC:515, 580, AO; Building Permit no. 361, 21 December 1888, RG 13, C 4, Box 1, CTA; CAB 1 (December 1888): after 6; College Street Baptist Church Minutes, 1886–1895, CBA; Robertson, *Landmarks* 4:454–5. The church is used now by a number of congregations, including the Overcomers Church.

67 HC:532, 806, AO; Building Permit no. 398, 15 November 1889, RG 13, C 4, Box 1, CTA; Champion, *Methodist Churches*, 246.

68 Carpenter and Joiner Specifications, Parkdale United Church, Histories File, VicUA; Robertson, *Landmarks* 4:378–9; *Globe*, 20 August 1890, 3; Parkdale United Church, *Diamond Jubilee*, 6, stating that Hart Massey laid the cornerstone in October 1889.

69 For First Baptist Church in Winnipeg of 1893 by Langley & Burke (demolished except for the tower), see HC:6, 590, AO; Minute Book, CBA; *Manitoba Free Press* (Winnipeg) 8 October 1892, 3; Grover, "440 Hargrave Street," both references courtesy of Giles Bugailiskis; "First Baptist Church, Winnipeg," 279–80 (reference courtesy of Randy Rostecki); "Old Calvary Temple," 1–2. Regarding Central Methodist Church, now Metropolitan United Church, London, 1896, by Burke & Horwood, see HC:775a, 779, 782, 835, 901, 956, 1191, Plan List, and Ledger, AO; *London Free Press*, 31 July 1895, 6. For Knox Presbyterian Church, Woodstock, 1896, by Burke & Horwood, see HC:530a, 788, 792a, 796, 902, 959, 1166 and Plan List, AO; "Knox Church, Woodstock," 12, ill.

70 HC:836, 858, 1661, Certificate Ledger, and Plan List, AO; Building Permit no. 728/301, 25 August 1902, RG 13, C 4.27, Box 4, CTA; Robertson, *Landmarks* 4:599–600. The facade and interior of what is now known as Riverside Church have been restored. See HC:1010, AO, for domed Byzantine scheme the firm prepared for Western Baptist on Lansdowne Avenue in 1909.

71 Fergusson, *History of Architecture*, 2:370–1.

72 For comparative examples, see Dendy, *Lost Toronto*, 112–13, 140–1. Involving its congregations full-time through facilities of this type was a longstanding concern for the Methodist church and parallels the concept behind the YMCA.

73 Davey, *Arts and Crafts Architecture*; Margaret Richardson, *Architects of the Arts and Crafts*; Girouard, *Sweetness and Light*.

74 Turak, *William Le Baron Jenney*, 207–22, quoting "A Rural Church," 20–3. In a paper on "John Danley Aitchison (Winnipeg)," presented before the Society for the Study of Architecture in Canada, 14 April 1989, Philip Haese noted similar works by Aitchison in the 1910s. Cox and Ford, *Parish Churches*, 50–1 and plate 47, indicate that wood and half-timbering were used in English parish examples, but normally for the bell-tower.

75 Douglas Richardson, "Hyperborean Gothic," 48–74, and "The Spirit of the Place," 23–5; Stanton, *Gothic Revival*, 163–5.

76 Mallory, "Three Henry Langley Churches," 1:9–25; Douglas Richardson, "Hyperborean Gothic," 48–74.

77 "Sketch for a Village Church," 11; HC:582, 585, AO.

78 Other Toronto half-timbered churches included

Clinton Street Methodist, Ossington Avenue Baptist, Broadview Congregational, Runneymede Presbyterian, St Savior's Anglican, St James Humber Bay, St Olave's Anglican and Olivet Baptist, Picture Collection, MTRL. See Arthur, *Toronto*, 260–1, for Strickland & Symons.

79 Scully, *Shingle Style*, 71–90.

80 Hines, *Burnham of Chicago*, 39–43.

81 HC:16, AO; Drawings for Baptist Church and Parsonage at Maskinongé, Quebec, "Facts Relating to Maskinongé Church," Scrapbook of Maskinongé; *Grande Ligne – Truth is Stranger than Fiction – Maskinongé*, pamphlet, n.d., Files of Baptist Chapel, Maskinongé, Quebec, CBA.

82 In 1912 Burke & Horwood also designed Kildonan Baptist Church, now St Anthony Church Hall, West Kildonan, near Winnipeg in clapboard and shingle, see HC:1155, AO. Other Shingle style churches in Toronto included Morningside Presbyterian, 1891, and the Anglican Church of St Michael and All Angels, 1907, which was shingle and stucco: Picture Collection, MTRL. Compare also A.E. Wells, "Design for a Village Church," in Committee on Church Architecture, *Designs for Village, Town, and Country Churches*, 6–7, which is distinctly English in derivation.

83 The design was published as part of W.H. Hodson's column, "How to Estimate," May 1892:49, June 1892:61; July 1892:69.

84 HC:558, 563, 595a, 846, 1059, 1127, AO; Building Permit no. 701, 24 February 1892, RG 13, C 4.10, Box 2, CTA; *Christmas 1892 Souvenir: The Opening Services of the Walmer Road Baptist Church* (1892), CBA.

85 HC:798, AO. See Brandon and Brandon, *Parish Churches*, not paginated; and Gebhard, "C.F.A. Voysey," 304–17.

86 HC:885, 887, AO; information from McMaster family.

87 Kaplan, *Art That is Life*, 112–14.

88 Cram, *Church Building*, 14, 22–5, 66.

89 HC:880, AO; Preston Baptist Church Minutes, 1895–1915, CBA. Compare HC:971, AO, for an undated *Design for a Village Chapel* along the same lines.

90 Cram, *Church Building*, 28–9.

91 All Saint's is illustrated in Kaplan, *Art That is Life*, 138.

92 The church is large, filling most of the suburban lot. Its Tudor motif coincides with a local stylistic affinity for half-timbering exemplified in the domestic works of local architect Samuel Maclure, described by Eaton, *Architecture of Samuel Maclure*; Segger, *Buildings of Samuel Maclure*.

93 Muccigrosso, *American Gothic*, 59–66; Cram *Church Building*, 13, 45; and H.B., "Pointed or English Style of Architecture," January 1891, 5–6; April 1891, 60; R.C. Sturgis, "Church Architecture," 153–4, which demonstrate the continuing interest in Gothic throughout the 1890s.

94 HC:1021, AO. See also Brosseau, *Gothic Revival*, 178–9; Kalman and Roaf, *Exploring Vancouver 2*, 129; Carmichael, *Autobiography of a Church*; by the same author *These Sixty Years*; *Province* (Vancouver) 10 February 1931, 1; Cram, *Church Building*, 25, on wooden roofs; and criticism in "An American Gothic Revival," 131–2.

95 HC:1057, 1058, 1080, 1111a, AO, for Murray Street Baptist; HC:1062, 1158, 1160, 1176, 1185, AO, for Trinity Methodist, Peterborough. Compare also HC:1070, AO, for both New Chalmers Church of 1911 on Vansittart Avenue in Woodstock and conventional interior J. Gibb Morton designed for the former Metropolitan Methodist in 1928–29. In both cases the Sunday School buildings abut without forming part of the church proper, as purists had long demanded.

96 See Brosseau, *Gothic Revival*, 176–7; Schuyler, "Works of Cram, Goodhue & Ferguson," 18; "The Cathedral of St Alban the Martyr, Toronto," 50–8.

97 "Fourth Annual Convention of the Royal Architectural Institute of Canada," 109.

98 Clippings, R.C. Windeyer Papers, Ms 488, AO; *AABN* 24 (17 November 1888):229; "The Cathedral of St Alban the Martyr," 50–8; chapter 8 for British role in Ottawa Departmental buildings competition after 1911.

CHAPTER FOUR

1 Mitchell's *Building Construction* was a text designed for students of building construction at Regent Street Polytechnic, London.

2 Burke, "Elements of Building Construction," 28–9.

3 Ibid. For the balloon frame, see Condit, *American Building*, 43–5; and Rempel, *Building with Wood*, 117–57. Field, "A Reexamination into the Invention of the Balloon Frame," 3–29, describes it as "an-

other symbol of America's love of getting things done quickly." For first example of balloon framing in 1832; see Sprague, "Origin of Balloon Framing," 311–19.

4 Crossman, *Architecture in Transition*, 109–35, regarding demands for a Canadian style of architecture.

5 Burke, "Elements of Building Construction," 28; Greenhill Macpherson and Richardson, *Ontario Towns*, chapter 1, on local constructional adaptations of the early nineteenth century.

6 Siddall, "Advancement of Public Taste in Architecture," 28.

7 Toronto Society of Architects, *Catalogue of the Sixth Exhibition* (1912), 9, offers the exhibition as proof that "our Architectural problems are being fairly faced, intelligently studied and worthily solved." The Society emphasized the artistic side of architecture, instead of the scientific approach advocated by Burke. But results could not have been achieved without both elements; see Toronto Architectural Eighteen, *Catalogue of the Fifth Exhibition* (1909), 12, for mission statement.

8 Burke, "Some Notes on House Planning," 55–7.

9 Osborne, *Notes on the Art of House Planning*, 8–9. Kerr's *Gentleman's House* was an earlier authority on the subject.

10 Burke, "Some Notes on House Planning," 55–7, paraphrasing Osborne, *Notes on the Art of House Planning*, 9. Burke's mechanistic metaphor anticipates by three decades Corbusier's *machine à habiter*.

11 McMordie, "The Cottage Idea," 19, quoting Wood the Younger, *Series of Plans for Cottages*: a designer "ideally places himself in the position of the person for whom he designs."

12 A.J. Downing, *Victorian Cottage Residences*, 10–12. For Greenough, see Tuckerman, *A Memorial to Horatio Greenough* (1853) reprinted Mumford, *Roots of Contemporary American Architecture*, 57. Also T. Brown, "Greenough, Paine, Emerson, and the Organic Aesthetic," 304–17.

13 See chapter 6.

14 Burke, "Some Notes on House Planning," 55–7; and Kerr, *Gentleman's House*, 61: "Another grievance (and one of universal prevalence) lies in the want of due consideration for the all-important question of Aspect ... Generally speaking, architects have to learn this golden rule – 'Take care of the inside, and

the outside ought to take care of itself.'" Also Osborne, *Notes on the Art of House Planning*, 53–5.

15 Brosseau, *Gothic Revival*, 18–19.

16 Arthur, *Toronto*, 149. Other examples by Gundry & Langley in McHugh, *Toronto Architecture*, 164–6, include the Blaikie/Alexander house, of 1863–64, at 400–404 Jarvis Street (altered), and the Arthur R. McMaster residence, of 1868, (attributed only), now the Keg Mansion Restaurant, at 515 Jarvis Street.

17 McHugh, *Toronto Architecture*, 165, for Thomas Thompson house at 471 Jarvis Street, of 1873–74, by Langley, Langley & Burke.

18 Cameron and Wright, *Second Empire Style*. For alteration of motifs in the North American context, see Hersey, "Replication Replicated," 21–48.

19 Dendy, *Lost Toronto*, 34–6; and by same author "Government House," 21–5. For early residential examples in Britain and the United States, see Hitchcock, "Second Empire 'Avant La Lettre'," 115–30; McKenna, "James Renwick, Jr," 97–101. See chapter 5 for Hay's mansards.

20 Langley, "Description of the Lieutenant Governor's Residence"; and Cameron and Wright, *Second Empire Style*, 30–3, for London's Paddington Station and Hotel of 1852 by Hardwick & Hardwick, and Design for the War Office in Whitehall of 1856–57 by Henry B. Garling, both of which were significantly different from the French precedents.

21 Collins, *Changing Ideals*, 122–3, credits Rev. J.L. Petit with ushering eclecticism at the Architectural Exhibition in 1861.

22 HC:500, AO; and A.S. Thompson, *Jarvis Street*, 157–60, on the now demolished Carruthers house.

23 Service, *Edwardian Architecture*, 14–23, illustrates brick town houses that combine Gothic vernacular with "Queen Anne" elements. The Carruthers house had American elements as well.

24 A.S. Thompson, *Jarvis Street*, discusses the general flavour of the neighbourhood.

25 HC:472, 617, AO (now demolished).

26 Girouard, *Sweetness and Light*, 2, reworks a description by Ridge in *Building News* 28 (13 March 1875):285.

27 Collins, *Changing Ideals*, 122–3; Stevenson, "On the Reaction of Taste," 689–91; Dixon and Muthesius, *Victorian Architecture*, 176–8.

28 Girouard, "Review of Andrew Saint," 195–6, distinguishes Shaw's Old English manner, exemplified by Leyswood, of 1868, from a narrowly defined

"Queen Anne" revival represented by the Old Swan House, of 1876. As interpreted in the nineteenth century, "Queen Anne" stood for the principle of eclecticism.

29 Scully, *Shingle Style*, 31, quoting Holly, "Modern Dwellings: Their Construction, Decoration, and Furniture," *Harper's* 52 (1875–76):855–67. Also S., "Concerning 'Queen Anne'," 403–4.

30 Peabody, "A Talk About 'Queen Anne'," 133–4; and J.M.B. "A Few More Words About 'Queen Anne'," 320–2.

31 Schuyler, "Concerning 'Queen Anne,'" in Jordy and Coe, *American Architecture*, 2:453–87.

32 *Minutes of ... the City of Toronto* (9 April 1874):95, By-law 627, s. 53, CTA. Scully, *Shingle Style*, 12, indicates Shaw's tile hangings and half-timber were applied over "perfectly sound brick walls," a method adopted by Burke to comply with the by-law.

33 For Simpson plan, see *AABN* 19 (20 February 1886): ill. no. 530, after 90, reference courtesy of Robert Hill. Also Scully, *Shingle Style*, 14–18 and plate 10, for Watts Sherman plan.

34 "Architectural Offices," 123.

35 HC:472, 617, AO; and Articles of Agreement, 4 December 1882, between Richard Horwood, John Charles Batstone Horwood, and Langley, Langley & Burke, HC: Add. 1, MU 3985, AO.

36 Burke, "Some Notes on House Planning," 55, refers to the client's involvement in the design process with obvious preference for those who know their own tastes and requirements.

37 Girouard, *Sweetness and Light*, 91, 163. Shaw's Kate Greenaway house at 39 Frognal, of 1884–85, is also comparable.

38 McHugh, *Toronto Architecture*, 226; Dendy and Kilbourn, *Toronto Observed*, 118–20, for the Lewis Lukes house at 37 Madison Avenue, of 1888–89, by E.J. Lennox, which is claimed to have provided the model for other Annex houses.

39 *Globe*, 23 August 1890, 3. The author also refers to the influence of American Romanesque and "southern" style, described only as requiring "plenty of room." For other examples, see *Saturday Globe*, 1 November 1890, 1; and 22 November 1890, 1.

40 A.S. Thompson, *Jarvis Street*, 153–6, 165–6. Also *CAB* 5 (April 1892): after 38, for W.H.A. Massey residence (demolished) by William Young of New York. For McKinnon house, of 1888, at 506 Jarvis Street, see McHugh, *Toronto Architecture*, 167.

41 HC:28a, 499, 543, 594b, 816, AO.

42 H.M. Brown, *Lanark Legacy*, 136–45; Reid, "The Rosamond Woolen Company of Almonte," 266; and Morgan, *Canadian Men and Women of the Time*, 880–1.

43 *CAB* 3 (February 1890):36. Burke suggested $5000-$12,000 for an architect-designed house in Burke, "Some Notes on House Planning," 56.

44 HC:28a, AO. Burke undertook alterations for Rosamond in April of 1894 while a sole practitioner. Neither Murray White nor John Horwood, who delineated the drawings in 1885, had yet joined his firm.

45 HC:506, 579, AO, bearing the initials C.H.A.B. and J.C.B.H.; and *CAB* 3 (November 1890):123, for a perspective of the elaborate shingle-hung mansion (now demolished).

46 Burke, "Some Notes on House Planning," 56.

47 The transmission of this idea to the United States is documented by Scully, *Shingle Style*, 5–18.

48 "Specialization as it Applies to Arts and Crafts," 78–9.

49 Burke, "Some Notes on House Planning," 56, observed that the "stairs should be so placed as not to expose the upper hall to view from the entrance." He also suggested that "where a hall fireplace is introduced it should be in a cosy nook away from the drafts." For similar examples of large halls, see Murray A. White, "TASC Competition for a Staircase in Wood"; Edmund Burke, "Staircase Hall in A.E. Kemp's House"; Burke & Horwood, "No. 123 St George Street, Toronto." Regarding Shaw's rediscovery of the inglenook, see Saint, *Richard Norman Shaw*; Girouard, "Review of Andrew Saint," 195–6.

50 HC:9, 42, AO, for Burke's plans of 1892–93 of the Charles J. Holman house, now the Women's Missionary Society of the Regular Baptists of Canada, at 75 Lowther Avenue. According to Parks Canada, Mrs Holman was president of Moulton College and founder of the Society which now owns the property. For illustration see, *CAB* 6 (December 1893):ill. delineated by Edward Langley, Jr, who began his articles with Burke that very year.

51 McHugh, *Toronto Architecture*, 237.

52 To compare more complex examples executed by Langley & Langley at 1 and 3 Elmsley Place in 1896, see McHugh, *Toronto Architecture*, 125.

53 A photograph of the house with its clay-tile roof was

published in *CAB* 15 (July 1892): ill; see also HC:522, AO, for another tile-hung residence built at the corner of Walmer Road and Lowther Avenue, in 1889, for the Reverend Elmore Harris.

54 *CAB* 15 (July 1902): suppl. ill.; Toronto Architectural Eighteen Club, *First Exhibition Catalogue* (1901), 53, for perspective under Horwood's name, similar to the firm's design for the Toronto Bible Training College of 1898 (demolished). Both resembled the residence of William Storrs Wells at Newport, Rhode Island, by G.E. Harding, see *AABN* (1 February 1890): no. 736.

55 See chapter 8.

56 "*Canadian Architect and Builder* Competition for a City House," 23–4, won by Arthur Wells. Runners-up were students in the Langley firm, Ernest Wilby whose "crisp and sparkling" rendering was "indicative of much facility and practice with the pen," and Murray White, who made "one or two unfortunate slips, due evidently to want of sufficient study."

57 HC:775, AO, for drawings stamped Burke & Horwood, dated April 1895. Building Permit no. 53, 1897, RG 13, C 4.17, Box 2, CTA, authorizes a large two-storey brick villa on Maple Avenue for H.H. Fudger, but does not specify the architect.

58 Saint, *Richard Norman Shaw*, 197, for illustration.

59 HC:864, 1076, AO, for later additions and several fine perspectives from 1902 by William F. Sparling.

60 Cleaveland, *Village and Farm Cottages 1856*, 14.

61 Newton, "Our Summer Resort Architecture," 297–318.

62 Ibid., 297–301. Newton mentions Virginia Hot Springs, and White Sulphur Springs in West Virginia, Ballston Spa, Richfield Springs, and Saratoga, all in northern New York state, and Rockaway on Long Island, as health resorts in the style of the European health spa, but "with more emphasis upon out-of-door exercise and recreation."

63 "Watering Places of the Lower St Lawrence," 9 April 1870, 362; 12 August 1871, 97; 26 August 1871, 130, where, at Cacouna, the reporter's room was above a bowling alley; 24 August 1872, 115.

64 Lorne Park Estates, *A Village Within a City*, 19–36. The original directors included John William Stockwell, William Richard Henderson, and George Leo Hillman, merchants; James Venn, jeweller; Peter McIntyre, steamboat agent; Rufus Shorey Neville,

barrister; James Bellingham Boustead, who had a successful fire insurance business; John Earls, general freight agent; and James Hewlett, broker. See also Toronto and Lorne Park, *Lorne Park Illustrated*, 10–11, for an advertisement that lists Langley & Burke as the Lorne Park architects and note that Burke himself was a director by 1890. Burke undertook the refitting of the hotel, which had been operating since 1879, see HC:532, AO.

65 Lorne Park Estates, *Village Within a City*, 29; and *Mail*, 22 May 1879, 2–3, regarding Toronto's other resort known as Victoria Park, located on Scarboro [sic] Heights, and owned by Shields, Smith & Co. Both offered band concerts several times a week, and promised well-policed grounds. Toronto Island also provided an escape from the city beginning in the 1830s, see Sward, *Toronto Islands*, 15; and Gibson, *More Than an Island*, 107, for cottages. See also HC:10, 501, AO, for Charles Goad cottages on Toronto Island, and Reverend Castle cottage in the Thousand Islands. Resorts like suburbs only flourished once their accessibility was assured by advances in transportation technology: Toronto and Lorne Park, *Lorne Park Illustrated*, 3.

66 Toronto and Lorne Park, *Lorne Park Illustrated*, 3.

67 HC:492, 571, 575, AO.

68 Toronto and Lorne Park, *Lorne Park Illustrated*, 11 and photograph of Burke's cottage. Drawings for the Lorne Park cottages are signed by delineators other than Burke, but it seems fair to assume that he supervised the project.

69 Ibid., 36, for restrictive covenants in the deed of sale and prohibitions on animals and intoxicating liquors; all water closets and privies had to be approved.

70 Lorne Park Estates, *A Village Within a City*, 37.

71 The average cost was $700, see HC:492, AO.

72 Toronto and Lorne Park, *Lorne Park Illustrated*, 7; Newton, "Our Summer Resort Architecture," 301, for verandas in American resort architecture; and King, *Bungalow*, for other examples worldwide.

73 A.J. Downing, *Victorian Cottage Residences*, 89.

74 Newton, "Our Summer Resort Architecture," 297–301, for early resort hotels of the 1830s in wood-frame construction; and Scully, *Shingle Style*, xxxix-lii.

75 A.J. Downing, *Architecture of Country Houses*, 163.

76 HC:520, AO, appears to follow the technique described by Wheeler, *Homes for the People*, 408–9.

77 Scully, *Shingle Style*, lvi-ii, says diagonal bracing was known by 1865.

78 Ibid., xlvi, regarding the angular profile and protruding wood skeleton.

79 Ibid., xliv; Condit, *American Building*, 43–5; and Rempel, *Building with Wood*, 99–171.

80 A.J. Downing, *Architecture of Country Houses*, 127; McMordie, "The Cottage Idea," 23, tracing the Swiss cottage motif to P.F. Robinson, *Rural Architecture; or a Series of Designs for Ornamental Cottages* (1823), design no. 8; illustrated also in Lancaster, *American Bungalow*, 30.

81 Cleaveland, *Village and Farm Cottages*, 92; Scully, *Shingle Style*, xlvi-liii, regarding Downing and Cleaveland.

82 HC:504, 505, 508–11, 520, AO. Scully, *Shingle Style*, liii, indicates the term "Swiss" continued long after the disappearance of the characteristic sawtooth bargeboards.

83 Sinclair and Lewis, *Victorious Victorians*, 46–7, for photographs of Oceanpathway in Ocean Grove, New Jersey. For other examples, see McAlester, *Field Guide to American Houses*, 311.

84 The Centennial Exhibition held in Philadelphia in 1876 popularized Japanese motifs in the United States, inspiring the Shingle style lattice work of McKim, Mead & White's Newport Casino of 1879–81, see Scully, *Shingle Style*, 21–2; "Japanese Building at the Centennial," 136; "The Habitations of Man in All Ages," 68–70; and Lancaster, "Japanese Buildings in the United States," 219–24. In Burke's library was a copy of Edward S. Morse, *Japanese Homes and Their Surroundings* (1886).

85 For seaside cottages or southern houses, see Comstock, *Victorian Domestic Architectural Plans and Details*; *Palliser's New Cottage Homes and Details*, plates 22 and 60; and Mitchell, *American Victoriana* for reproductions from *Scientific American*.

86 Wheeler, *Homes for the People*, 3.

87 Scully, *Shingle Style*, 78, on the use of the round tower by Bruce Price in "The Craigs," of 1879–80. At Lorne Park polygonal turrets were a feature of the Paul Campbell cottage, of 1887 (HC:493, 495, 584, 593, AO), and the A.H. Gilbert cottage, of 1888 (HC:513, AO). Wheeler, *Homes for the People*, 42, notes that towers were best placed "on undulating land, where … a distant view or other loveliness can be looked upon, provided the elevation is sufficient."

88 HC:22, 573, AO. The McMaster project antedates Horwood's return from the United States. Compare Richardson's Codman project of 1869–71 (based on the Elizabethan living hall), and the Victor Newcomb House in Elberon, New Jersey, of 1880–81, by McKim, Mead & White (influenced by the open interiors of the Japanese): Scully, *Shingle Style*, 5–12, 135–43.

89 Newton, "Our Summer Resort Architecture," 297.

90 *Historical Sketch of the Grande Ligne Mission*, 1–22, for the Baptist mission established since 1835, and its pentecostal school recently reconstructed following a fire. Grande Ligne was linked with the Baptist mission at Maskinongé.

91 HC:14, AO.

92 Peabody, "A Talk About 'Queen Anne,'" 133–4; "Georgian" [pseud. R.S. Peabody], "Georgian Homes of New England," 338–9; Scully, *Shingle Style*, 42–4.

93 Marianna Richardson, *Ontario Association of Architects Centennial Collection*, 36.

94 *Allisonia* (Sackville), November 1904.

95 Now known as the Black house and owned by Mount Allison University: *CAB* 10 (February 1897):37.

96 Macaulay, "John Hammond," in Stacey, *Lives and Works of the Canadian Artists*; Rombout, "John Hammond," 24–5; and Sackville Art Association, *John Hammond* (copy courtesy of Lynda Jessup, Queen's University, Kingston).

97 *CAB* 12 (November 1899):213, ill. Rombout, "John Hammond," indicates the artist was in the Far East between 1899 and 1901; Interview #21, dated 11 May 1977, with K. Hammond Krug of Waterloo, Acc. #8226, MAUA, states that Hammond designed his own residences. Burke & Horwood planned the house for Hammond, but his tenure was short. Also Maitland, "Queen Anne Revival," 44–8, and *Queen Anne Revival Style*, 102.

98 *CAB* 12 (November 1899):213, ill. Railway magnate Sir William Van Horne was Hammond's chief patron and is said to have designed the fireplace in the artist's studio.

99 Burke, "Some Notes on House Planning," 55–7.

100 Contrast, "Design for a Villa Costing $3,500," 3–7, with a Shingle-style example by Buffalo architect Edward A. Kent in which the main interior space is a living hall that opens directly onto a veranda.

101 According to J. Lawrence Black, son of the original owner, this house is now owned by Canadian artist David Silverberg.

102 *CAB* 5 (March 1892):111, ill.

103 Now the residence of Arthur Moyter, according to information provided by the Black family.

104 Gowans, *Comfortable House*, 84, quoting Aladdin's catalogue for the Williamette model. See also HC:817, AO, for a page torn from *Ladies Home Journal* reviewing a series of articles for a prize-winning house from 1897–98.

105 Now the residence of Dr Marion Trenholme, according to Donna Beal, Archives Assistant, MAUA. In 1909, Burke, Horwood & White executed another residence for John Hammond in Sackville, see HC:1029(21), AO, but it cannot be considered among the Shingle-style works of this period.

106 Gowans, *Comfortable House*, 201, for Sears "Modern Home, 109" from the catalogue of 1908.

107 *An Act relating to Young Avenue in the City of Halifax*, Statutes of Nova Scotia, 1896, 59 Vic., chap. 28, sec. 1.

108 *McAlpine's Halifax City Directory for 1900–1901*, 702.

109 "Citizens of Halifax who Aim to Keep Homes Beautiful," *Morning Chronicle* (Halifax), 24 May 1909, 5.

110 It may not be coincidence that Langley & Burke had entered the 1890 competition for the Confederation Life building in Toronto, see HC:564, AO.

111 *McAlpine's Halifax City Directory for 1900–01*, 702, 257, with address as 56 Young Avenue and 126 Young Avenue respectively. By 1903 the latter was occupied by Robert Leslie a commercial merchant, who is mentioned in *Halifax, Nova Scotia and Its Attractions* (c. 1902). In 1914 the same property, then 114 Young Avenue, was occupied by building contractor Samuel M. Brookfield, president of S.M. Brookfield, Ltd and Halifax Graving Dock, see *McAlpine's Halifax City Directory for 1914*, 161; *CAB* 18 (January 1905):16.

112 The bays were later enlarged, see Building Permit no. 3698, 8 May 1914, RG 35–102, Series 39, Section I-59, Archives of Nova Scotia, Halifax.

113 HC:842, AO.

114 Osborne, *Notes on Art of House Planning*, 9.

115 Burke, "Some Notes on House Planning," 55.

CHAPTER FIVE

1 "Hospital," *Canadian Encyclopedia*, 2:1009.

2 Arthur, *Toronto*, 115, for Toronto General Hospital (demolished); and Dendy, *Lost Toronto*, 120–1, for the House of Providence (demolished). See also Cameron and Wright, *Second Empire Style*, 30–1, 40–1, regarding the history of the mansard roof. Hitchcock, "Second Empire," 115–30, describes mansarded examples prior to 1852; and Roth, *Concise History of American Architecture*, 128, enumerates early Second Empire examples in the United States, including James Renwick's Charity Hospital on Blackwell's Island, New York City of 1854–57. Also McKenna, "James Renwick, Jr," 97–101.

3 "The Editor's Shanty," 211–13, for a description of Toronto General Hospital. St Aidan's College is described as "Domestic Gothic" of the fifteenth or sixteenth century: *Builder* 8 (6 April 1850):162.

4 Hellmuth College also had hot and cold running water on each floor, see LC:198–207, MTRL; Tausky and DiStephano, *Victorian Architecture*, 144–9; "Educational Intelligence: Hellmuth Ladies' College," 141–3; "Hellmuth College," 316; "Hellmuth Ladies College," 171–2. Also "The Boys' Home," 83, 92.

5 C.M. Johnston, *McMaster University*, 1:48. The purposes for which the institution was endowed are noted by Rawlyk, *Canadian Baptists*, 33.

6 HC:611, 622, AO, for contract drawings dated 14 July 1880; C.M. Johnston, *McMaster University*, 1:18–44, on the founding of Toronto Baptist College (later McMaster University); and Rawlyk, *Canadian Baptists*, 31–62. For current use by Royal Conservatory of Music, see McHugh, *Toronto Architecture*, 122.

7 Burke, "McMaster University Buildings," 154–60 (reference courtesy of Judith Colwell, Archivist of CBA). C.M. Johnston, *McMaster University*, 1:22; Robertson, *Landmarks*, 4:579–80.

8 For Trinity College of 1851–52 by Kivas Tully, St Michael's College of 1855–56 by William Hay, Knox College of 1873–75 by Smith & Gemmell, see Arthur, *Toronto*, 120–1, 126–7, 138–43, 220. University College of 1856–59 by Cumberland & Storm integrated High Victorian Gothic and

Norman round-arched elements, while Wycliffe College of 1881 by William Storm was Romanesque. In Britain the Gothic was rejected by nonconformist institutions, which associated the style with Church of England schools, see Malcolm Seabourne in Robson, *School Architecture*, 20.

9 Architectural vocabularies of Baptist colleges in the United States varied greatly according to their date, as indicated by illustrations in Cathcart, *Baptist Encyclopaedia*.

10 Ibid., 152–4, for Newton Theological Centre, 844–5, for Brown University; Henderson, *Harvard: An Architectural History*, 297, n.29, 301, n.19, for the Episcopal Theological College, Cambridge.

11 For an excellent colour photograph of the facade, see McKelvey, *Toronto Carved in Stone*, 97.

12 Maltby, Macdonald, and Cunningham, *Alfred Waterhouse*, 9, have pointed out that Waterhouse specifically rejected "Queen Anne." See also Hobhouse, *Lost London*, for description of St Paul's as "indigestible in the carbolic red of its material." Contrast Robson, *School Architecture*, who champions "Queen Anne." Also on Waterhouse, see Dixon and Muthesius, *Victorian Architecture*, 242–3; and Fawcett, *Seven Victorian Architects*, 102–21.

13 Landau, "Tall Office Building Artistically Reconsidered," 136–64. See also Robson, *School Architecture*, 62–3, 77, for French and German examples with continuous round arches.

14 Cathcart, *Baptist Encyclopaedia*, 212–24; C.M. Johnston, *McMaster University*, 1:90–113. Compare F. Kimball's design for the Connecticut Theological Institute and changes made in the course of construction; see *AABN* 6 (13 September 1879): 85, ill.; (15 November 1879):no. 203.

15 Tausky and DiStephano, *Victorian Architecture*, 337–40; Dendy, *Lost Toronto*, 188–9; *Dominion Illustrated* (Montreal) Special Edition on Toronto, 1892, 8; and "Toronto – The Commercial Metropolis of Ontario," *Saturday Globe*, 14 June 1890, 1.

16 Richard Waite of Buffalo had just introduced the single-storey round arch to Toronto in his Western Life Assurance building of 1880, see Crossman, *Architecture in Transition*, 9–27. Meeks, "Romanesque Before Richardson in the United States," 17–33, explores the early transmission of the round-arch motif from Germany and elsewhere.

17 *Act to Unite Toronto Baptist College and Woodstock College under the Name of McMaster University*, 50 Vic. (1887), chap. 5; C.M. Johnston, *McMaster University*, 1:46–7, 65.

18 HC:2, 12, 46, 561, 562, Plan List, AO; Burke, "McMaster University Buildings," 158.

19 Blueprints and Architects Drawings nos. 1–12 (1894) and nos. 1–4 (1899), CBA; HC:826a, 832, and Ledger, AO; Burke, "McMaster University Buildings," 158–60.

20 In 1904–6 a second fireproof addition housing science laboratories was built at the rear of McMaster Hall; see HC:862, AO; Progress Photographs, McMaster Files, CBA.

21 The Canadian Literary Institute offered co-educational facilities from the 1860s, and in 1873 erected a Ladies' Building. This facility later moved to Toronto as Moulton College; see Department of Travel and Publicity Press Release, 23 September 1960, courtesy of the Woodstock Museum, Woodstock; and C.M. Johnston, *McMaster University*, 1:16–17, on the liberal admission policies of this nominally Baptist institution.

22 The name is variously reported as David White and Paul White, but it has not been possible to verify any link to Murray A. and Melville P. White; see Rev. W. Gordon Carder on "Woodstock College, 1857–1926," Speech before the Oxford Historical Society, 27 May 1981, quoting *Oxford and Norfolk Gazetteer* (1867); and W. Gordon Carder, "Decision Made 100 Years Ago Ended Dream of University," *Daily Sentinel Review* (Woodstock), 26 March 1988, 4 (copies courtesy of Sheila A. Johnson, Curator of the Woodstock Museum). See also "Baptist Institute, Woodstock," 28.

23 HC:461, AO, for 1871 drawings, signed Henry Langley per "E.B." This mansarded addition to the Canadian Literary Institute is noted by C.M. Johnston, *McMaster University*, 1:15–16; and "Baptist Institute, Woodstock," 35. For the 1886 Dining Hall plans, see HC:486a, 512, 595, AO, including a perspective bearing the initials "JCBH." In 1905 Burke & Horwood also designed a gymnasium: HC:869, Ledger, and Plan List, AO.

24 Another Romanesque scheme was prepared the following year by Langley & Burke for the Victoria College competition, see *Christian Guardian* (Toronto) 9 November 1887, 71 (reference courtesy of Stephen A. Otto).

25 Burke, "Sub-Surface Irrigation Drainage," 12–13, notes the technology was transferred to North

America by Colonel George Waring of Newport. For other plumbing advice, see Burke & Horwood, "The Intercepting Trap," 149.

26 Storm had been retained since 1856, but Law Society of Upper Canada Minutes, 1867-68, Michelmas Term, 44 Vic., Law Society of Upper Canada Archives, Toronto, record one earlier occasion on which the firm of Gundry & Langley also acted.

27 Law Society of Upper Canada Minutes, 21 May 1894, Law Society of Upper Canada Archives, Toronto, inviting submissions from Burke, E.J. Lennox, Frank Darling, and Beaumont Jarvis.

28 HC:25, 790, 814, 1666, Add. 5, Box 1, and Plan List, AO; Arthur, *Toronto*, 104, for illustrations.

29 HC:24, 33, 773, Plan List, and Ledger, AO, for drawings bearing signature of Burke as well as E. Burke per J.B. Horwood. Melville P. White, who executed the illustrated perspective, later joined his brother Murray A. White in Chicago, returning in 1907 to work as the manager of the Architectural Iron Department of the Canada Foundry Company, see Archindont Index, MTRL. For further information on the American Room, see also Law Society of Upper Canada Minutes, 31 January and 30 November 1894, Law Society of Upper Canada Archives, Toronto; and *CAB* 10 (April 1897):71, ill.

30 Irving, "Owens Museum of Fine Arts," MAUA; and Sackville Art Association, *John Hammond*, unpaginated, for information regarding the purchase of the John Owens collection. See also Board of Regents of Mount Allison University Minutes, 31 May and 8 August 1893, 1:324, 445, MAUA; and *Argosy* (January 1894), 14. General information on the town's architecture is recorded by DeGrace, "An Architectural History of Sackville, New Brunswick."

31 Kostof, *Architect*, chapter 8.

32 D.H. Crook, "Louis Sullivan and the Golden Doorway," 250-8; Tselos, "Chicago Fair and the Myth of the 'Lost Cause,'" 259-68; Karlowitz, "D. H. Burnham's Role in the Selection of Architects for the World's Columbian Exposition," 247-54; Moore, *Daniel Hudson Burnham*, 1:39, regarding Burnham's invitation to eastern architects, their choice of stylistic expression for the World's Fair, and its future impact. Among those who participated were Richard Morris Hunt, who designed the *néo-grec* Lenox Library in New York in 1877, and McKim, Mead & White, whose Villard Houses, of

1883-85, in New York and Boston Public Library, of 1888-92, had already launched the Beaux-Arts manner in the United States.

33 HC:19, 19a, 47a, AO; *CAB* 7 (April 1894):51, for elevation by William Ford Howland. The original roof was replaced in order to accommodate a second storey in the attic. Final cost of the structure was $25,000, including architect's fees, see Board of Regents of Mount Allison University Minutes, 27 May 1896, 1:473, MAUA.

34 A perspective of the Shepley, Rutan & Coolidge design was exhibited at the World's Fair: "Architecture at the World's Columbian Exhibition, Part 3," 17.

35 "Ontario Association of Architects," February 1894, 31-2, for Burke's observations of the World's Fair.

36 This building was in turn destroyed by fire on 11 January 1941. Plans in HC:817a, 960, Plan List and Ledger, AO; and *CAB* 13 (December 1900):233, ill. Also *Morning Chronicle*, 22 June 1899, 3; and *Argosy*, November 1893, 10; October 1899, 2-3, 30; November 1899, 21-2; January 1900, 16-17, 24; October 1900, 2.

37 "The New Addition to the Ladies College," 33-6; "The Opening of the New Addition," 53-4; "Reminiscences of Mount Allison," 67-72, 78. Now demolished, the building was known as Borden Hall.

38 *CAB* 18 (March 1905):xv, for advertisement by Sackville Freestone Co., Limited; *Catalogue of the Mount Allison Ladies College* (Sackville, 1906), 66-8, for materials.

39 Quotation from "Fawcett Hall," 103-4. See also "Our College," January 1906, 45-8; March 1906, ill. opp. 74-7; May 1906, opp. 125. Board of Regents of Mount Allison University Minutes, 3 June 1909, 2:127, 132, 142, 149-56, MAUA, indicate an expenditure of $53,000 including the architects' fee of $1600. Burke represented the firm before the Board despite Horwood's involvement with the design. See also Blueprints, 24 June 1909; Agreement between University of Mount Allison College, the Methodist Church, and the Trustees of the Last Will and Testament of Jarius Hart, 13 August 1909, Legal/Financial File 0106 (1980), no. 17, MAUA.

40 The building stood on the site now occupied by Hydro Place. HC:824, 824a, 955, Plan List, and

Ledger, AO; Building Permit no. 82, 20 May 1899, RG 13, C 4.20, Box 3, CTA; Toronto Conservatory of Music, *Twenty-Fourth Year Book*, 11–13.

41 See Pierson, "Richard Upjohn and the American Rundbogenstil," 223–42; Toronto Conservatory of Music, *Twenty-Fourth Year Book*, 14.

42 HC:805a, 962, 962a, Plan List and Ledger, AO. C.M. Johnston, *McMaster University*, 1:91; Robertson, *Landmarks*, 4:458–9, 585, for the Toronto Bible Training School (demolished); Building Permit no. 63, 30 March 1898, RG 13, C 4.18, Box 3, CTA; *CAB* 14 (January 1901):ill.

43 "Bible Schools," *Canadian Encyclopedia*, 1:212.

44 Baker, *Richard Morris Hunt*, 298–9; King and McLean, *Vanderbilt Homes*, 46–55.

45 See chapter 3, above; Toronto Architectural Eighteen Club, *First Annual Exhibition Catalogue* (1901), 20, 159, for the Harris house under Horwood's name and the Toronto Bible Training School under the firm name of Burke & Horwood. See also [J.C.B. Horwood], "Architecture in New York," 6, regarding the wealth of ornament on the buildings in New York.

46 Maxwell, "Architectural Education in Canada," 51.

47 This was about the time that the Federal government appointed Burke, then president of the Ontario Association of Architects, along with Alcide Chaussé, Province of Quebec Association of Architects president, and David Ewart of the Department of Public Works, to the board of assessors for the Departmental Buildings competition of 1906–07; see chapter 8; and Crossman, *Architecture in Transition*, 137, 139–40.

48 Stupart, "Meteorology in Canada," 75–87, for Toronto Observatories.

49 For plans of Ottawa Observatory, see HC:935, AO; Kalman and Roaf, *Exploring Ottawa*, 164.

50 HC:929, 935, 946, 999, and Ledger, AO; Department of Public Works (Canada) Files, RG 11m, 79003/42, items 4746–69 and 4776–8; RG 11, B 2(b), vv. 1908–9, NA; Building Permit no. 9987, 31 January 1908, RG 13, C 4.79, Box 12, CTA.

51 McKelvey, *Toronto Carved in Stone*, 64, 99, for type of stone. See also Burke, Horwood & White to Chief Architect, Report 322424, 28 September 1909, Department of Public Works (Canada) Files, RG 11, B 2(b), v. 1909, NA; and Physical Plant File

A75–0027, Box 602, no. 12, University of Toronto, UofTA, Toronto.

52 HC:991, 1009, 1287, 1698, Plan List, and Certificate Ledger, AO; Physical Plant File, A75–0027, Box 602, no. 42, University of Toronto, UofTA, Toronto; Building Permit no. 12403, 1 September 1908, RG 13, C 4.89, Box 14, CTA. See also tender call in *Contract Record* 23, 4 (27 January 1909):20. For the history of the college and earlier buildings: Willmott, "The Royal College of Dental Surgeons of Ontario," 216–18; Webster, "Canadian Dentistry," 400–2.

53 King, *King's Handbook of New York*, 377–9.

54 HC:1009, AO, for structural steel and ornamental iron by McGregor & McIntyre Limited.

55 King, *King's Handbook of New York*, 253.

56 Roth, *Architecture of McKim, Mead & White*, 22; Roth, *McKim, Mead & White, Architects*, 150–1, 214–17.

57 Burnett, " 'Here Let the Fires of Friendship Burn' "; and "YMCA," 323–4. The Montreal branch erected a Gothic revival structure on Victoria Square at the same period, see Cross, *One Hundred Years of Service*, 110–13; "YMCA Montreal," 1.

58 Robertson, *Landmarks*, 4:566–71.

59 Regarding the reluctance of the Canadian Association to place a priority on fitness facilities, see Ross, *YMCA in Canada*, 86–90. For early examples of YMCA buildings in the United States, see "Design for the YMCA Building, Philadelphia," 397; "Building for the Young Men's Christian Association in Germantown, Pennsylvania," 100. Later Romanesque examples include, "Accepted Design for the YMCA Building, Richmond, Va.," 234; "Building of the Young Men's Christian Association, Worcester, Mass," 271; "Young Men's Christian Association Building, Utica, New York," 307; "Design for a YMCA Building," 182; and "YMCA Building in Bridgeport, Conn.," 219. See also, *CAB* 1 (March 1888):3, for new YMCA building in Detroit by Mason & Rice.

60 *Globe*, 13 December 1890, 3, indicates the group was organized in 1879 to serve the Canadian Pacific Railway workers at Credit Valley station. See also *CAB* 2 (August 1889):95, regarding the subscription of funds.

61 For the second YMCA building in Montreal, see Cross, *One Hundred Years of Service*, 162–77; and

AABN 32 (18 April 1891):44. Burke, "Elements of Building Construction," 28, refers to the collapse of the Montreal building.

62 [Horwood], "Architecture in New York," 6.

63 "Editorial: Smuggling," 37–9. An article dealing with recent Association buildings identifies the YMCA in Ottawa as having been erected by Jackson & Rosencrans of New York, see Wood, "Working Plants for Young Men's Christian Associations," 159–72.

64 *Contract Record* 24 (12 January 1910):22; (2 February 1910):22, indicate that Harry Ryrie, a long-time client related by marriage to Edmund Burke, was on the executive of the Toronto Association at this date, and that the YMCA proposed to erect four new buildings across the city.

65 For neo-Georgian YMCA buildings in the United States, see Stern, Gilmartin, et al., *New York 1900*, 245; "Exterior and Interior of the YMCA Building, San Francisco, Cal.," 30. In 1906 Sproatt & Rolph had adopted a similar motif for the National Club in Toronto.

66 "A Typical YMCA: The Broadview YMCA, Toronto," 56–60; *Contract Record* 25 (1 February 1911):28.

67 HC:1063, 1064, 1072, AO; Building Permit no. 26051, 31 March 1911, RG 13, C 4.144, Box 23, CTA (building since demolished).

68 HC:1048, 1058a, 1067, AO; Building Permit no. 27902, 6 June 1911, RG 13, C 4.151, Box 24, CTA; "The New West End YMCA Building, Toronto," 19–25.

69 Wood, "Working Plants for Young Men's Christian Associations," 159–72. It seems that American examples were influential more than British neo-Georgian examples of the same period. For Lutyens' 7 St James Square of 1911, see Butler, Hussey, et al., *Architecture of Sir Edwin Lutyens*, 15–16.

70 "New West End YMCA Building, Toronto," 19; "New Look for YMCA," 26–9, for changes to the building by Brook, Carruthers & Shaw.

71 McKee, *Jubilee History of the Ontario Woman's Christian Temperance Union*, 5–7.

72 Ibid., 134–5; *Allisonia* 3 (November 1905):222, notes that Frances Willard had immortalized her name by founding the WCTU in 1873. See also HC:1117, AO, for perspective of Willard Hall; *Contract Record* 24 (1 June 1910):25; and Building Permit no. 30387, 19 September 1911, RG 13,

C 4.161, Box 26, CTA. Also "WCTU Building, Toronto," 184–7.

73 "WCTU Building, Toronto," 185; McKee, *Jubilee History of the Women's Christian Temperance Union*, 134–5.

74 HC:1082a, 1151, Add. 5, Box 1, AO.

75 HC:1115, 1150, 1184, 1255, 1289, and Ledger, AO; Building Permit no. 33146, 10 April 1912, RG 13, C 4.127, Box 27, CTA; Ratcliffe, "Central YMCA Building, Toronto," 51–60; *Globe*, 2 August 1911, 9.

76 Wood, "Working Plants for Young Men's Christian Associations," 159–72.

77 Abramson, "The Planning of a Young Men's Christian Association Building," *Brickbuilder* 22 (March 1913): 49–54; (April 1913):77–80, (June 1913):127–31.

CHAPTER SIX

1 "Ontario Association of Architects," February 1894, 29–31. The structures Gambier-Bousfield considered unsuitable for commercial purposes were in the Romanesque Revival style of American architect Henry Hobson Richardson.

2 Ibid., for W.R. Gregg. Regarding the Golden Lion, see Thompson, *Toronto in the Camera*, plate 42; Arthur, *Toronto*, 158–9; Dendy, *Lost Toronto*, 74–7.

3 Amicus, "Notes on Modern Shop Fronts," 299–301. See also Hay, "Architecture for the Meridian of Canada," 252: "The fashionable shop front, with its wall of glass, supporting in appearance several stories of substantial masonry, creates in the mind a tremulous feeling of anxiety, which the known fact of the secret agency of some wirey pillar can scarcely dispel."

4 "Ontario Association of Architects," February 1894, 30: Gregg describes but does not identify this building in Ottawa in which oriels of plate glass are carried to the eaves. Nor does he mention that the configuration was facilitated by steel beams supported on brick piers to carry the weight of the floors. See also "Ottawa and the Parliament of Canada," 112; and Kalman and Roaf, *Exploring Ottawa*, 44, for John James Browne. Concerning Peter Ellis, see Woodward, "History," 268–70, on construction of "cast-iron frame with flat brick

arches, the spandrels of which are filled with concrete"; Hughes, *Seaport*, 57–65 (latter reference and measured drawings of Oriel Chambers and 16 Cook Street also by Ellis courtesy of Michael King, City Conservation Office, Liverpool).

5 "Ontario Association of Architects," February 1894, 29–31 (emphasis added).

6 Ibid., 29. It was half a century since a writer identified only as M, "On the Effect Which Should Result to Architecture, from the General Introduction of Iron in the Construction of Buildings," 277–87, had observed that "the great use now made of iron in our buildings ... renders it more desireable that architects should qualify themselves, not less to adapt their designs to the new material, than the new material to their designs."

7 "Ontario Association of Architects," February 1894, 29–31.

8 "The Late Mr Henry Langley," 14, for attribution; Timperlake, *Illustrated Toronto*, 311, for date. See also Arthur, *Toronto*, 149; Dendy, *Lost Toronto*, 64–5, for additions that doubled the length of the Wellington Street facade in 1878, and the Front Street facade in 1882, as well as demolition 1964–65.

9 "Toronto: The Commercial Metropolis of Ontario," 30; *Globe*, 1 January 1891, 5, regarding Ohio sandstone and Oswego brown stone trimming. See also Douglas Richardson, *Gothic Revival Architecture in Ireland*, 2:376, 413–15, for Hibernian monumental of Deane & Woodward's Crown Life office in New Bridge Street, Blackfriar's, 1856–57 (demolished), as well as the unexecuted design of 1857 for the Foreign Office. Also Blau, *Ruskinian Gothic*, 100–8; Brooks, *John Ruskin and Victorian Architecture*, 135–7.

10 "Progress of Toronto – New Wholesale Warehouses," 581, identifies this warehouse as the first of a new trend in the city.

11 Timperlake, *Illustrated Toronto*, 311; *Globe*, 30 May 1891, 15, notes goods were received on the basement level, while the upper five floors were given over to linens and staples, woolens, silks and dress goods, haberdashery, and carpets respectively. Each flat was served by two freight and two passenger elevators. See also *Toronto World*, 5 May 1892, 1, for similar arrangement in James A. Skinner & Co. warehouse on Wellington at Bay.

12 *Globe*, 1 January 1891, 5.

13 Museum of Modern Art, *Architecture of Richard Morris Hunt*, 102–5, for David van Zanten's comments on this type of commercial architecture in the United States, which he believes was influenced by Ruskinian models, as well as French Gothic rationalism and *néo-grec*.

14 For building at 26–30 Toronto Street (demolished), see "Toronto – the Queen City of the West," 338–9; and "The Late Mr. Henry Langley," 14. Also Dendy, *Lost Toronto*, 83, for photograph showing scale in relation to earlier structures. According to de Wit, *Louis Sullivan*, 25, quoting Levine, "The Idea of Frank Furness' Buildings," (Master's thesis, Yale University, 1967), French *néo-grec* inspired the overscaling of Gothic commercial buildings.

15 Regarding original scheme, see chapter 1, and HC:623, AO, for perspective initialled "E.B." prepared for People's Insurance Co. on King Street, according to Douglas Richardson, "Glory of Toronto," no. 24. See also Ontario Society of Artists, *Catalogue* (1879), no. 196, regarding a *Design for Offices*.

16 HC:624(1), AO, for second perspective by an unidentified draughtsman – possibly Frank Burke. As late as the 1890s "The Royal Academy Exhibition," 64–5, noted: "If instead of looking merely for style our shop front designers would take a hint from the Flemish they ought to find the most characteristic fronts, which are simply mullions and glass from end to end, serviceable models for the store which is to be well-lighted on each floor."

17 Schuyler, "The Works of the Late Richard Morris Hunt," in Jordy and Coe, *American Architecture*, 502–55, describes Hunt's work as *néo-grec*. Neil Levine, who coined the term "crypto-Gothic," is quoted by Sarah Bradford Landau in her assessment of this work as a fusion of High Victorian Gothic and *néo-grec* rationalism, see Museum of Modern Art, *Richard Morris Hunt*, 51, 56. Hunt's early use of the triple-window bay in the Tribune building is also noted. The neo-Gothic and *néo-grec* hybrid is also referred to in de Wit, *Louis Sullivan*, 23, quoting Sims, "Architectural Fashions," *Penn Monthly* 7 (1876):700–11. For the significance of Hunt's New York Tribune building of 1873–75 (demolished) and George B. Post's slightly earlier Western Union Telegraph building erected in 1873–74 (demolished), both in New York, see Weisman, "New York and the Problem of the First Skyscraper," 13–21.

18 Van Brunt, "Greek Lines, Part 2," 85.

19 HC:311b, AO, for Langley, Langley & Burke perspective, initialled "J.A.F." Drawings of the Building and Loan offices were exhibited: Ontario Society of Artists, *Catalogue* (1879), nos. 194 and 195. For a second competition entry signed "Bona Fide," attributed to D.B. Dick, see HC:311a, AO. The building (demolished) was located at 13–15 Toronto Street, see Douglas Richardson, "Glory of Toronto," no. 23. For a brief biography of Joseph Ades Fowler, see Arthur, *Toronto*, 247.

20 For incised linear ornament and stylized geometric forms of American *néo-grec*, see Baker, *Richard Morris Hunt*, 474–5.

21 "Toronto – The Queen City of the West," 339.

22 Of thirty-three tenders advertised by the firm in the *Daily Globe* in 1874, eleven related to commercial projects.

23 HC:48, AO, for perspective by Frank Burke, illustrated in Weir, *Lost Craft of Ornamented Architecture*, plate 27; *Daily Globe*, 17 February 1874, 3, for tender call on cut stone, brickwork, iron founder, and galvanized iron.

24 In North America *néo-grec* was a largely ornamental style, according to Baker, *Richard Morris Hunt*, 474–5. He describes the incised linear ornament, stylized geometric forms, and broad linear relief on pilasters and columns as characteristic of the mode. See also Museum of Modern Art, *Richard Morris Hunt*, 58, for Landau's comment on this "bony, hard-edged, crisply detailed commercial mode"; de Wit, *Louis Sullivan*, 18–19, on its abstract quality; O'Gorman, *Architecture of Frank Furness*.

25 Hay, "Architecture for the Meridian of Canada," 252, two decades earlier had rejected the applied facade, "A fine *front*, which exhibits a dazzling display of enrichment, perhaps genuine sculptures, looses much of its grandeur, when, on turning the corner, it is discovered to be but a thin veneering of architecture tacked on to an unsightly brick block."

26 *Daily Globe*, 16 June 1874, 3, tenders call for a stone-fronted building on Adelaide Street near the Post Office. *Toronto City Directory for 1889*, 10, lists nineteen tenants of the building.

27 Dendy, *Lost Toronto*, 86–7; Wright, "Thomas Seaton Scott," 207, for the dependence of Langley's design upon Mullett's model. See also Dewe to Department of Public Works, 4 March 1870, Registered Correspondence, 1859–74, Department of Public Works (Canada), RG 11, B 1 (a), v. 307, subject 881, 933 (7)-(11), no. 9884, NA; Rubidge to Langley, 7 November 1870, v. 313, subject 883, 62–3, no. T 762, NA. For general information on Second Empire style and Alfred Mullett, see Cameron and Wright, *Second Empire Style*, 9–16.

28 Godfrey, *Italian Architecture up to 1750*, 213.

29 Douglas Richardson, "Glory of Toronto," no. 39; and Building Permit, no. 124/796, 4 March 1903, RG 13, C 4.28, Box 4, CTA, for the change in location of the entrance. Also Dendy and Kilbourn, *Toronto Observed*, 100–1.

30 Langley & Burke Ledger, 85–6, 197–8, LC, MTRL, for payments on 133–5 and 129–33 King Street East.

31 I am indebted to Douglas Richardson for information confirming the date of this structure.

32 Building Permit no. 128, 26 April 1889, RG 13, CTA (courtesy of Alec Keefer).

33 Architectural Draughtsmen's Association Minutes, 10 January and 7 February 1887, Ontario Association of Architects Papers, MU 2734, AO, record a debate on "What Style of Architecture is Best Adapted to this Country" in which "Romanesque met with the most approval." The next discussion dealing with "Uses and Abuses of the Romanesque Style" seems to have been presented by John Horwood. For a list of Romanesque office buildings of this period, see Gad and Holdsworth, "Building for City, Region, and Nation," 272–321.

34 See discussion following article by Horwood, "Some Observations on Fireproof Building in New York," 38.

35 For Richard A. Waite, see Crossman, *Architecture in Transition*, 13–14, 18–20; Arthur, *Toronto*, 262–3. Though English-born, Waite was trained entirely in the United States, establishing himself in Buffalo in the 1870s. He made his mark in Toronto in 1880 with a *néo-grec* design for the *Toronto Mail* at King and Bay, and a Romanesque revival scheme for Western Life Assurance on Wellington Street.

36 Cameron and McMordie, "Architecture, Development of," *Canadian Encyclopedia*, for Equity Chambers, which in 1856 was the first building in the city to install an elevator. The MacDonald warehouse and Union Loan were also equipped with

passenger lifts. For Canada Life and economic developments coinciding with this type of building, see Gad and Holdsworth, "Corporate Capitalism and the Emergence of the High-Rise Office Building," 212–31.

37 *Toronto World*, 10 January 1891, 1; *Globe*, 31 January 1891, 1. Regarding the Home Insurance building of 1883–85 by Chicago architect William Le Baron Jenney, see Condit, *Chicago School of Architecture*, 80–8; Turak, "Rememberances of the Home Insurance Building," 60–5.

38 Dendy, *Lost Toronto*, 94–5; "The Bank of Commerce New Building," 903; MacKimmie, "About Banks and Bank Buildings: Part 2," 395.

39 For Freehold Loan, see "Our Illustrations," *CAB* 2 (December 1889):143; "To Iron Founders and Blacksmiths," *CAB* 3 (March 1890):36, regarding tenders on cast iron columns and wrought iron beams as well as iron staircases; and Calculations of Cubic Foot Cost, RG 15, E-1, v. 27, file 2, AO, at $0.29/cubic foot.

40 Other works, see Arthur, *Toronto*, 183, 190–4; Sobolak, "A Lennox Folly," 13–18.

41 Burke, "Elements of Building Construction," 28–9.

42 *Inland Architect & News Record* 27 (March 1896):16.

43 Crossman, *Architecture in Transition*, 17–19; "Our Illustrations," *CAB* 1 (February 1888):4; Marsan, *Montreal in Evolution*, 245; Abbott, *Story of NYLIC*, 118–19, for description of world-wide expansion from 1884 on, during which company offices were to give "an impression of solidity and permanency." For information on John Pierce Hill's Henry Morgan & Co. (now The Bay) of 1889–91, John Murphy's Store of 1894 (the structure of which is so far documented only by exterior photographs), and the original Ogilvy's of 1896, attributed to David Ogilvy, see Pinard, *Montreal*, 5:440–52; Communauté urbaine de Montréal, *Architecture Commerciale III*, 205–15. A controversy over the competition for the Morgan's store is also recorded in "Montreal," 32.

44 Abacus, "Notes of a Trip to the West," 17, could rightfully claim, "The treatment of our modern mercantile and business structures, particularly those ten or twelve stories in height, is more successful than any other work of the kind in the world; the planning of our office buildings is unrivalled anywhere ...

many details of American construction such as the encased iron framing and isolated pier foundations of the Chicago architects, and the heating and ventilating systems in use everywhere here, are far in advance of foreign practice."

45 Arthur, *Toronto*, 252, indicates that James & James emigrated to New York from England. Also Stanford, *To Serve the Community*, 49–52; "Conditions of the Board of Trade Building Competition," 4; "Toronto Board of Trade Building Competition," 4; Board of Trade Council Minute Book, 25 January 1887 to 31 January 1894, and Report of the Building Committee, 19 February 1888, Toronto Board of Trade Papers, MG 28, III 56, NA.

46 "Description of the Home of the Board of Trade of the City of Toronto," in Toronto Board of Trade, *Annual Report* (1891), 35, Toronto Board of Trade Papers, MG 28, III 56, NA.

47 *Globe*, 21 March 1890, 8; 22 March 1890, 20; *CAB* 3 (May 1890):53; Report of Building Committee for 22 December 1890, Toronto Board of Trade Papers, MG 28, III 56, v. 4, NA, for appointment of Kent.

48 *Globe*, 2 April 1890, 10; Report of Building Committee, 22 December 1890, Toronto Board of Trade Papers, MG 28, III 56, v. 4, NA. Also "Canada," 19 April 1890, 39–40; "Canada," 21 June 1890, 180–1.

49 *CAB* 3 (May 1890):53. See also Burke, "Elements of Building Construction," 28, for collapse of the Montreal YMCA designed by an American architect. A second notorious failure occurred in 1895 during construction of the Montreal Street Railway building by E.C. & J.W. Hopkins of Montreal; see "Building in Canada in 1894," 8.

50 Windeyer Papers, MS 488, AO, for clippings of letters from various newspapers, many of which verge on the "poison pen." One unidentified item referring specifically to the Toronto *Mail* building executed by Waite in 1880, questions the wisdom of placing confidence in an American architect.

51 *CAB* 1 (November 1888):4–5.

52 H.R. Ives & Co., "The Advantages (?) of Employing an American Architect," 75.

53 Canadian, "The Necessity for a Canadian School of Architecture," 70.

54 Crossman, *Architecture in Transition*, 11–17, for an account of events; and Incoming Correspondence on

the Parliament Buildings, 1880–86 and 1887–95, Office of the Architect Construction Accounts, 1856–1916, Chief Architect's Files, Public Works Department (Ontario), RG 15, E-1, v. 27, files 1–2, AO.

55 The final cost of Waite's building was $1.25 million or $.1666/cubic foot. This was less expensive than the Municipal buildings by E.J. Lennox and the Parliament buildings in Quebec, see Calculations of Cubic Foot Cost, Department of Public Works (Ontario), RG 15, E-1, v. 27, file 2, AO. For a broadside claiming the cost of Waite's building might exceed $2 million; see Broadside Collection, Baldwin Room, MTRL.

56 Report of the Hon. Alexander MacKenzie, William George Storm, and Richard Waite, 15 November 1880, Department of Public Works (Ontario), RG 15, E-1, v. 27, file 1, AO, awarding the competition to "Detur Dignion," "Waterloo," and "Nox." Darling & Pearson and Gordon & Helliwell later prepared specifications for the project.

57 Aylesworth, "The Need of Organization," 7–8.

58 "Canada," 16 February 1889, 81.

59 Correspondence, Wm Edwards to Waite, 27 November 1885, and Frank Darling to Commissioner, 25 March 1887, Department of Public Works (Ontario), RG 15, S-6, v. 3, files 282–300, 309, AO. Also CAB 3 (May 1890):53, notes a recent letter in the Globe under the pseudonym "Canadian."

60 Globe, 13 August 1886, 5; and "The New Parliament Buildings," 6.

61 "New Parliament Buildings," 6.

62 "Canada," 18 May 1889, 236.

63 Crossman, Architecture in Transition, 18, enumerates "innovations" including the multi-storey office building, metal framing techniques, and the Romanesque Revival style.

64 The government not only believed Waite, it published a pamphlet six years later which claimed that the American had gained "the appointment after a fair competition." Fortunately the Canadian profession had not forgotten the truth; see CAB 3 (May 1890):51–2.

65 For example, Birkmire, Architectural Iron and Steel; and by the same author, Skeleton Construction in Buildings (which was in the library collection of Burke, Horwood & White). See also Willett, "Skeleton Structures in Building," 47–8, for reviews of Skeleton Construction and Freitag, Architectur-al Engineering, with Special Reference to High Building Construction (1895). Viollet-Le-Duc, Lectures on Architecture, is listed as part of the Burke library.

66 Burke, "Elements of Building Construction," 28–9.

67 Ibid., quoting Professor Aitchison.

68 Horwood, "Some Observations on Fireproof Building in New York," 36–8.

69 Ibid., for closing remarks by Curry.

70 "Illustrations," CAB 8 (January 1895):12–13, suppl. ill.; (February 1895): suppl. ill.

71 Ibid. Also HC:26, 29, 30 (1)-(5), and Ledger, AO; Building Permit nos. 1249 and 1613, 4 April 1893 and 7 May 1894, RG 13, C 4.12, Box 2, CTA, for a six-storey brick store worth $80,000 on the southwest corner of Queen and Yonge Streets.

72 "Composition for Rendering Buildings Fire-proof," 327; and letter by Hutton, "Fireproof Construction," 111. Burke must have known this was a less than ideal solution.

73 Evening Star (Toronto), 4 March 1895, 1–2; 15 March 1895, 4; 28 March 1895, 3; 13 April 1895, 6; and Globe, 4 March 1895, 1; 15 March 1895, 2.

74 Aylesworth, "Departmental Store Buildings," 48.

75 Ibid. Also "Building Construction in its Relation to Fire Protection," 38–9, indicates that the Ontario Association of Architects appointed a committee of architects to study possible by-law changes. An amendment was proposed so that structures over seventy feet high would be fireproofed with specific materials. Architects were reminded that iron framing was not fireproof and only served to secure larger floor area and better lighting.

76 Globe, 4 March 1895, 1.

77 HC:27, 30(6), 771a, 780, 781, and Plan List, AO. Horwood became Burke's partner in January of 1895, and contributed significantly in the rebuilding. His curriculum vitae, filed in Vancouver in 1913 when he was working on the Hudson's Bay store, lists Simpson's among his credentials (he was certainly responsible for later additions); see Old Hudson's Bay Company File, Vancouver City Hall, Vancouver. Building Permit no. 1922, 31 May 1895, RG 13, C 4.14, Box 2, CTA, lists Edmund Burke as the architect for the new $200,000 structure.

78 "Popular Impressions vs. Fact," 54; "The Simpson Departmental Store," 115.

79 Burton, *A Sense of Urgency*, 75.

80 Art Institute of Chicago, *Chicago Architecture*, 39–90.

81 *CAB* 7 (February 1894):29: a free-standing metal frame with protective cladding was used only in the second Simpson's store, of 1895, but the curtain-wall concept was implicit in the first design.

82 Ibid., 31–2. See also Schuyler, "Last Words About the Fair," in Jordy and Coe, *American Architecture*, 2:556–74.

83 Burke, "Elements of Building Construction," 28; Condit, *Chicago School*, 54.

84 Douglas Richardson, "Glory of Toronto," no. 41, regarding White's tenure in Chicago.

85 Sullivan, "The Tall Office Building Artistically Considered," 203–9. Sullivan rejects the term "tripartite" and the "base-shaft-capital" analogy in favour of the organic theory that "form follows function," proposing a below-grade power plant, with an ample ground floor and accessible mezzanine of corresponding liberality for business establishments, surmounted by an infinite number of identical cell-like offices, and topped by an attic housing ventilation and plumbing. The architect's Wainwright building of 1890 in St Louis is the archetype for this analysis, but the tract itself was not published until after Simpson's store was built. Consequently, it is more correct to describe Burke's scheme as "tripartite," according to the standard terminology of the day, see Schuyler, "The 'Skyscraper' Up-To-Date," 231–57, and "The Skyscraper Problem," 2:437–41, 442–52, citing George Post's Union Trust of 1889–90 as the first major example of this type. Also Ferree, "The Modern Office Building," 45–6, for the Aristotelian concept of beginning, middle, and end.

86 Baigell, "John Haviland in Pottsville," 4, observes that iron founder Daniel Badger purported to create a building entirely of iron, but apparently resorted to timbers for the interior. See also Bannister, "Bogardus Revisited – Part 1," 12–22, on iron founder James Bogardus' claims to have patented the first complete cast-iron building in America.

87 For early works like the Laing stores, New York, of 1849, by James Bogardus, see Bannister, "The First Iron-Framed Buildings"; Bannister, "Bogardus Revisited – Part 1," 12–22.

88 W.K. Sturgis, *Origins of Cast Iron Architecture*, reprinting Badger's "Illustrations of Iron Architecture made by the Architectural Iron Works of the City of New York," of 1865; and Bogardus' "Cast Iron Buildings: Their Construction and Advantages," of 1856.

89 Bannister, "Bogardus Revisited – Part 1," 13–15, casts doubt on the validity of Bogardus' claims; but see also Huxtable, "Harper & Brothers Building – 1854," 153–4.

90 Burnham, "Last Look at a Structural Landmark," 273–9; Gayle and Gillon, *Cast-Iron Architecture*, 160–1; T. Hamlin, *Forms and Functions*, 4:37–8.

91 For example the Jayne building, Philadelphia, 1849, by William Johnston: Weisman, "Philadelphia Functionalism," 3–19; R.C. Smith, "Antebellum Skyscraper," 25, 27–8; and Editor, "The Jayne Building Again," 25. See also Pevsner, *Pioneers of Modern Design*, 125; Condit, *Chicago School*, 6; Marsan, *Montreal in Evolution*, 228–42. Oriel Chambers, Liverpool, discussed above, is one of the few examples in which the facade is directly related to structure, see Woodward, "History," 268–70. For the similar technology in France: Steiner, *French Iron Architecture*.

92 German architect Friedrich Schinkel had devised a similar motif for a "department store" as early as 1827, see Art Institute of Chicago, *Chicago Architecture*, 97–9; and Grisebach, *Carl Friedrich Schinkel*, 132, for illustration of the original perspective in the collection of the Staatliche Museum zu Berlin. For the development of the department store in Europe and North America: T. Hamlin, *Forms and Functions*, 4:36–83; Giedion, *Space, Time, and Architecture*, 168–77; Artley, *Golden Age of Shop Design*.

93 Art Institute of Chicago, *Chicago Architecture*, 48; "Shillito Store," 328–30.

94 Art Institute of Chicago, *Chicago Architecture*, 49, quoting Peter B. Wight.

95 Elmer C. Jensen Drawings, Art Institute of Chicago, Chicago; Condit, *Chicago School*, 79–80; Turak, "Ecole Centrale and Modern Architecture," and by the same author, *William Le Baron Jenney*.

96 Elmer C. Jensen Drawings Collection, Art Institute of Chicago; Condit, *Chicago School*, 80–8; J.C. Webster, "Skyscraper: Logical and Historical Considerations," 138–9; Turak, "Rememberances of the Home Insurance Building," 60–5; Larson and Geraniotis, "Toward a Better Understanding of the Evolution of the Iron Skeleton Frame in Chicago,"

39–48. The metal frame of the Home Insurance building, which was iron below the sixth floor and steel above, was balanced on load-bearing masonry at the second storey. It is credited as the first sky-scraper construction because the frame was self-sustaining, and fully embedded in the masonry piers that were carried from floor to floor despite the absence of flanges. Also Bannister, "Bogardus Revisited – Part 2," 11–19.

97 Elmer C. Jensen Drawings Collection, Art Institute of Chicago; Condit, *Chicago School*, 83–4.

98 Condit, *Chicago School*, 90–1.

99 HC: Add. 5, for page from *Inland Architect & News Record* illustrating this project; and discussion by de Wit, *Louis Sullivan*, 90–8.

100 "Royal Canadian Academy Exhibition," May 1895, 65.

CHAPTER SEVEN

1 *CAB* 7 (December 1894):156.

2 [Horwood], "Architecture in New York," 6, for observations on the ornateness of the architecture. See also Horwood Sketchbooks and Photographs, dated 12 June-10 August 1894, HC: Add. 1, Acc. 14018, MU 3979–3985, AO, for items collected during visits to Venice, Padua, Rome, Spoleto, Siena, Florence, Bologna, Perugia, Foligno, and Verona.

3 "Globe in its New Home," *Saturday Globe*, 13 September 1890, 1–5, on how Knox & Elliott gutted the former Hughes Brothers warehouse, installing new concrete foundations and iron columns cast by St Lawrence Foundry. The front was refaced with Portage sandstone in a style identified as "Elizabethan." Building Permit no. 9, 3 February 1890, RG 13, C 4, Box 1, CTA, authorized an additional storey and alterations to the warehouse at Yonge and Melinda Streets.

4 Arthur, *Toronto*, 253, for Wilm Knox and John Elliot, who moved to Chicago in 1892, and then on to Cleveland where they carried on business until 1915.

5 Horwood, "Some Observations of Fireproof Building," 36.

6 "First 'Skeleton' Building," 239, records the Columbia building by Youngs & Cable as the third steel-skeleton structure in the city. Plans were filed on 2 January 1890, and P. Minturn Smith, President of Union Iron Works prepared framing details for owner Spencer Aldrich. See also King, *King's*

Handbook of New York City, 768–9, for a short summary. The site is now occupied by a thirty-one storey Art Deco building, according to Willensky and White, *AIA Guide*, 11.

7 HC:774, 1257, Plan List, Ledger, and Certificate Ledger, AO.

8 "New Globe Building," 143, notes the office portion at the rear was conventional construction in the interests of economy. See also Building Permit nos. 1875 and 1993, 19 April and 30 July 1895, RG 13, C 4.14, Box 2, CTA, for a three-storey printing house worth $21,000, and three-storey brick office building worth $11,000. For further details of the Globe building (demolished), see Richardson, "Glory of Toronto," no. 37. The Simpson's store was destroyed in March 1895, and by December, contrary to this report, had been rebuilt with floor beams embedded in cement.

9 Knox & Elliott had covered the walls and ceilings of the Globe offices with thin plate steel, but Burke & Horwood finished their interior with plaster. Fire doors enclosed the mechanical departments where the risk of combustion was particularly great, see "New Globe Building," 143.

10 Burke & Horwood to Dr Oronhyatekha of the Independent Order of Foresters, HC:925 (11)-(16), 6, AO, for details of plans prepared between February and March 1895; and HC:968, AO.

11 For Gouinlock, see Building Permit no. 1886, 27 April 1895, RG 13, C 4.14, Box 2, CTA; *CAB* 8 (June 1895):81; Douglas Richardson, *Romanesque Toronto*, 14–15; Arthur, *Toronto*, 188–9, 208; Dendy, *Lost Toronto*, 102–3.

12 For rebuilding the Robert Simpson store, see Building Permit no. 1922, 31 May 1895, RG 13, C 4.14, Box 2, CTA.

13 Horwood to Pierson, 5 June 1923, Winnipeg Dead Dossier, no. 216, HBCA, Winnipeg, states Burke was responsible for office management by 1911. See also Burke & Horwood to the Robert Simpson Co. Limited, 23 November 1907, HC:Add. 1, file 2, AO, for the client's discussion with Horwood about the possibility of installing a light well in the new building. Burke is obviously the one who intervened, graphically evoking the potential for disaster: "Smoke ascending through the various flats from even a small fire would asphyxiate the occupants before relief could arrive – minutes, even seconds sealing their doom."

14 For Horwood's interest in architectural ornament,

see [Horwood], "Architecture in New York," 5. In 1923, after Burke's death, when Horwood & White executed their last addition to the Robert Simpson Company store, the round-arched motif was used again, "Robert Simpson Company's Store Addition, Toronto," 77–81.

15 Landau, "Tall Office Building Artistically Reconsidered," 136–64.

16 [Horwood], "Architecture in New York," 6, for reference to the iron work and fireproofing of the 42nd Street Mission. Horwood, "Some Observations on Fireproof Building in New York," 37, illustrates the attachment of the building's terra-cotta cornice. Details of the building are recorded in King, *King's Handbook of New York*, 324–5. The arcaded DeVinne Press building on Lafayette Place by Babb, Cook & Willard is also noted in Horwood, "American Architectural Methods from the Standpoint of a Canadian," 8, as "one of the most instructive buildings" he had ever seen. Also for DeVinne Press, see R. Sturgis, "Warehouse and the Factory in Architecture," 1–17.

17 HC:1173, 1122a and Ledger, AO. Building Permit no. 537, 25 May 1904, RG 13, C 4.36, Box 6, CTA, for repairs to buildings at Yonge and Shuter; no. 14381, 26 March 1909, C 4.97, Box 15, for alterations to 235 Yonge Street; no. 2591, 25 March 1913, C 4.202, Box 32, for a five-storey store and office building valued at $125,000, CTA. Also *Contract Record* 27 (3 September 1913):73.

18 *Ryrie Building* (c.1913); HC:1173 (149), AO, records Burke, Horwood & White among the building's first tenants. Toronto Local Stone Cutters, *Toronto Building and Ornamental Stones*, 27, describes Ryrie facade trim as Portage sandstone.

19 Burke, "Slow-Burning Construction," 22.

20 [Horwood], "Architecture in New York," 6, is his first recorded communication from New York. See also Burke, "Elements of Building Construction," 28–9.

21 Contrast this with Shaw and Jackson, who in *Architecture, A Profession or an Art?* defend the concept of architecture as a fine art. For a discussion of the scientific and artistic aspects of architecture in the context of the OAA registration controversy, see chapter 8.

22 For example, Horwood, "Some Observations on Fireproof Building in New York," 36–8; [Horwood], "Architecture in New York," 6; Horwood, "American Architectural Methods," 8–9, which concentrates

on the details of metal framing rather than the more crucial question of protective cladding.

23 Burke, "Elements of Building Construction," 28–9; "Building Construction and Its Relation to Fire Protection," 38–9.

24 "Popular Impressions vs. Fact," 54–5. See also "Home Life Building Fire – An Object Lesson," 864–5, which notes the lack of concrete filling on top of wooden sleepers contributed to the building's destruction. Also "Success of Fireproof Construction," 907.

25 Burke, "Two Questions in Connection With Steel Construction," 31–4; and by the same author, "Qualities of Fire-Proofing Materials," 68.

26 The protective qualities of these materials were the subject of long-standing debate, see "What is Fireproof Construction?" 275–6; "Northcroft's System of Fireproof Construction," 60; Hutton, "Fireproof Construction," 1 April 1876, 111; 5 February 1876, 43. For Canadian tests of terra cotta, see "Tests of Fireproofing Material," 78–9; "Terra cotta as a Building Material," 15.

27 Burke, "Reducing the Fire Loss in Building," 52–4. A plea for stringent building by-laws had appeared a decade earlier in "Fire Prevention," 123–4. As for slow-burning construction, see Burke, "Slow-Burning Construction," 22. A late example of this type is noted in a letter from Burke, Horwood & White to A.P. Stradling of Philadelphia Fire Underwriters, 3 October 1912, HC:Add. 5, Box 3, AO, regarding the Samuel & Benjamin warehouse of 1908.

28 American insurance underwriters were considering fire-resistant features in 1890, see AABN 24 (19 July 1890):34. Burke's analysis is entirely in keeping with contemporary American thinking, see "All Kinds of a Store," 286–303.

29 "Some Special Features of Traders Bank Building, Toronto," 91–3; *Construction* 3 (January 1910):48; "American Architects in Canada," 51–3.

30 "American Architects in Canada," 51–3.

31 "Messrs. Carrère & Hastings Reply," 41–2.

32 HC:1622, 1623, and perspective file, AO, the latter displayed at "The Loan Exhibit of Architectural Drawings by the Ontario Association of Architects," 56.

33 For the Havemeyer building, see Weisman, "The Commercial Architecture of George B. Post," 176–203; Horwood, "Some Observations on Fireproof Building in New York," 36.

34 Maxwell, "Dominion Express Building, Montreal, Quebec," 47–9; Canadian Centre for Architecture, *Montréal*, item 1, Dominion Express, 215 rue Saint-Jacques, completed 1912.

35 For information on Burnham's role, see Art Institute of Chicago, *Chicago Architecture*, 155, note 39; Burnham to Burbidge, 10 February 1911, Burnham Letters, v. 18, Art Institute of Chicago, in which the Chicago architect advises that "the sort of building mentioned by you is strictly in our line." See also Horwood to Pierson, 5 June 1923, Winnipeg Dead Dossier 216, and Burbidge to Ingrams, 30 January 1914, Calgary A.12/S.509/3, no. S.595, HBCA, Winnipeg, for the appointment of Burke, Horwood & White on 13 February 1911.

36 Burbidge to HBC Secretary William Ware, 25 February 1911, Calgary A.12/S.509/2, no. S.182, and Burbidge to Chairman, 9 July 1923, Winnipeg Dead Dossier 216, HBCA. Horwood could claim Simpson's as his own because of the 1908 Simpson's addition. Early records identify the Simpson's store of 1895 as the work of Edmund Burke, see Building Permit no. 1922, 31 May 1895, RG 13, C 4.14, Box 2, CTA. The senior partner's role in the Hudson's Bay projects is limited, although he did obtain a licentiate from the Royal Institute of British Architects on 13 March 1911, see HC: Add. 1, Box 2, AO.

37 Burbidge to HBC Acting Secretary F.C. Ingrams, 19 April 1911, Calgary A.12/S.509/2, no. S.206, HBCA.

38 Ibid.; Horwood to Braidwood, 9 May 1922, Winnipeg Dead Dossier 216, HBCA, indicating the "plain wall" design was presented to the London Committee by Horwood in March 1912.

39 Ware to Burbidge, 11 March 1911, Calgary A.12/S.509/2, no. S.208, HBCA.

40 Ibid., Burbidge to Ingrams, 19 April 1911, no. S.206, HBCA.

41 Ibid., Burbidge also contemplated gaining a major market share of the mail-order business controlled by Toronto retailers T. Eaton Company and the Robert Simpson Company.

42 Always a barometer of the city's economic growth, the company built a frame store in 1884 a year after the arrival of the railway. By 1891 it had relocated in a two-storey sandstone structure at the corner of Centre Street and Eighth Avenue; see "Calgary and the Company," 42; and "Calgary," 96. For early sandstone buildings in the city, see Cunliffe, *Calgary – In Sandstone*.

43 Ingrams to Burbidge, 10 May 1911 and 22 November 1911, Calgary A.12/S.509/2, nos. S.256 and S.397, HBCA, accuses Burbidge of overstepping his authority and demands to know why he committed the company to the structural steel contract.

44 Secretary to H.E. Burbidge, 16 March 1912, Calgary A.12/S.509/3, no. S.479, and Horwood to Braidwood, 9 May 1922, Winnipeg Dead Dossier, HBCA (my emphasis), refers to the "Englishman's love of columns."

45 Elevation of the Hudson's Bay Store, Calgary, signed Burke, Horwood & White and marked "*London, England, 6 March 1912,*" in HC:Add. 5, AO (reference courtesy of William Cooper, HC Archivist). See also HC:Add. 5, for illustration of Selfridge's from the pages of *Builder* (3 April 1909); and "Modern Business Premises in London," 37–47, for contemporary Canadian publication. Other drawings for the project include, HC:1084a, 1085, 1089, 1090, 1101, 1102(1), 1124, 1264a, AO; Calgary B.6/1–34, MS Blueprint, HBCA.

46 Art Institute of Chicago, *Chicago Architecture*, 146–7, 154, note 34 quoting "Selling Selfridge," *Saturday Evening Post* 208 (10 August 1935): 66–70, identifies Francis Swales as the draughtsman of the original concept, D.H. Burnham & Co. as consulting architects, Sir Frank Atkinson as local architect, and Albert Miller and J.J. Burnet as engineers. Also Service, *Edwardian Architecture*, 168.

47 For an illustration of the Paris Bourse from *Builder* (10 December 1903) among the firm's files, see HC:Add. 5, AO.

48 Art Institute of Chicago, *Chicago Architecture*, 146–7, 154, note 34, quoting "Selling Selfridge," *Saturday Evening Post* 208 (10 August 1935): 66–70.

49 For illustration of the Opéra, Montgomery-Massingberd, *Royal Palaces of Europe*, 22–3.

50 Drexler, *Architecture of the Ecole des Beaux-Arts*; R. Middleton, *Beaux-Arts*; Kostof, *Architect*, 209–37.

51 Dendy, *Lost Toronto*, 68–9, records the demolition of this landmark to make way for the Toronto-Dominion Centre.

52 Melnyk, *Calgary Builds*, 32–6, describes the pre-war boom years.

53 "Building Activity at Calgary," 20.

54 Melnyk, *Calgary Builds*, 143–6, for the Grain Exchange, which is still in use.

55 Francis, "Reinforced Concrete Construction," 47–8, details the history of hydraulic cement and reinforced concrete. An anonymous article entitled "The Reinforcement of Concrete Beams," 114, records the early use of reinforced concrete beams in the museum at Stamford University and the California Academy of Sciences, as well as experimental testing.

56 Detroit Institute of Arts, *Legacy of Albert Kahn*, 40–54; Ritchie, *Canada Builds*, 229–51, regarding concrete.

57 Condit, *American Building*, 240–50, for a discussion of the earliest concrete skyscrapers. See also "Ontario Association of Architects," January 1903, 3–29, regarding attempts by Elzner & Anderson to secure a building permit.

58 Haas, "Reinforced Concrete Designing," 14–15, 24, indicates that reinforced concrete buildings had boomed in Canada over the previous two years. See also "Rapid Work on Reinforced Concrete," 60, regarding its use in Montreal. Also "By-laws Governing Reinforced Concrete Construction in Toronto," 10–11; "Concrete Building Code," August 1907, xii–xiii. For publications, see "Marsh's Reinforced Concrete," 35–6; "Review of *Principles of Reinforced Concrete Construction* by F.E. Turneaure," 25. Cameron and McMordie, "Architecture, Development of" in *Canadian Encyclopedia* claim that 60 Front Street West, built c.1900, was the first reinforced concrete building in Toronto.

59 Plans, William Stanley Bates Papers, 1902–1948, file 94, Glenbow, Calgary. The architects were then known as Hodgson, Bates & Beattie: see Melnyk, *Calgary Builds*, 136–8. See also "Calgary," 44. Patricia Jasen, "The Burns Building in Calgary," 12–13 (courtesy of John Gilpin, Historic Sites Service, Alberta Culture) notes the similarity in shape of the Grain Exchange and Burns building. See also "Burns Building, Calgary," 32–3, on the renovation and alteration by A.J. Diamond & Partners.

60 Art Institute of Chicago, *Chicago Architecture*, 294–5, says the dream of the "alabaster city" inspired by the Chicago World's Fair prompted explorations of white terra cotta by architects like Charles Atwood of Burnham & Co., who completed Root's design for the Reliance building in 1895.

61 See Bates Papers, 1902–1948, file 60, Glenbow; Melnyk, *Calgary Builds*, 138–41, who describes this as a Chicago-style building. For the dominance of the Beaux-Arts in both Chicago and New York, see Art Institute of Chicago, *Chicago and New York*. Regarding arcades, see Landau, "The Tall Office Building Artistically Reconsidered," 136–64.

62 For the McLeod building by John K. Dow of Seattle, see Edmonton Historical Board, *Edmonton's Threatened Heritage*, 2–3, and by the same authors, *Evaluation of the Heritage Building List*, 22–3. The Lancaster building by James C. Teague, also of Seattle, is detailed in "Amalgamated Contracting Interests at Calgary," 52–3; Boddy, "Pastiche versus Plastique," 18–23; Ingles and McMordie, "Preserving the Past," 17–21. See also Bates Papers, 1902–48, file 55, Glenbow. For details of the Calgary store and other buildings, see *Construction* 6, 10 (October 1913):374, 379–80.

63 Specifications for Vancouver, 20 September 1912, refer to both concrete and Bessemer steel framing. See also Harrods Ltd to Sir Thomas Skinner, 13 December 1912, for savings in the use of ferro-concrete, Ingrams to Burbidge, 15 January 1913, on the issue of ferro-concrete, Vancouver A.12/s.537/2[a], no. s.5594, HBCA. When the Company enlarged the Calgary store in 1928, the issue came up again, but consistency necessitated the use of structural steel: Doe to Governor and Committee, 8 January 1929, Calgary Dead Dossier 55, C.C. no. 5507 for views of store manager Mr Parker and controller of construction A.H. Doe both favourable to steel construction, pending an estimate of the increased cost; also Sketches and Specifications for 1929 Extension, June 1929, Calgary Dead Dossier 55; for linkage of the old section with the new: Doe to NLT Beaver London, 11.1.29, and Hubaycomte to Winnipeg, 12.1.29, Calgary Dead Dossier 55, nos. 2643 and 2425, HBCA.

64 Burbidge to Ware, 1 April 1901, Calgary A.12/s.509/2, unnumbered, HBCA.

65 Horwood to Braidwood, 9 May 1922, Winnipeg Dead Dossier 216, HBCA, indicates the foundations were already laid.

66 "Calgary," 12 February 1913, 44.

67 Viollet-le-Duc, *Lectures on Architecture*, 1:212, discusses the true principles of the Greeks as opposed to the superimposed ornament of the Romans, "To erect, as in the great Basilica of the Giants at Agrigentum, columns as stable points of support – piers or buttresses supporting the entablature and roofing – and to shut in all or part of the intercolum-

nations with a slighter construction – a simple enclosure, in fact – was to reason most wisely; but to take as the Romans did at a later day, the voids for solids, the partitions for the part of strength, and the buttresses for a mere decoration, was – with all due respect for the Romans, and for those who copy them without serious examination – to reason barbarously." This passage was also quoted with reference to New York's Knickerbocker Trust Company of 1902–4 by Schuyler, "A Modern Classic," 431–44.

68 C.H. Walker, "Artistic Expansion of Steel and Concrete," 21–3.

69 Strictly speaking there is a minor variation, but it is not significant enough to be noticeable, see Doe to NLT Beaver London, 11 June 1929, no. 2643, Calgary Dead Dossier 55, HBCA, which states that the existing end pier of the 1912–13 building had to be replaced with a slightly narrower upright to maintain the consistency of the facade.

70 For example, the Second Leiter and Fair stores by Chicago architect William Le Baron Jenney, noted in previous chapter.

71 "Elevator Buildings," 794.

72 Melnyk, *Calgary Builds*, 109–12; "Boston Architect's Design Selected for Calgary Library," 29. The latter notes that the same problem occurred in Regina when a Chicago firm, called in to adjudicate, submitted its own plans for the project instead.

73 "Why Not Patronize Canadian Architects?" 18, regarding the Canadian Northern and Grand Trunk railway station in Winnipeg. See also *Early Buildings of Manitoba*, 73, for what is now Union Station designed in 1909–11 by New York architects Warren & Wetmore. Two decades earlier the same problem arose when Bruce Price planned the Viger and Windsor stations in Montreal, see Marsan, *Montreal in Evolution*, 225. Also "Canadian Buildings Erected by American Contractors," 252.

74 "Sight-Seeing the Calgary Store," 420, describes the fabric of the arcade as polished granite. Horwood to Braidwood, 9 May 1922, Winnipeg Dead Dossier 216, HBCA, indicates an arcade was first suggested for Winnipeg in 1920 by Edward Fitzgerald, Deputy Chairman of the Canadian Committee, who had seen something similar in Brussels. To make way for this extension, the Alexander building at the corner of Eighth Avenue and First Street West was demolished in May 1929. See also HC:1253a, 1703(1), 1707(8) and Ledger, AO; as well as Calgary

A.12/S.509/1, Calgary B.7/1–31, MS Blueprint, and Calgary B.9/1–4, Set C, HBCA.

75 "Victoria and Calgary Store Fronts," 9.

76 Charles V. Sale to P.J. Parker, 6 March 1929, Calgary Dead Dossier 55, BCS no. 88, HBCA. HC:1707, AO, includes the floor plans of a number of major stores across Europe and North America.

77 Vancouver B.31/1–10, August 1911, and B.32/1–42, MS Blueprints, September 1912, HBCA. See also HC: Add. MSS 787, VCA; HC:1088, 1095, 1121, 1122, 1125, 1159, 1212, 1224a, AO. A perspective delineated by "J.E. Sampson" known only from a photographic reproduction illustrates the ten-storey option, see HC:Add. 1, AO; Horwood to Pierson, 5 June 1923, Winnipeg Dead Dossier 216, HBCA, 17, confirms this perspective was prepared at the outset along with plans for the store's extension to Granville St. Also Segger, *Victoria*, 73.

78 Burbidge to Ingrams, 15 September, 5 November 1913, 30 January 1914, 21 March 1916, Vancouver A.12/S.537/2[a], nos. S.530, S.551, S.602, S.808, HBCA.

79 "Vancouver and the Company," 32–7. Additional details are set out in "First H.B.C. Store in Vancouver," 57.

80 Kalman and Roaf, *Exploring Vancouver* 2, 23, 35, for Hotel Europe as well as details of Parr & Fee. See also Carker, "The Europe Hotel," 33–7.

81 Kalman and Roaf, *Exploring Vancouver* 2, 38–9, 94, 112–13, 268, regarding Woodward's store of 1908, the Province, Winch, and Dominion buildings of the same year, all of which were steel frame, and the Bauer (now Pemberton) building of 1910 by W. M. Somervell, and the Birks Building of 1912–13 by Somervell & Putnam (demolished), both of which used reinforced concrete.

82 Ibid., 83, 85, 268, for the Vancouver Block of 1910–12, the Rogers Building of 1911–12, and the Birks Building (already mentioned) all clad with white-glazed terra cotta. See also Gillespie, "Reinforced Concrete," 51–63. Concerns about the safety of concrete were a continuing issue, see Horwood to Braidwood, 9 May 1922, Winnipeg Dead Dossier 216, HBCA, on a collapse resulting from poorly designed concrete reinforcing.

83 For perspectives depicting the extensions, see HC:787, folder 6, CVA, delineated by S.H. Maw, and displayed at the Ontario Association of Architects, *Exhibition of Architecture and Allied Arts* (1927).

For photographs and plans relating to the additions see HC: Add. 1, AO. Also "Our Imposing Store in Vancouver," 68; "Vancouver Store," 10–11; and Vancouver B.33/1–166, MS Blueprints, Vancouver A.92/153/3, Vancouver A.92/17/101, Vancouver Dead Dossier 206, HBCA; HC:Add. MSS 787, folders 2–5, VCA; Horwood to Pierson, 5 June 1923, Winnipeg Dead Dossier 216, HBCA.

84 Like the old section, the new part of the building was built to carry a ten-storey load; see "Our Imposing Store at Vancouver," 68. Regarding retail design, see "All Kinds of a Store," 292.

85 Doe to Sale, 22 September 1925, and Doe(?) to Governor and Committee, 7 December 1925, Vancouver Dead Dossier 206, nos. 118 and 143, HBCA.

86 StJ.B. Smith, "Children's Promotional Features – Vancouver Store," 361–2, speaks of "the good-will we are now establishing" for ten, twenty, or thirty years hence. The company's good corporate citizenship was also demonstrated in its employment stategies. Two graduate nurses attended the physical and psychological well-being of employees, while management remarked on the importance of offering "sympathy and inspiration." See "Romance 'At Home,' Vancouver Store," 356–60. The logic behind community involvement is apparent from "Notes on Morgan's Store," 6 July 1925, Vancouver A.93/19, HBCA, in which the Montreal retailer is recorded as having rented its top floor for an automobile show attended by 125,000 people. The Bay promoted itself as assisting the development of Western Canada and the "upbuilding" of the Dominion when it installed a roof-top beacon to guide pilots, see "Vancouver," 133.

87 "Company in Victoria," 4–9; Segger, *Victoria*, 70–3; Victoria A.12/S 539/1[a], and B.34/1, 17–46, MS Blueprint, HBCA; HC:1125, 1152, 1161, 1165, and 1190, AO; *Daily Colonist* (Victoria) 30 July 1913, 1.

88 "Company in Victoria," 4–9; *Daily Colonist*, 18 September 1913, 2.

89 *Daily Colonist*, 3 September 1913, 1.

90 HC:1181 (52)-(56), AO; Horwood to FitzGerald, 22 May 1922, Winnipeg Dead Dossier 216, HBCA.

91 City of Victoria Heritage Advisory Committee, *This Old Town*, 57.

92 *Daily Colonist*, 19 September 1913, 1, for excavation; *Victoria Daily Times*, 7 April 1919, 3; 21 April 1919, 17; *Daily Colonist* 11 September 1921, 1, on store opening. See also HC:1180, 1181 and 1261, AO. It is not clear if Horwood & White were involved in a 1929 extension at the rear, see HC:1165, 1295, AO.

93 Burbidge to Governor and Committee, 1 August 1918, and Secretary to Burbidge, 24 October 1918, Winnipeg A.12/S 543/2, nos. S.1040 and S.1073, HBCA.

94 Governor and Committee to Burbidge, 12 November 1918, Winnipeg A.12/S 543/2, no. S.1074, and Horwood to Braidwood, 9 May 1922, Winnipeg Dead Dossier 216, HBCA, point out that the committee had proposed Altman's in New York as an appropriate model.

95 Burbidge to Governor and Committee, 17 February 1919, Winnipeg A.12/S 543/2, no. S.1087; Horwood to Braidwood, 9 May 1922, Governor and Committee to Secretary of the Canadian Advisory Committee, 22 June 1922, and Pierson to Messrs Burke, Horwood & White, 23 December 1922, Winnipeg Dead Dossier 216, HBCA.

96 Horwood to Pierson, 5 June 1923, Burbidge to Chairman of Canadian Committee, 9 July 1923, Acting Secretary Canadian Committee to Messrs Burke, Horwood & White, 2 August and 30 November 1923, file S-24, Horwood to Pierson, 14 June 1924, Fitzgerald to Messrs Burke, Horwood & White, 13 August 1924, file S-24, Doe to Governor and Committee, 28 October 1925, no. X 131, Winnipeg Dead Dossier 216, HBCA.

97 Sup't of Buildings to General Manager, 2 June 1937, Winnipeg, RG 2, Series 8 – 806.2.1., HBCA. The memorandum bears a note that Vancouver, Calgary and Victoria cost $0.65/square foot, whereas Winnipeg was only $0.49, and Bon Marché in Seattle $0.35.

98 "Methodist Book Room, Toronto," 8–14; "Thomas Ogilvie & Sons' New Warehouse," 22. The red brick and stone is reminiscent of Shaw's New Scotland Yard of 1887–88 or George B. Post's Western Union of 1873–75, pictured in Silver, *Lost New York*, 162.

CHAPTER EIGHT

1 Architectural Guild of Toronto Minutes, 3 October 1887, Ontario Association of Architects Papers, MU 2734, AO. See also Crossman, *Architecture in Transition*, 19–20, 30; Simmins, *Ontario*

Association of Architects, 20–6; Card, *Ontario Association of Architects*, 10–13.

2 For historical background on architectural organizations, see Arthur, *Toronto*, 237–41; Tausky and DiStephano, *Victorian Architecture*, 61–4; Constans Fides, "An Appeal for Organization," 3.

3 Architectural Guild of Toronto Minutes, 3 October 1887, Ontario Association of Architects Papers, MU 2734, AO.

4 *CAB* I (January 1888):1.

5 Architectural Guild of Toronto Minutes, 12 July, 11 October 1888, Ontario Association of Architects Papers, MU 2734, AO; "Ontario Association of Architects," February 1892, 10.

6 Aylesworth, "Need of Organization," 7–8; "The Inception and Progress of the Ontario Association of Architects," 137.

7 Architectural Guild of Toronto Minutes, 8 November 1888, Ontario Association of Architects Papers, MU 2734, AO.

8 Ontario Association of Architects before Incorporation, Proceedings of 21 March 1889, Ontario Association of Architects Papers, MU 2734, AO. Other members of the organizing committee of the Guild included D.B. Dick, Frank Darling, Walter Strickland and William Langton. Also "Proposed Canadian Architectural Association," 19–20; "Draft Constitution of Proposed Ontario Association of Architects," 26, 29–30.

9 Because of the relatively recent emergence of the distinction between builders and architects, the Association's by-laws defined the term "architect" as "A professional person whose occupation consists in the supplying of drawings, specifications and other data preliminary to the material construction and completion of buildings, in exercising administrative control over the operations of contractors supplying material and labour incidental to the construction and completion of buildings, and in officiating as arbitrator of contracts, stipulating terms of obligations and fulfillment between the proprietor and the contractor"; see Ontario Association of Architects before Incorporation, Proceedings of 21 March 1889, Ontario Association of Architects Papers, MU 2734, AO. No such definition appeared in the act itself: "Ontario Architects Act, April 1890, 40–2; and August 1891, 80, for provisions and reaction from the *Australasian Builder*.

10 Weaver, "The Modern City Realized: Toronto Civic Affairs, 1880–1915," Artibise and Stelter, *Usable Urban Past*, 40–9.

11 Ontario Association of Architects before Incorporation, Proceedings of 21 March and 19 June 1889, Ontario Association of Architects Papers, MU 2734, AO.

12 "Ontario Association of Architects," December 1889, 139–40.

13 Ibid., 137, 140.

14 Five Per Cent, "Dishonourable Practice," 111. The same year D.B. Dick charged that certain members of the Guild were not acting honourably regarding fees and a mechanism was set up to deal with disputes among members: see Architectural Guild of Toronto Minutes, 10 April 1890, Ontario Association of Architects Papers, MU 2734, AO.

15 Burke & Horwood, "Attempt to Bribe Architects," 217; "Wolves in Sheep's Clothing," 37; Langton, "Professional Ethics," 345.

16 "Ontario Architects' Act," April 1890, 40–2.

17 For educational requirements, see "Ontario Association of Architects," December 1890, 135; "Ontario Association of Architects Students Examinations," June 1892, 57–61.

18 "Ontario Association of Architects," December 1890, 135.

19 "Ontario Association of Architects," January 1896, 17–19; January 1898, 9; January 1898, 8; "The Ontario Architects Act," November 1896, 174–6; "Ontario Association of Architects Examinations," June 1897, 115–16; Burke to *CAB* Editor, 11 November 1899, *CAB* 12 (November 1899):214. The Province of Quebec Association of Architects became a closed corporation in 1898, and Illinois also passed a statutory license law at the same time. The Ontario Association of Architects did not achieve this status until 1931.

20 Simmins, *Ontario Association of Architects*, 47–64; Card, *Ontario Association of Architects*, 20–22; J.P Hynes, "Notes on the History of the Toronto Architectural Eighteen Club," Ontario Association of Architects Papers, MU 2734, AO.

21 "Ontario Association of Architects," January 1899, 10–17; January 1900, 8–19; "Canada," 3 March 1900, 67–8.

22 Toronto Architectural Eighteen Club (later Toronto Society of Architects), *Exhibition Catalogues*

(1901–2, 1905, 1909, 1912), particularly 1909, 9–12, for history, MTRL. See also Crossman, *Architecture in Transition*, 85–99.

23 "Ontario Association of Architects," January 1899, 10–17.

24 E. Smith, "Architectural Education–1900," 109; "Educational Work of the Ontario Association of Architects," 153–4; "Ontario Association of Architects," January 1902, 5, 8; February 1901, 33, 35–8; January 1903, 6, 9; February 1904, 33.

25 "Ontario Association of Architects," January 1905, 10; January 1906, 8–9.

26 "Twentieth Annual Convention of the Ontario Association of Architects," January 1908, 28; Horwood, "Licence Law Strongly Opposed," 36B, 38–40, 70; E. Smith, "Compulsory Architectural Education Opposed," 67; "J.C.B. Horwood Has More to Say on Proposed Licensing Act," 42; June 1909, 49. For withdrawal of legislation, see "Editorial," May 1908, 26–7; "Provincial Board of Examiners," November 1908, 30; February 1909, 30. Regarding merger of Ontario Association of Architects and Toronto Architectural Eighteen Club, see "Amalgamation," 55.

27 By-law 2948, *Minutes of the Proceedings of the Council of the Corporation of the City of Toronto* (1891), App. B, 595–7; "Toronto Technical School," October 1892, 101; November 1893, 113; March 1894, 39–40; November 1895, 130.

28 "Toronto Technical School," March 1894, 39.

29 "Toronto Technical School," November 1895, 130–1; Architectural Guild of Toronto Minutes, 10 December 1891, 13 October and 5 December 1893, 4 December 1894, 3 December 1895, 7 January 1896, and 1 December 1896, Ontario Association of Architects Papers, MU 2734, AO, for appointments to the board.

30 "Ontario Association of Architects," February 1895, 21–8. Final Report of the Committee on Fire and Light, *Minutes of the Proceedings of the Council of the Corporation of the City of Toronto* (1895), App. C, 506, lists the Globe, Osgoodby, and Simpson buildings as year's major fire losses.

31 "Ontario Association of Architects," February 1895, 24; By-law 152, City of Toronto, CTA, passed 28 January 1850.

32 "Building Construction in its Relation to Fire Protection," 38; By-law 2434, *Minutes of the Proceedings of the Council of the Corporation of the City of Toronto* (1890).

33 "Ontario Association of Architects," February 1895, 25; "Building Construction and its Relation to Fire Protection," 38–9; *Minutes of the Proceedings of the Council of the Corporation of the City of Toronto* (1895), items 57, 193.

34 "Building Construction and its Relation to Fire Protection," 38–9; By-laws 3340 and 3384, *Minutes of the Proceedings of the Council of the Corporation of the City of Toronto* (1895–96).

35 "Ontario Association of Architects," January 1896, 21, 29–32, for comments by H.B. Gordon on patching up the old by-law, and his address to the convention on the subject of "Municipal Building Laws."

36 "Ontario Association of Architects," February 1895, 21–8. The Province of Quebec Association of Architects placed a resolution before the Montreal City Council every year for three years beginning in 1897, but the initiative was rejected; see Wolfe, "Montréal: Des Plans d'Embellissement," 25; and by the same author "The City Beautiful Movement in Montreal." See also "The New York Art Commission," 3, for the establishment of the Municipal Art Commission in New York in 1898; "League for the Adornment of the City of Chicago," 160.

37 "Ontario Association of Architects," February 1895, 21–8.

38 "Ontario Association of Architects," January 1896, 20; January 1897, 12; January 1898, 18; Card, *Ontario Association of Architects*, 19, for committee report.

39 "Guild History," 2–3, notes the Civic Guild was founded on 21 May 1897 by Sir Edmund Walker, E.F.B. Johnston, Bernard McEvoy, Professor James Mavor, artists Lucius O'Brien and G.A. Reid, and architect William Langton.

40 Ibid., pinpointing the role of the Toronto Architectural Eighteen Club and the involvement of the Ontario Society of Artist, Ontario Association of Architects, Canadian Institute, Engineer's Club, Board of Trade, Canadian Manufacturers Association, Civic Victorian Memorial Committee, and Public School Art League; also "Ontario Association of Architects," January 1902, 5, 9; and Toronto Society of Architects (formerly Toronto Architectural Eighteen Club), *Fifth Exhibition Catalogue*

(1909), 10. For Albert E. Kelsey, "Modern City Making," 80; "Architectural League of America," 73.

41 "Ontario Association of Architects," January 1906, 5–12; Langton, "Plan of Improvements to Toronto," 26–8; Weaver, "Modern City Realized," in Artibise and Stelter, *Usable Urban Past*, 60.

42 B.E. Walker, "Plan of Improvements to Toronto," 18–19; by the same author, "Comprehensive Plan for Toronto," in Rutherford, *Saving the Canadian City*, 221–6. Contrast opinions expressed in "Civic Art Pays," 54.

43 Service, *Edwardian Architecture*, 166–7.

44 Lemon, "Plans for Early 20th-Century Toronto," 11–31; "Guild History," 2–3.

45 Toronto Civic Guild Minutes, 4 December 1908, 215, Toronto Civic Guild Papers, s 48, MTRL.

46 Burke, "Some Notes on a Flying Visit to Washington, Baltimore, and Philadelphia," 71–2.

47 "Ontario Association of Architects," January 1905, 10; Toronto Civic Guild, *Report on a Comprehensive Plan* (1909). Also see "Ontario Association of Architects," February 1904, 36; January 1905, 11; January 1906, 5; *Minutes of the Proceedings of the Council for the Corporation of the City of Toronto* (1903), items 697, 751, 816, CTA.

48 National Conference on Civic Planning held annual meetings every year from 1907 on. For Philadelphia, see "Conference on City Planning," 945–6.

49 Choay, *Modern City*, 15–22, 125; Benevolo, *Origins of Modern Town Planning*.

50 Hines, *Burnham of Chicago*, 73–124, 139–216; Art Institute of Chicago, *Chicago Architecture*, 107–19; by the same institution, *Plan of Chicago* for various city plans prepared by Burnham; and Bach, "Reconsideration of the 1909 'Plan of Chicago,'" 132–41, for difference between Burnham's ideas, and German or British models.

51 Correspondence File, Toronto Civic Guild Papers, s. 48, MTRL; "Diagonal Streets," May 1911, 3; February 1912, 1–8.

52 Reps, *Making of Urban America*; Fein, *Frederick Law Olmsted*; W.H. Wilson, *City Beautiful Movement*, 1–6, on Olmsted's place in the city planning movement.

53 There were two methods of widening streets, the "homologous line" (which resulted in the pocketing of new properties behind the newly designated street line), or the excess-expropriation technique (which established wide road allowances from the outset), see "An Example of Excess Expropriation," 5.

54 Lemon, "Plans for Early 20th Century Toronto," 11–19; Report No. 12 of the Committee on Legislation and Reception, *Minutes of the Proceedings of the Council of the Corporation of the City of Toronto* (1910), App. A, 1483, CTA, for the city's refusal to set up a Civic Improvement Trust to acquire parkland.

55 Interim Report, 26 May 1911, *Minutes of the Proceedings of the Council of the Corporation of the City of Toronto* (1911), App. A, 1240; Final Report, 28 December 1911, Civic Improvement Committee Files, RG 242, CTA.

56 Lyle was consulting architect to the city's Civic Improvement Committee, see "Proposed Federal and Municipal Scheme for Toronto," 51; "Description of Proposed Federal Square and Federal Avenue," 4; Hunt, *John M. Lyle*, 83–5; Dendy, *Lost Toronto*, 142–4.

57 "Ontario Association of Architects," February 1901, 40–3.

58 Burke, "Improvement of the Grounds," 29.

59 Ibid. L'Enfant's 1791 plan for Washington with its wide processional boulevards linking chief points of interest was also mentioned. Burnham & Co. were in the process of rehabilitating L'Enfant's scheme, see Art Institute of Chicago, *Chicago Architecture*, 109–10.

60 Fifteenth and Final Report of the Committee on Parks and Exhibitions, 3 December 1903, *Minutes of the Proceedings of the Council of the Corporation of the City of Toronto* (1903), App. C, 703, CTA; "Ontario Association of Architects," January 1903, 9.

61 "Notes of the Toronto Exhibition," ix; *Globe*, 11 August 1911, 9; 28 August 1911, 1 and 3.

62 Werner, "Bridging Politics," 2–4, CTA, referring to a Report on Transit of 25 August 1910; "Bloor-Danforth Viaduct," 3 December 1911, 4–8.

63 "Recent Work of the Civic Guild," 1 May 1911, 6.

64 Report of the City Engineer, 17 November 1911, *Minutes of the Proceedings of the Council of the Corporation of the City of Toronto*, App. A, 1889; Interim Report, 12 October 1911, and Final Report, 28 December 1911, Civic Improvement Committee Files, RG 242, CTA; "Bloor-Danforth Viaduct," 1 September 1911, 6, 1; 3 December 1911, 4–8; 1

June 1912, 2; 1 July 1912, 6–7; November 1912, 1–2; December 1912, 3.

65 Market Gallery, *Architecture of Public Works*, 14–17; "The Bloor-Danforth Viaduct," July 1913, 7; February 1914, 2; "Editorial," *Construction* 5 (December 1911):46; 8 (July 1912):45; 9 (August 1912):44–5; "Danforth Avenue and Bloor St. Connection," 61–4; "Don Section, Bloor St Viaduct," 902–3; "Progress of Bloor St Viaduct, Toronto," 278–82; "Bloor St. Viaduct Progress," 682; Steel Joined at Bloor St Viaduct, Toronto,"400–12; City Engineer's Department Photographs, RG 8, CTA. For concrete scheme, ''Proposed Henry Hudson Memorial Bridge,"29–31.

66 "Work of the Guild," 1 March 1912, 1; Executive Committee Minutes, 29 December 1913, Toronto Civic Guild Papers, S 48, MTRL; HC:1052, 1162, 1146, AO, for plans of St Clair, Yonge, and Adelaide Streets.

67 Crossman, *Architecture in Transition*, 11–23; Minutes of Architectural Guild of Toronto, 12 April, 3, 16, 17 May and 14 June 1888, Ontario Association of Architects Papers, MU 2734, AO, regarding Toronto Board of Trade, Oxford Courthouse, Harbord Collegiate Institute, and the Montreal Board of Trade competitions.

68 "Ontario Association of Architects," February 1892, 15.

69 "Ontario Association of Architects," February 1901, 39; Report of Assessors for Proposed New Departmental and Justice Buildings for the Dominion of Canada in Ottawa, Ontario, and Documents Submitted to the Minister of Public Works, Department of Public Works (Canada) files, RG 11, V. 4239, file 1298–1, NA; Crossman, *Architecture in Transition*, 137–42. For Tarsney Act: Hines, *Burnham of Chicago*, 126–32.

70 Report of the Assessors, Department Public Works (Canada), RG 11, V. 4239, file 1298–1, NA.

71 Ibid., Documents Submitted to the Minister of Public Works; *House of Commons Debates* (1907), col. 3619, National Library.

72 Report of Assessors, Department of Public Works (Canada) Files, RG 11, V. 4239, 1298–1; "Editorial," October 1907, 17–18, for criticism of competition.

73 *House of Commons Debates* (1909), col. 1251 and (1909–10), V. 1, col. 556, National Library; "Prize Designs, Proposed Departmental and Justice Buildings, Ottawa," October 1907, 42–4, 48–9,

178–9; "Ottawa Government Building Competition," November 1907, 15–20; December 1907, 15–19.

74 Documents Submitted to the Minister of Public Works, Department of Public Works (Canada) Files, RG 11, V. 4239, file 1298–1, NA.

75 *House of Commons Debates* (1911–12), V. 1, col. 1333, National Library; and letter dated 18 January 1912 from E. & W.S. Maxwell to Hon. F.D. Monk, Department of Public Works (Canada) Files, RG 11, V. 4239, file 1298–1, NA.

76 Kalman and Roaf, *Exploring Ottawa*, 29, for Connaught building. See also, "Editorial," December 1911, 43–4; April 1912, 45–6; Bland, "The Landscape Architecture of Frederick Todd," 111–13. A new competition was organized according to suggestions by Hynes, "More About Competitions," 58, on site now occupied by the Confederation and Justice buildings. Also "Editorial," October 1912, 56; "Proposed Departmental Buildings, Ottawa," February 1913, 61; "New Departmental Buildings, Ottawa," May 1913, 169; "Plans Showing Scheme for New Departmental and Court Buildings," September 1913, 331; February 1914, 75.

77 Baillargé, "Reasons for a Dominion Association of Architects," 2–3; Fitzpatrick, "The Canadian Institute of Architects," 45; Chaussé, "Incorporation of the Canadian Institute of Architects," 33–6, 43. For Province of Quebec Association of Architects, see CAB 22 (January 1908):9, 15–16; (March 1908):10.

78 Horwood, "Institute of Architects of Canada," 24; CAB 21 (December 1907):9–10; "Editorial," and "Would the Registration of Architects be a Menace to the Profession?" *Construction* 1 (January 1908): 15, 39–41.

79 "Architectural Institute of Canada," March 1908, 19; "Editorial," March 1908, 21–4; "National Assembly of Architects," 32–6.

CONCLUSION

1 Jones, *Grammar of Ornament*.

2 "First Annual House Number," 47.

3 Gargoyle, *Five Sins of the Architect*, 104, from Burke's library includes this well-marked passage: "A man is certainly at fault in failing to keep his work on the highest plane of his possibilities."

4 For Burke's views, see J.E. Middleton, *Municipality of Toronto*, 2:41, 278; Morgan, *Canadian Men and Women of the Time*, 173.

5 Surrogate Court Files no. 37398, 6 February 1919, MS 584, AO.

Bibliography

MANUSCRIPT SOURCES

ARCHIVES OF ONTARIO, TORONTO (AO)
William Gregg Papers
Horwood Collection (HC)
Measured Drawings Collection
Ontario Association of Architects Papers
Ontario Society of Artists Papers
Partnership Records
Picture Collection
Public Works Department (Ontario)
R.C. Windeyer Papers

ARCHIVES NATIONALES DE QUÉBEC À MONTRÉAL
(ANQM)
Collection des Plans d'Architecture

ART INSTITUTE OF CHICAGO
Burnham Letters
Elmer C. Jensen Collection (microfilm)
Picture Collection

BROOKLYN MUSEUM ARCHIVES

CANADIAN BAPTIST ARCHIVES MCMASTER
UNIVERSITY, HAMILTON (CBA)
Baptist Church Files
Blueprints

CHICAGO HISTORICAL SOCIETY
Picture Collection

CITY MUSEUM OF NEW YORK
Picture Collection

CITY OF TORONTO ARCHIVES, TORONTO (CTA)
Assessment Rolls
Building Permits
City Engineer's Department Files
Civic Improvement Committee Files
Insurance Atlases
*Minutes of the Proceedings of the Council of the
   Corporation of the City of Toronto*
Picture Collection
Salmon Collection (SC)

GLENBOW ALBERTA INSTITUTE OF ART, CALGARY,
ALBERTA (GLENBOW)
Insurance Atlases
Picture Collection
William Stanley Bates Papers

HISTORIC AMERICAN BUILDINGS SURVEY (HABS)
LIBRARY OF CONGRESS WASHINGTON (DC)
Picture Collection

HUDSON'S BAY COMPANY ARCHIVES, WINNIPEG
Blueprints
Company Files

LAW SOCIETY OF UPPER CANADA ARCHIVES,
OSGOODE HALL, TORONTO
Minutes of the Law Society of Upper Canada

METROPOLITAN TORONTO REFERENCE LIBRARY,
TORONTO (MTRL)
Archindont Index
Broadside Collection
John Ross Robertson Collection
Langley Collection (LC)
Picture Collection
Toronto City Directories
Toronto Civic Guild Papers

MOUNT ALLISON UNIVERSITY ARCHIVES, SACKVILLE
(MAUA)
Interview #21 with J. Hammond Krug of Waterloo
Legal/Financial Files
Minutes of the Board of Regents

NATIONAL ARCHIVES OF CANADA, OTTAWA (NA)
Census Returns
Department of Public Works (Canada) Papers
House of Commons Debates
Toronto Board of Trade Papers

NEW YORK HISTORICAL SOCIETY, NEW YORK CITY
Picture Collection

PRESBYTERIAN CHURCH OF CANADA ARCHIVES, KNOX
COLLEGE, UNIVERSITY OF TORONTO, TORONTO
Presbyterian Church Files
Toronto Academy Papers

PROVINCIAL ARCHIVES OF MANITOBA, WINNIPEG
Insurance Atlases
Picture Collection

PUBLIC ARCHIVES OF NOVA SCOTIA, HALIFAX
Architectural Drawings Collection
Building Permits
By-laws
City Directories
Picture Collection

UNITED CHURCH OF CANADA ARCHIVES, VICTORIA
UNIVERSITY, UNIVERSITY OF TORONTO, TORONTO
(VicUA)
Methodist Church Files
Minutes of Committee on Church Architecture
Minutes of the Toronto Conference of the Methodist
  Church of Canada

UNIVERSITY OF TORONTO ARCHIVES, TORONTO
(UofTA)
University of Toronto Physical Plant Files
Upper Canada College (UCC) Files

VANCOUVER CITY ARCHIVES, VANCOUVER (VCA)
Horwood Collection (HC)
Picture Collection

VANCOUVER CITY HALL, VANCOUVER
Building Permits and Plans
Insurance Atlases
Old Hudson's Bay Company File

PERIODICALS

Allisonia (Sackville)
American Architect and Building News (AABN)
Architectural Magazine and Journal (London)
Architectural Record (New York)
Argosy (Sackville)
Beaver (Winnipeg)
Building News (London)

Canadian Agriculturalist (Toronto)
Canadian Architect (Toronto)
Canadian Architect and Builder (CAB) (Toronto)
Canadian Illustrated News (Montreal)
Canadian Methodist Magazine (Toronto)
Christian Guardian (Toronto)
Construction (Toronto)
Contract Record (Toronto)
Daily Colonist (Victoria)
Daily Sentinel Review (Woodstock)
Daily Spectator (Hamilton)
Dominion Illustrated (Montreal)
Ecclesiologist (Cambridge)
Globe and *Saturday Globe* (Toronto)
Illustrated London News (London)
Inland Architect and News Record (Chicago)
Morning Chronicle (Halifax)
*Journal and Transactions of the Board of Agriculture of
  Upper Canada* (Toronto)
Journal of Education for Upper Canada (Toronto)
London Free Press (London, Ontario)
Mail (Toronto)
Manitoba Free Press (Winnipeg)
Monetary & Commercial Times (Toronto)
Morning Chronicle (Sackville)
Province (Vancouver)
Real Estate Record and Guide (New York)
Star and *Evening Star* (Toronto)
Toronto Civic Guild Monthly Bulletin (Toronto)
Toronto World (Toronto)
Victoria Daily Times (Victoria)
Wesleyan Methodist Magazine (London)

GENERAL

Abacus. "Notes of a Trip to the West." AABN 27
  (11 January 1890):17.

Abbott, Lawrence. *The Story of NYLIC: A History of the
  Origin and Development of the New York Life
  Insurance Company from 1845 to 1929.* New York:
  NYLIC, 1930.

Abramson, Louis Allen. "The Planning of a Young Men's
  Christian Association Building." *Brickbuilder* 22
  (March 1913):49–54; (April 1913):77–80; (June
  1913):127–31.

"The Academy's Unwritten Laws as to Architectural
  Drawings" *Building News* 32 (11 May 1877):479.

"Accepted Design for the YMCA Building, Richmond,
  Va." AABN 18 (14 November 1885):234.

Ackerman, James S. *Nineteenth and Twentieth Century Architecture*. New York: Garland, 1976.

Adams, Maurice B. "Free Church Architecture." *Building News* 33 (9 November 1877):473.

Akron Regional Church Planning Office. *The Church in Akron, an Interpretive Analysis*. Cleveland, 1963.

"All Kinds of a Store." *Architectural Record* 12 (August 1902):286–303.

"Amalgamated Contracting Interests at Calgary." *Contract Record* 28 (19 February 1913):52–3.

"Amalgamation." *Construction* 5 (October 1912):55.

"American Architects in Canada." *Construction* 3 (July 1910):51–3.

"An American Gothic Revival." *CAB* 18 (September 1905):131–2.

Amicus. "Notes on Modern Shop Fronts." *Architectural Magazine and Journal* 4 (June 1837):299–301.

Andrews, Wayne. *Architecture in Chicago and Mid-America: A Photographic History*. New York: Atheneum, 1968.

"Annual Banquet." *Construction* 2 (January 1909):43.

"Architects' Eighteen Club." *CAB* 12 (September 1899):181.

"Architectural Association." *Building News* 32 (29 June 1877):643.

"The Architectural Draughtsman's Association." *CAB* 1 (January 1888):4; (February 1888):4; (April 1888):8; (November 1888):5.

"Architectural Drawing in Pen and Ink." *Construction* 5 (March 1912):71.

"Architectural Education in the United States, Parts 1–4." *AABN* 24 (4 August 1888):43; (1 September 1888):95; 6 (October 1888):155; (1 December 1888):251, 330.

"Architectural Eighteen Club." *CAB* 19 (December 1906):ix.

"Architectural Exhibition." *CAB* 15 (May 1902):64.

"Architectural Institute of Canada." *CAB* 22 (March 1908):19.

"Architectural League of America." *CAB* 15 (June 1902):73.

"Architectural Offices." *CAB* 3 (November 1890):123.

"The Architectural Students Club." *CAB* 14 (May 1901):96.

"Architecture at the World's Columbian Exhibition, Part 3." *Inland Architect & News Record* 22 (September 1893):17.

Armstrong, Frederick H. *A City in the Making: Progress, People & Perils in Victorian Toronto*. Toronto: Dundurn, 1988.

Art Gallery of Ontario. *100 Years: Evolution of the Ontario College of Art*. Toronto: AGO, 1976.

Arthur, Eric. *Toronto: No Mean City*. 3rd ed., rev. Stephen A. Otto. Toronto: University of Toronto Press, 1986.

Artibise, Alan F.J., and Gilbert Stelter. *The Canadian City: Essays in Urban and Social History*. Ottawa: Carleton University Press, 1984.

– *Shaping the Urban Landscape: Aspects of the Canadian City-Building Process*. Ottawa: Carleton University Press, 1982.

– *The Usable Urban Past: Planning and Politics in the Modern Canadian City*. Toronto: Macmillan, 1979.

Art Institute of Chicago. *Chicago and New York: Architectural Interactions*. Ed. John Zukowsky. Chicago: AIC, 1984.

– *Chicago Architecture, 1872–1922*. ed. John Zukowsky. Munich: Prestel-Verlag, 1987–88.

– *The Plan of Chicago: 1909–1979*. Chicago: Burnham Library of Architecture, 1979–80.

Artley, Alexandra, ed. *The Golden Age of Shop Design: European Shop Interiors, 1880–1939*. London: The Architectural Press, 1975.

Aylesworth, Marshall B. "Departmental Store Buildings." *CAB* 8 (March 1895):48.

– "The Need of Organization." *CAB* 1 (June 1888):7–8.

B___, H. "The Pointed or English Style of Architecture." *CAB* 4 (January 1891):5–6; (April 1891):60.

B___, J.M. "A Few More Words About 'Queen Anne.'" *AABN* 2 (6 October 1877):320–2.

Bach, Ira. "A Reconsideration of the 1909 'Plan of Chicago.'" *Chicago History* 2 (1973):132–41.

Baigell, Matthew. "John Havilland in Pottsville." *Journal of the Society of Architectural Historians* 26 (1968):4.

Bailey, Thomas M., ed. *Dictionary of Hamilton Biography*. Hamilton: W.L. Griffin, 1981.

Baillargé, Charles. "Reasons for the Dominion Association of Architects." *CAB* 10 (January 1897):2–3.

Baker, F.S. "An Appreciation." *Construction* 16 (June 1923):206–7.

Baker, Richard R. *Richard Morris Hunt*. Cambridge, MA: MIT Press, 1980.

Balston, Thomas. *James Whatman, Father and Son*. London: Methuen, 1957.

– *William Balston: Paper Maker*. London: Methuen, 1954.

"The Bank of Commerce New Building." *Monetary and Commercial Times* 23 (1889–90):903.

Bannister, C. Turpin. "Bogardus Revisited – Part 1: The

Iron Fronts." *Journal of the Society of Architectural Historians* 15 (December 1956):12–22.

– "Bogardus Revisited – Part 2: The Iron Towers." *Journal of the Society of Architectural Historians* 16 (March 1957):11–19.

– "The First Iron-Framed Building." In *Nineteenth and Twentieth Century Architecture*. Ed. James Ackerman. New York: Garland, 1976, 231–46.

"Baptist Institute, Woodstock." *Canadian Illustrated News* 6 (13 July 1872):28, 35

Benevolo, Leonardo. *The Origins of Modern Town Planning*. London: Routledge & Kegan Paul, 1967.

Beszedits, Stephen. *Eminent Toronto Architects of the Past: Their Lives and Works*. Toronto: B&L Information Services, 1983.

Betjeman, John. "Nonconformist Architecture." *Architectural Review* 88 (December 1940):161–74.

Birkmire, William H. *Architectural Iron and Steel*. New York: John Wiley & Sons, 1891.

– *Skeleton Construction in Buildings*. New York: John Wiley & Sons, 1893.

Bland, John. "The Landscape Architecture of Frederick Todd." *RACAR* 7, no. 1/2 (1980):111–13.

Blau, Eve. *Ruskinian Gothic: The Architecture of Deane and Woodward, 1845–1861*. Princeton: Princeton University Press, 1982.

Blomfield, Reginald. *Architectural Drawings and Draughtsmen*. London: Cassell, 1912.

"Bloor-Danforth Viaduct." *Toronto Civic Guild Monthly Bulletin* 1 (1 September 1911):1, 6; (3 December 1911):4–8; (1 June 1912):2; (1 July 1912):6–7; 2 (November 1912):1–2; (December 1912):3; (July 1913):7; 3 (February 1914):2.

"Bloor St. Viaduct Progress." *Contract Record* 30 (12 July 1916):682.

Boddy, Trevor. "Pastiche versus Plastique: Two Renovations Examined." *Canadian Architect* 25 (June 1980):18–23.

Bond, C.H. Acton. "Notes from St John's, NF" *CAB* 7 (January 1894):9.

The Book of Canada. Montreal, 1905.

"Boston Architect's Design Selected for Calgary Library." *Construction* 2 (December 1908):29.

"Boys' Home." *Canadian Illustrated News* 3 (11 February 1871):83, 92.

Brandon, Raphael, and J. Arthur Brandon. *Parish Churches; Being Perspective Views of English Ecclesiastical Structures: Accompanied by Plans Drawn to a Uniform Scale and Letter-Press Descriptions*. London: George Bell, 1858.

Brooks, Michael W. *John Ruskin and Victorian Architecture*. London: Rutgers University Press, 1987.

Brosseau, Mathilde. *Gothic Revival in Canadian Architecture*. Ottawa: Parks Canada, 1980.

Brown, Howard Morton. *Lanark Legacy: Nineteenth Century Glimpses of an Ontario County*. Perth: County of Lanark, 1984.

Brown, Theodore M. "Greenough, Paine, Emerson, and the Organic Aesthetic." *Journal of Aesthetics & Art Criticism* 14 (1956):304–17.

"Building Activity at Calgary." *CAB* 22 (April 1908):20.

"Building Construction and its Relation to Fire Protection." *CAB* 8 (March 1895):38–9.

"Building for the Young Men's Christian Association in Germantown, Pennsylvania." *AABN* 5 (29 March 1879):100.

"Building of the Young Men's Christian Association, Worcester, Mass." *AABN* 21 (4 June 1887):271.

"Building in Canada in 1894." *CAB* 7 (January 1894):8.

Burges, William. "Architectural Drawing." *Royal Institute of British Architects Transactions* (1860–61):15–28.

Burke, Edmund. "Elements of Building Construction – Structural Iron Work." *CAB* 5 (March 1892):28–9.

– "Improvement of the Grounds of the Toronto Industrial Exhibition." *CAB* 15 (February 1902):29.

– "McMaster University Buildings." *McMaster University Monthly* (January 1902):154–60.

– "Qualities of Fireproofing Materials." *CAB* 11 (April 1898):68.

– "Reducing the Fire Loss in Building." *CAB* 14 (March 1901):52–4.

– "Slow Burning Construction." *CAB* 4 (February 1891):22.

– "Some Notes on a Flying Visit to Washington, Baltimore, and Philadelphia." *CAB* 18 (May 1905):71–2.

– "Some Notes on House Planning." *CAB* 3 (May 1890):55–7.

– "Staircase Hall in A.E. Kemp's House." *CAB* 8 (September 1895): ill.

– "Sub-Surface Irrigation Drainage." *CAB* 2 (January 1889):12–13.

– "Two Questions in Connection With Steel Construction in Buildings." *CAB* 11 (February 1898):31–4.

Burke to *CAB* Editor, 11 November 1899. *CAB* 12 (November 1899):214.

Burke & Horwood. "An Attempt to Bribe Architects." *CAB* 13 (November 1900):217.

– "The Intercepting Trap." *CAB* 13 (August 1900):149.

– "No 123 St George Street, Toronto." *CAB* 18 (January 1905): ill.

Burnett, Terry. "'Here Let the Fires of Friendship Burn': The Toronto YMCA Buildings of Burke, Horwood & White." Research Paper, University of Toronto, 1986.

Burnham, Alan. "Last Look at a Structural Landmark." *Architectural Record* 120 (September 1956):273–9.

"Burns Building, Calgary." *Canadian Architect* 32 (November 1987):32–3.

Burton, Charles Luther. *A Sense of Urgency: Memoirs of A Canadian Merchant.* Toronto: Clarke, Irwin, 1952.

Butler, A.S.G., Stewart Hussey and Christopher Hussey. *Architecture of Sir Edwin Lutyens.* Woodbridge, Suffolk: Country Life, 1950.

"By-laws Governing Reinforced Concrete Construction in Toronto." *CAB* 20 (January 1907):10–11.

"Calgary." *Beaver* 5 (March 1925):96.

"Calgary." *Contract Record* 27 (12 February 1913):44.

"Calgary and the Company." *Beaver* 271 (March 1941):42.

Cameron, Christina, and Janet Wright. *Second Empire Style in Canadian Architecture.* Ottawa: Parks Canada, 1977.

Cameron, Christina, and Michael McMordie. "Architecture, Development of." *Canadian Encyclopedia.* Edmonton: Hurtig, 1988.

"Canada." *AABN* 14 (16 February 1889):81; (18 May 1889): 236; 28 (19 April 1890):39–40; (21 June 1890):180–1; 67 (3 March 1900):67–68.

Canadian. "The Necessity for a Canadian School of Architecture." *CAB* 7 (May 1894):70.

"*Canadian Architect and Builder* Competition for a City House." *CAB* 4 (February 1891):23–4.

"Canadian Buildings Erected by American Contractors." *Construction* 6 (July 1913):252.

Canadian Centre for Architecture. *Montréal: Centre-Ville, Maisons du flanc de la montagne, Université McGill, Porjet Milton Parc, Square Saint-Louis.* Montreal: CCA, n.d.

Canadian Encyclopedia. 4 vols. Edmonton: Hurtig Publishers, 1988.

Capper, Stewart H. "Architecture in the University." *CAB* 9 (November 1896):179–82.

– "University Training in Architecture." *CAB* 15 (January 1902):15.

Card, Raymond. *The Ontario Association of Architects.* Pamphlet. Toronto: OAA, 1950.

Carder, W. Gordon. "Woodstock College, 1857–1926." Speech before the Oxford Historical Society, 27 May 1981.

Carker, Helen. "The Europe Hotel." *Habitat* 26/27 (1983–84):33–7.

Catalogue of the Mount Allison Ladies College. Sackville, 1906.

Catalogue of the Third Annual Exhibition of the Department of Architecture of the Brooklyn Institute of Arts and Sciences. Brooklyn: Brooklyn Institute of Arts and Sciences, 1894.

Carmichael, William. *The Autobiography of a Church: Being a History of the First Baptist Church, Vancouver, British Columbia.* Vancouver, 1937.

– *These Sixty Years, 1887–1947.* Vancouver: Capitol Printers, 1947.

Cathcart, William, ed. *The Baptist Encylopaedia.* Philadelphia: Louis H. Everts, 1881.

"The Cathedral of St Alban the Martyr, Toronto." *Construction* 6 (January 1912):50–8.

"Cemeteries and Cemetery Chapels." *Ecclesiologist* 4 (January 1845):9–13.

Champion, Thomas Edward. *The Methodist Churches of Toronto.* Toronto: G.M. Rose & Sons Company, 1899.

Chapman, Alfred. "The Development of Architectural Design in Canada." *Construction* 10 (October 1917): 352.

Chaussé, Alcide. "Incorporation of the Canadian Institute of Architects." *Construction* 1 (November 1907): 33–6, 43.

Choay, Francoise. *The Modern City: Planning in the Nineteenth Century.* New York: George Brazillier, 1969.

Christmas 1892 Souvenir: The Opening Service of the Walmer Road Baptist Church. Toronto 1892.

"Church of St Simon, Rosedale, Toronto." *CAB* 1 (May 1888): ill.

City of Victoria Heritage Advisory Committee. *This Old Town.* Victoria, 1983.

"Civic Art Pays." *CAB* 18 (April 1905):54.

Cleaveland, Henry W. *Village and Farm Cottages 1856.* New York: Appleton, 1856. Reprint Watkins Glen, NY: American Life Foundation, 1976.

Cole, David. *The Work of Sir Gilbert Scott.* London: Architectural Press, 1980.

Collins, Peter. *Changing Ideals in Modern Architecture.* Montreal: McGill University Press, 1965.

Committee on Church Architecture of the Presbyterian Church in Canada. *Designs for Village, Town, and Country Churches.* Toronto: Canadian Architect and Builder Press, 1893.

Communauté urbaine de Montréal. *Répertoire d'architec-*

ture traditionnelle: Architecture commerciale III, Les Magasins, Les Cinémas. Montréal: Communauté urbaine de Montréal, 1985.

"Company in Victoria." Beaver 272 (September 1941): 4–9.

"Composition for Rendering Buildings Fire-proof." Architectural Magazine and Journal 5 (1838):327.

Comstock, William T. Victorian Domestic Architectural Plans and Details. New York: William T. Comstock, 1881. Reprint New York: Dover Publications, 1987.

"Concrete Building Code." CAB 20 (August 1907): xii-xiii.

Condit, Carl. American Building: Materials and Techniques from the Beginning of the Colonial Settlements to the Present. Chicago: University of Chicago Press, 1982.

– The Chicago School of Architecture: A History of Commercial and Public Building in the Chicago Area, 1875–1925. Chicago: The University of Chicago Press, 1964.

"Conditions of the Board of Trade Building Competition." CAB 1 (July 1888):4.

"Conference on City Planning." Real Estate Record & Guide 87 (20 May 1911):945–6.

Conover, Elbert M. Building the House of God. New York: Methodist Book Concern, 1928.

Constans Fides. "An Appeal for Organization." CAB 1 (February 1888):3.

Cox, J.B. and C.B. Ford. Parish Churches. London: Batsford, 1961.

Cram, Ralph Adams. Church Building: A Study of the Principles of Architecture in Their Relation to the Church. Boston: Small, Maynard, 1901.

Croly, Herbert. "What is Civic Art?" Architectural Record 16 (July 1904):47–52.

Crook, David H. "Louis Sullivan and the Golden Doorway." Journal of the Society of Architectural Historians 26 (December 1967):250–8.

Crook, J. Morduant. The Greek Revival. London: RIBA Drawings Series, 1968.

Cross, Harold, C. One Hundred Years of Service with Youth: The Story of the Montreal YMCA. Pamphlet. Montreal: YMCA, 1951.

Crossman, Kelly. Architecture in Transition: From Art to Practice, 1885–1906. Kingston: McGill-Queen's University Press, 1987.

Cunliffe, Richard. Calgary – In Sandstone. Calgary: Historical Society of Alberta, 1969.

Curran, Kathleen. "The German Rundbogenstil and Reflections on the American Round-Arch Style." Journal of the Society of Architectural Historians 47 (December 1988):351–73.

"Danforth Avenue and Bloor St Connection." Construction 5 (February 1912):61–4.

Davey, Peter. Arts and Crafts Architecture: The Search for the Earthly Paradise. London: Architectural Press, 1980.

"Decoration of Trinity Church, Boston." AABN 5 (24 May 1879):164–5.

DeGrace, William. "An Architectural History of Sackville, New Brunswick." Hons. B.A. paper, Mount Allison University, May 1975.

Dendy, William. "Government House, Toronto, 1866–70." Canadian Collector 12 (September/October 1977):21–5.

– Lost Toronto. Toronto: Oxford University Press, 1978.

– and William Kilbourn. Toronto Observed. Toronto: Oxford University Press, 1986.

Denison, Merrill. This is Simpson's. Toronto, 1947.

"Description of Proposed Federal Square and Federal Avenue." Saturday Night, 2 January 1928, 4.

"Design for a Villa Costing $3,500." CAB 1 (April 1888):3–7.

"Design for a Village Church." CAB 6 (June 1893):68.

"Design for a YMCA Building." AABN 24 (20 October 1888):182.

"Design for the YMCA Building, Philadelphia." AABN 1 (9 December 1876):397.

"Designers and Draughtsmen." Building News 33 (2 November 1877):428–9.

Detroit Institute of Arts. The Legacy of Albert Kahn. Detroit: DIA, 1970.

de Wit, Wim, ed. Louis Sullivan: The Function of Ornament. Chicago: Chicago Historical Society, 1986.

"Diagonal Streets." Toronto Civic Guild Monthly Bulletin 1 (May 1911):3; (February 1912):1–8.

Dickson, George, and G. Mercer Adam. A History of Upper Canada College 1829–92 with Contributions by Old Upper Canada Boys. Toronto: Rowsell & Hutchinson, 1893.

Dictionary of Canadian Biography. Toronto: University of Toronto Press, 1966–.

Dixon, Roger, and Stefan Muthesius. Victorian Architecture. London: Thames and Hudson, 1978.

Dolby, George W. The Architectural Expression of Methodism. London: Epworth, 1964.

"Don Section, Bloor St Viaduct." *Contract Record* 28 (15 July 1914):902–3.

Downing, Andrew Jackson. *The Architecture of Country Houses.* New York: Appleton, 1854.

– *Victorian Cottage Residences.* Reprint of 1873 ed. by New York: Dover Publications, 1981.

Downing, Antoinette, and Vincent Scully. *The Architectural Heritage of Newport, Rhode Island.* Cambridge, MA: Harvard University Press, 1952.

"Draft Constitution of Proposed Ontario Association of Architects." *CAB* 2 (March 1889):26, 29–30.

"Drawing at the Eighteen Club Exhibition, Toronto." *CAB* 18 (February 1905):19.

Drexler, Arthur, ed. *The Architecture of the Ecole des Beaux-Arts.* New York: Museum of Modern Art, 1977.

Drummond, Andrew. *The Church Architecture of Protestantism.* Edinburgh: T.& T. Clark, 1934.

Eaton, Leonard K. *The Architecture of Samuel MacLure.* Victoria: Art Gallery of Greater Victoria, 1971.

Early Buildings of Manitoba. Winnipeg: Peguis Publishers, 1973.

"Ecclesiastical Architecture: Village Churches." *Anglo-American Magazine* 4 (January 1854):21–2.

Editor. "The Jayne Building Again." *Journal of the Society of Architectural Historians* 10 (March 1951): 25.

"The Editor's Shanty." *Anglo-American Magazine* 4 (1854):211–13.

"Editorial." *Construction* 1 (October 1907):17–18; (January 1908):15; (March 1908):21–4; (May 1908):26–7; 5 (December 1911):43–6; 8 (July 1912): 45; 9 (April 1912):45–6; (August 1912):44–5; (October 1912):56.

"Editorial: Smuggling," *Construction* 2 (February 1909):37–9.

Edmondson, Ernest. *A History of Sherbourne Street Wesleyan Methodist Church, 1871–1959: To Commemorate the 100th Anniversary of the Present Church Buildings, 1887–1987.* Toronto, 1987.

Edmonton Historical Board. *Edmonton's Threatened Heritage.* Edmonton, 1980.

– *Evaluation of the Heritage Building List in the Downtown Area Redevelopment Plan By-law.* Edmonton, 1982.

"Educational Intelligence: Hellmuth Ladies' College," *Journal of Education for Ontario* 21 (September 1868):141–3.

"An Educational Standard for Architects." *CAB* 9 (November 1896):173–4.

"Educational Work of the Ontario Association of Architects." *CAB* 13 (August 1900):153–4.

"Eighteen Club Exhibition." *CAB* 18 (January 1905):2.

Egbert, Donald Drew. *The Beaux-Arts Tradition in French Architecture: Illustrated by the Grands Prix de Rome.* Princeton: Princeton University Press, 1980.

"Elevator Buildings." *Real Estate Record & Guide* 88 (25 November 1911):794.

"An Example of Excess Expropriation." *Toronto Civic Guild Monthly Bulletin* 1 (1 July 1912):5.

"Exhibition of Architectural Drawings." *CAB* 13 (November 1900):219.

"Exterior and Interior of the YMCA Building, San Francisco, Cal." *AABN* 48 (20 April 1895):30.

F___, J.A. "Modern Church Building, Part 2." *AABN* 5 (1 March 1879):66–7.

"Fawcett Hall." *Allisonia* 7 (May 1910):103–4.

Fawcett, Jane, ed. *Seven Victorian Architects.* University Park: Pennsylvania State University Press, 1977.

Fein, Albert. *Frederick Law Olmsted and the American Environmental Tradition.* New York: George Braziller, 1972.

Fergusson, James. *History of Architecture in all Countries from the Earliest Times to the Present Day.* 2 vols. London: John Murray, 1874.

Ferree, Barr. "The Modern Office Building." *IANR* 27 (June 1896):45–6.

Field, Walker. "A Re-examination into the Invention of the Balloon Frame." *Journal of the Society of Architectural Historians* 2 (October 1942):3–29.

"Fire Prevention." *CAB* 3 (November 1890):123–4.

"First Annual House Number." *Construction* 2 (June 1909):47.

"First Baptist Church, Winnipeg." *Colonist* 10 (June 1895):279–80.

"First HBC Store in Vancouver." *Beaver* 257, 4 (March 1927):57.

"First 'Skeleton' Building." *Real Estate Record & Guide* 64 (12 August 1899):239.

Fitzpatrick, J.W. "The Canadian Institute of Architects." *Construction* 1 (October 1907):45.

Five Per Cent. "Dishonourable Practice." *CAB* 3 (October 1890):111.

"Fourth Annual Convention of the Royal Architectural Institute of Canada." *Construction* 4 (November 1911):109.

Fox, William Sherwood, ed. *Letters of William Davies, Toronto, 1854–1861*. Toronto: University of Toronto Press, 1945.

Francis, Walter J. "Reinforced Concrete Construction." *Construction* 2 (March 1909):47–8.

"Fredericton Cathedral." *Ecclesiologist* 5 (February 1846):81.

Freeman, John Crosby. "Thomas Mawson: Imperial Missionary of British Town-Planning." RACAR 2, no. 2 (1975):37–47.

Gad, Gunter, and Deryck Holdsworth. "Building for City, Region, and Nation: Office Development in Toronto, 1834–1984." In *Forging a Consensus: Essays on Historical Toronto*, ed. V.L. Russell, 272–319. Toronto: University of Toronto Press, 1984.

– "Corporate Capitalism and the Emergence of the High-Rise Office Building." *Urban Geography* 8 (May-June 1987):212–31.

Gambier-Bousfield, R.W. "Architectural Education in Canada." CAB 4 (April 1891):46.

Gargoyle, Solomon. *Five Sins of the Architect*. Riverton: Riverton Press, 1895.

Gayle, Margot, and Edmund V. Gillon, Jr. *Cast-Iron Architecture in New York*. New York: Dover Publications, 1974.

Gebhard, David. "C.F.A. Voysey: To and From America." JSAH 30 (December 1971):304–17.

Gersowitz, Julia. "Montreal Architects, 1870–1914." Paper for Columbia University, 1980.

Gibson, Sally. *More Than an Island: A History of the Toronto Island*. Toronto: Irwin, 1984.

Giedion, Siegfried. *Space, Time, and Architecture*. Cambridge, MA: Harvard University Press, 1941.

Gifford, John. *Edinburgh*. Harmondsworth: Penguin, 1984.

Gillespie, Peter. "Reinforced Concrete: Its Advantages and Limitations." *Construction* 10/11 (March 1911): 51–63.

Gillon, Edmund V., Jr, and Christopher Little. *Elegant New York: The Builders and the Buildings, 1885–1915*. New York: Abbeville, 1985.

Girouard, Mark. "Review of Andrew Saint, *Richard Norman Shaw*." *Journal of the Society of Architectural Historians* 35 (1976):195–6.

– *Sweetness and Light: the 'Queen Anne' Movement, 1860–1900*. Oxford: Clarendon, 1977.

Godfrey, F.M. *Italian Architecture up to 1750*. London: Alec Trecanti, 1971.

Goldberger, Paul. *A Monograph on the Works of McKim, Mead & White, 1879–1915*. New York: Da Capo, 1985.

Goodhart-Rendel, H.S. "Architectural Draughtsmanship of the Past." *Royal Institute of British Architects Journal* 58 (February 1951):127–37.

Gowans, Alan. *The Comfortable House: North American Suburban Architecture, 1890–1930*. Cambridge, MA: MIT Press, 1986.

Grant, John Webster. *A Profusion of Spires: Religion in Nineteenth-Century Ontario*. Toronto: University of Toronto Press, 1988.

Greenhill, Ralph, Ken Macpherson, and Douglas Richardson. *Ontario Towns*. Ottawa: Oberon, 1974.

Grisebach, August. *Carl Friedrich Schinkel*. Leipzig: Insel-Verlag, 1924.

Grover, Shiela. "440 Hargrave Street, Winnipeg: Calvary Temple (formerly First Baptist)." Research Paper for the Historical Buildings Committee, Winnipeg, March 1984.

"Guild History." *Toronto Civic Guild Monthly Bulletin* 1 (1 May 1911):2–3

H.R. Ives & Co. "The Advantages(?) of Employing an American Architect." CAB 3 (July 1890):75.

Haas, R.H. "Reinforced Concrete Designing." CAB 22 (April 1908):14–15, 24.

"The Habitations of Man in All Ages." AABN 1 (26 February 1876):68–70.

Haese, Philip. "John Danley Aitchison." Paper presented to the Society for the Study of Architecture in Canada, Montreal, 14 April 1989.

Halifax, Nova Scotia and Its Attractions. Halifax: Howard & Kutsche, c. 1902.

Hamlin, A.D.F. "The Influence of the Ecole des Beaux-Arts on Our Architectural Education." *Architectural Record* 23 (April 1908):5.

Hamlin, Talbot. *Forms and Functions of Twentieth Century Architecture*. New York: Columbia University Press, 1952.

Harbeson, John. *The Study of Architectural Design with Special Reference to the Program of the Beaux-Arts Institute of Design*. New York: Pencil Points Press, 1926.

Harmon, Nolan, ed. *Encyclopedia of World Methodism*. Nashville: United Methodist Publishing House, 1974.

Harper, J. Russell. "Ontario Painters, 1846–1867." *National Gallery of Canada Bulletin* 1 (May 1963): 16–32.

Hay, William. "Architecture for the Meridian of Canada." *Anglo-American Magazine* 2 (1853):253–5

– "The Late Mr Pugin and the Revival of Christian Architecture." *Anglo-American Magazine* 2 (1853): 70–3.

"Hellmuth College." *Canadian Illustrated News* 1 (19 March 1870):316.

"Hellmuth Ladies College." *Canadian Illustrated News* 2 (10 September 1870):171–2.

Henderson, Margaret, ed. *Harvard: An Architectural History*. Cambridge, MA: Belknap, 1985.

Hersey, George. "Replication Replicated, or Notes on American Bastardy." *Perspecta* 9/10 (1965):21–48.

Hill, Robert, ed., comp. *The Biographical Dictionary of Architects in Canada, 1800–1950*. Forthcoming.

Hines, Thomas S. *Burnham of Chicago: Architect and Planner*. New York: Oxford University Press, 1974.

Historical Sketch of the Grande Ligne Mission. Montreal: Morton, Philips, 1898.

Hitchcock, Henry-Russell. *Architecture: Nineteenth and Twentieth Centuries*. 4th ed. Harmondsworth, Middlesex: Penguin, 1981.

– "Ruskin and American Architecture, or Regeneration Long Delayed." In *Concerning Architecture*, ed. John Summerson. London: Allen Lane, 1968.

– "Second Empire 'Avant La Lettre.'" *Gazette des Beaux-Arts* 42 (August 1953):115–30.

Hobhouse, Hermione. *Lost London*. London: Macmillan, 1971.

Hodson, W.H. "How to Estimate." *CAB* 5 (May 1892): 49, (June 1892):61; (July 1892):69.

"Home Life Building Fire – An Object Lesson." *Real Estate Record & Guide* 62 (10 December 1898): 864–5.

Horwood, John C.B. "American Architectural Methods from the Standpoint of a Canadian." *CAB* 5 (January 1893):8–9.

– "Architecture in New York." *CAB* 4 (January 1891):6.

– "Institute of Architects of Canada." *CAB* 21 (November 1907):24.

– "J.C.B. Horwood Has More To Say on Proposed Licensing Act." *Construction* 2, 5 (March 1909):42; 8 (June 1909):49.

– "Licence Law Strongly Opposed." *Construction* 2 (January 1909):36B, 38–40, 70

– "Some Observations on Fireproof Building in New York." *CAB* 6 (March 1893):36–8.

Hughes, Quentin. *Seaport: Architecture and Townscape in Liverpool*. London: Lund Humphries, 1964.

Huls, Mary Ellen. "YMCA and YWCA Architecture: A Bibliography." *Vance Bibliographies*. Architecture Series: Bibliography #A 1586. Monticello, Illinois.

Hunt, Geoffrey. *John M. Lyle: Toward a Canadian Architecture*. Kingston: Agnes Etherington Centre, Queen's University, 1982.

Hutton, N.H. "Fireproof Construction." *AABN* 1 (5 February 1876):43; (1 April 1876):111.

Huxtable, Ada Louise. "Harper & Brothers Building – 1854." *Progressive Architecture* 38 (February 1957): 153–4.

Hynes, J.P. "More About Competitions." *Construction* 1 (October 1907):45.

"The Inception and Progress of the Ontario Association of Architects." *CAB* 3 (December 1890):137.

Ingles, Ernest, and Michael McMordie. "Preserving the Past: The Canadian Architectural Archives." *Canadian Architect* 23 (July 1978):17–21.

Irving, William Henry. "Owens Museum of Fine Arts." Sackville: Mount Allison University Archives, no date.

Jameson, Anna. *Winter Studies and Summer Rambles*. London: Saunders and Otley, 1838.

"Japanese Building at the Centennial." *AABN* 1 (1876):136.

Jasen, Patricia. "The Burns Building, Calgary." Calgary, 1986.

Jenkins, Frank. *Architect and Patron*. London: Oxford University Press, 1961.

Johnston, Charles M. *McMaster University: The Toronto Years*. 2 vols. Toronto: University of Toronto Press, 1976.

Johnston, Patricia J., and Paul R.L. Chenier, *Index of the Canadian Architect and Builder, 1888–1908*. Ottawa: Society for the Study of Architecture in Canada, n.d.

Jones, Owen. *The Grammar of Ornament*. London, 1856.

Jordy, William, and Frank Coe, eds. *American Architecture and Other Writings*. 2 vols. Cambridge, MA: Belknap, 1961.

Kalman, Harold, and John Roaf. *Exploring Ottawa*. Toronto: University of Toronto Press, 1983.

– *Exploring Vancouver 2: Ten Tours of the City and its Buildings*. Vancouver: University of British Columbia Press, 1978.

Kaplan, Wendy. *"The Art that is Life": The Arts and Crafts Movement in America, 1875–1920*. Boston: Museum of Fine Arts, 1987.

Karlowitz, Titus. "D.H. Burnham's Role in the Selection of Architects for the World's Columbian Exposition."

Journal of the Society of Architectural Historians 29 (December 1970):247–54.

Kaye, Barrington. *The Development of the Architectural Profession in Britain*. London: Allen & Unwin, 1960.

Kelsey, Albert E. "Modern City Making." *CAB* 14 (April 1901):80.

Kerr, Robert. *The Gentleman's House*. London: John Murray, 1865.

Kidder, F.E. *Churches and Chapels: Their Arrangements, Construction, and Equipment, Supplemented by Plans, Interior, and Exterior Views of Numerous Churches of Different Denominations and Cost*. 4th ed. New York: William T. Comstock, 1910.

King, Anthony D. *The Bungalow: The Production of a Global Culture*. London: Routledge & Kegan Paul, 1984.

King, Moses. *King's Handbook of New York*. Boston: Moses King, 1892.

King, Robert B., with Charles O. McLean. *The Vanderbilt Homes*. New York: Rizzoli, 1989.

"Knox Church, Woodstock." *CAB* 10 (December 1897):12, ill.

Kostof, Spiro, ed. *The Architect: Chapters in the History of the Profession*. New York: Oxford University Press, 1977.

Lancaster, Clay. *The American Bungalow, 1880–1930*. New York: Abbeville Press, 1985.

– "Japanese Buildings in the United States Before 1900: Their Influence Upon American Domestic Architecture." *Art Bulletin* 35 (1953):219–24.

Landau, Sarah Bradford. "Tall Office Building Artistically Reconsidered." In *In Search of Modern Architecture: A Tribute to Henry-Russell Hitchcock*, ed. Helen Searing. New York: The Architectural History Foundation, 1982, 136–64.

Langley, Henry. "Description of the Lieutenant-Govenor's Residence." In *Report of the Commissioner of Public Works, 1869*. Toronto: Government of Ontario, 1870.

Langton, William. "On the Architect's Part in His Work." *CAB* 13 (February 1900):28–9.

– "The Plan of Improvements to Toronto." *CAB* 19 (February 1906):26–8.

– "Professional Ethics." *Construction* 10 (October 1917):345.

Larson, Gerald, and R.M. Geraniotis. "Toward a Better Understanding of the Evolution of the Iron Skeleton Frame in Chicago." *Journal of the Society of Architectural Historians* 46 (March 1987):39–48.

"The Late Mr Henry Langley." *CAB* 20 (January 1907):14.

"The Late Mr Wm Hay, Architect." *CAB* 1 (July 1888):11.

"League for the Adornment of the City of Chicago." *CAB* 7 (December 1894):160.

Lemon, James. "Plans for Early 20th-Century Toronto: Lost in Management." *Urban History Review* 18 (June 1989):11–31.

– "Tracy Deavin LeMay: Toronto's First Planning Commissioner, 1930–1954." *City Planning* (Winter 1984):4–7, 36.

– and J. Simmons. "A Guide to Data on Nineteenth-Century Toronto." Toronto, 1977.

Lever, Jill, and Margaret Richardson. *The Architect as Artist*. New York: Rizzoli, 1984.

"The Loan Exhibit of Architectural Drawings by the Ontario Association of Architects." *Construction* 3 (September 1910):56.

Logan, Thomas H. "The Americanization of German Zoning." *Journal of American Institute of Planners* 42 (1976):377–85.

Lorne Park Estates Historical Committee. *A Village Within a City: The Story of Lorne Park Estates*. Guelph: Boston Mills Press, 1980.

Lowrey, Carol. "The Society of Artists and Amateurs, 1834: Toronto's First Art Exhibition and its Antecedents." *RACAR* 8 (1981):99–118.

– "The Toronto Society of Arts, 1847–48: Patriotism and the Pursuit of Culture in Canada West." *RACAR* 12 (1985):3–44.

McAlester, Virginia, and Lee McAlester. *A Field Guide to American Houses*. New York: Knopf, 1988.

McHugh, Patricia. *Toronto Architecture: A City Guide*. Toronto: Mercury, 1985.

McKee, S.G.E. *Jubilee History of the Women's Christian Temperence Union*. Whitby: C.A. Goodfellow & Son, 1927.

McKelvey, Margaret E., and Merilyn McKelvey. *Toronto Carved in Stone*. Toronto: Fitzhenry & Whiteside, 1984.

McKenna, Rosalie Thorne. "James Renwick, Jr and the Second Empire Style in the United States." *Magazine of Art* 44 (1951):97–101.

MacKimmie, G.W. "About Banks and Bank Buildings, 1837–1937: Part 2." *Monetary and Commercial Times* 23 (1889–90):903.

McMordie, Michael. "The Cottage Idea." *RACAR* 6 (1979):17–27.

MacRae, Marion, and Anthony Adamson. *Hallowed*

Walls: Church Architecture of Upper Canada. Toronto: Clarke, Irwin, 1975.

M___. "On the Effect Which Should Result to Architecture, from the General Introduction of Iron in the Construction of Buildings." *Architectural Magazine and Journal* 4 (1837):277-87.

Maddex, Diane. *Historic Buildings of Washington, DC.* Pittsburgh: Ober Park Associates, 1973.

Maitland, Leslie. "Queen Anne Revival." *Canadian Collector* 21 (1986):44-8.

- *Queen Anne Revival Style in Canadian Architecture.* Ottawa: Parks Canada, 1990.

Mallory, Mary Louise. "Three Henry Langley Churches: Victorian Gothic Architecture and the Diversity of Sects in Ontario." 2 vols. Master's thesis, University of Toronto, 1979.

Maltby, Sally, Sally Macdonald, and Colin Cunningham. *Alfred Waterhouse, 1830-1905.* RIBA Series. London: Heinz Gallery, 1983.

Markell, H.K. *A Short History of the Presbyterian Church in Canada.* Toronto: Presbyterian Publications, 1965.

Market Gallery. *The Architecture of Public Works: R.C. Harris, Commissioner, 1912-45.* Toronto: Market Gallery, 1982.

Marsan, Jean-Claude. *Montreal in Evolution.* Montreal: McGill-Queen's University Press, 1974.

"Marsh's Reinforced Concrete." *CAB* 18 (March 1905):35-6.

Mawson, Thomas. *Calgary: A Preliminary Scheme for Controlling the Economic Growth of the City.* Calgary: City Planning Commission, 1912.

Maxwell, W., and E.S Maxwell. "The Dominion Express Building, Montreal, Quebec." *Construction* 5 (November 1912):47-9.

Maxwell, W.S. "Architectural Education," *CAB* 22 (January 1908):21-5.

Meeks, Carroll L.V. "Romanesque Before Richardson." *Art Bulletin* 35 (March 1953):17-33.

Melnyck, Brian P. *Calgary Builds: The Emergence of an Urban Landscape.* Calgary: Alberta Culture/Plains Research Centre, 1985.

"Messrs. Carrère & Hastings Reply." *Construction* 3 (September 1910):41-2.

"Methodist Book Room, Toronto." *Construction* 9 (January 1916):8-14.

Michels, Eileen. "Late Nineteenth-Century Published American Perspective Drawing." *Journal of the Society of Architectural Historians* 31 (December 1972): 291-308.

Middleton, Jesse Edgar. *The Municipality of Toronto: A History.* 3 vols. Toronto: Dominion Publishing, 1923.

Middleton, Robin, ed. *The Beaux-Arts and Nineteenth-Century French Architecture.* Cambridge, MA: MIT Press, 1982.

Millard, Rodney. *The Master Spirit of the Age: Canadian Engineers and the Politics of Professionalism, 1887-1922.* Toronto: University of Toronto Press, 1988.

Mitchell, Charles F. *Building Construction.* London: B.T. Batsford, 1888.

Mitchell, Eugene. *American Victoriana: Floor Plans and Renderings From the Gilded Age.* San Francisco: Chronicle Books, 1979.

"Modern Business Premises in London." *Construction* 2 (December 1908):37-47.

Montgomery-Massingberd, Hugh. *Royal Palaces of Europe.* New York: Vendome, 1983.

"Montreal." *CAB* 2 (March 1889):32.

Moore, Charles. *Daniel Hudson Burnham, Architect and Planner of Cities.* New York: Da Capo, 1964.

Morgan, Henry James. *Canadian Men and Women of the Time: A Handbook of Canadian Biography.* Toronto: William Briggs, 1898, 1913.

Morrison, Hugh. *Early American Architecture: First Colonial Settlements to National Period.* New York: Oxford University Press, 1952.

Morriss, Shirley. "The Nine-Year Odyssey of a High Victorian Goth: Three Churches by Fred Cumberland." *Journal of Canadian Art History* 2 (Summer 1975): 42-53.

Morse, Edward. Japanese Homes and their Surroundings. Salem, MA: Peabody Academy of Sciences, 1886.

"Mr Petit's *Remarks on Church Architecture.*" *Ecclesiologist* 1 (April 1842):81-3.

Muccigrosso, Robert. *American Gothic: The Mind and Art of Ralph Adams Cram.* Washington: University Press of America, 1980.

Mumford, Lewis. *Roots of Contemporary American Architecture.* New York: Dover, 1972.

Murray, Joan. *Ontario Society of Artists, 1872-1972.* Toronto: Art Gallery of Ontario, 1972.

Museum of Modern Art. *The Architecture of Richard Morris Hunt.* New York: Museum of Modern Art, 1986.

"National Assembly of Architects." *Construction* 1 (September 1908):32-6.

"New Addition to the Ladies College." *Allisonia* 1 (January 1904):33-6.

"New Departmental Buildings, Ottawa." *Construction* 6 (May 1913):169.

"New Globe Building." *CAB* 8 (December 1895):143.

"New Look for YMCA." *Canadian Architect* 27 (September 1982):26–9.

"The New Parliament Buildings." *CAB* 1 (July 1888):6.

"The New West End YMCA Building, Toronto." *Construction* 6 (January 1913):19–25.

"New York Art Commission." *Toronto Civic Guild Monthly Bulletin* 2, 2 (November 1912):3.

Newton, Roger Hale. "Our Summer Resort Architecture – An American Phenomenum and Social Document." *Art Quarterly* 4 (Autumn 1941):297–318.

Nobbs, Percy. "The Late Frank Darling." *Construction* 16 (June 1923):205–6.

"Northcroft's System of Fireproof Construction." *Building News* 32 (19 January 1877):60.

"Notes of the Toronto Exhibition." *CAB* 15 (September 1902): ix.

Ochsner, Jeffrey Carl. *H.H. Richardson: Complete Architectural Works*. Cambridge, MA: MIT Press, 1982.

O'Gorman, James F. *H.H. Richardson and his Office, Selected Drawings: A Centennial of his Move to Boston*. Boston: Harvard College Library and Henry Godine, 1974.

– *The Architecture of Frank Furness*. Philadelphia: Philadelphia Museum of Art, 1973.

"Old Calvary Temple." *Winnipeg Real Estate News*. 14 June 1985, 1–2.

"On the Reluctance of Well-Known American Architects to Publish Their Plans." *AABN* 27 (11 January 1890):17.

"On Simplicity of Composition, Especially in Churches of the Early English." *Ecclesiologist* 2 (April 1843): 118–22.

"On Some of the Differences Between Cathedral and Parish Churches." *Ecclesiologist* 1 (August 1842): 181–3.

"Ontario." *Royal Architectural Institute of Canada Journal* (June 1940):108.

"Ontario Architects' Act." *CAB* 3 (August 1890):40–2; 4 (August 1891):80; 9 (November 1896):174–6.

"Ontario Architects' Convention." *Construction* 2 (February 1909):40.

"Ontario Association of Architects." *CAB* 2 (December 1889):139–40; 3 (December 1890):135; 5 (February 1892):10, 15; 7 (February 1894):29–32; 8 (February 1895):21–8; 9 (January 1896):17–19, 21, 29–32; 10 (January 1897):9, 12; 11 (January 1898):8, 18; 12 (January 1899):10–17; 13 (January 1900):8–19; 14 (February 1901):33, 35–43; 15 (January 1902):5, 8, 9; 16 (January 1903):3–29; 17 (February 1904):33–6; 18 (January 1905):10–11; 19 (January 1906):5–12.

Ontario Association of Architects. *Catalogue of the Exhibition of Architecture and Allied Arts*. Toronto: Art Gallery of Toronto, 1927, 1935.

"Ontario Association of Architects Examinations." *CAB* 5 (June 1892):57–61; 10 (June 1897): 115–16.

Ontario Society of Artists. *Annual Exhibition Catalogue*. Toronto: OSA, 1873–89.

"Opening of the New Addition." *Allisonia* 1 (January 1904):53–4.

"The Organization of an Architect's Office. Nos. 1–8." *Engineering Record* 21 (1890):83, 165, 181, 195; 22 (1890):5, 180; 24 (1891):362–3; 25 (1892):4–5.

Osborne, C. Francis. *Notes on the Art of House Planning*. New York: Comstock, 1888.

"Ottawa and the Parliament of Canada." *Dominion Illustrated* (Montreal) Special Edition (1891):112.

"Ottawa Government Building Competition." *CAB* 20 (November 1907):15–20; (December 1907):15–19.

Otto, Stephen A. "Press Kit for the Horwood Collection." Toronto, 1979.

"Our College." *Allisonia* 3 (January 1906):45–8; 3 (March 1906): ill. opp. 74–7; 3 (May 1906): opp. 125.

"Our Imposing Store in Vancouver." *Beaver* 5, 2 (March 1925):68.

"Our Office Table: Architecture at the Royal Academy." *Building News* 26 (13 March 1874):301.

Palliser's New Cottage Homes and Details. New York: Palliser, 1887. Reprint New York: Da Capo Press, 1975.

Parkdale United Church. *Diamond Jubilee, 1878 to 1938*. Toronto, 1938.

Peabody, R.S. [Georgian, pseud.]. "Georgian Homes of New England." *AABN* 2 (1877):338–9.

– "A Talk About 'Queen Anne.'" *AABN* 2 (28 April 1877):133–4.

Petit, John Louis. *Remarks on Church Architecture*. 2 vols. London: James Burns, 1841.

Pevsner, Nicholas. *Pioneers of Modern Design*. Harmondsworth, Middlesex: Penguin, 1987.

Pierson, William H., Jr. "Richard Upjohn and the American *Rundbogenstil*." *Winterthur Portfolio* 21 (1986):223–42.

Pinard, Guy. *Montréal: Son Histoire, Son Architecture*. vol. 5. Montréal: Editions du Méridien, 1992.

Placzek, Adolf, ed. *Macmillan Encyclopedia of Architects.* New York: Collier Macmillan, 1982.

"Plans Showing Scheme for New Departmental and Court Buildings." *Construction* 6 (September 1913):331; 7 (February 1914):75.

"Popular Impressions vs Fact." CAB 8 (April 1895): 54.

"Prize Designs, Proposed Departmental and Justice Buildings, Ottawa." CAB 20 (October 1907):42–4, 48–9, 178–9.

"Progress of Bloor St Viaduct, Toronto." *Contract Record* 29 (15 December 1915):1278–82.

"Progress of Toronto – New Wholesale Warehouses." *Monetary & Commercial Times* 3, 37 (29 April 1870):581.

"Proposed Canadian Architectural Association." CAB 2 (February 1889):19–20.

"Proposed Departmental Buildings, Ottawa." *Contract Record* 27 (February 1913):61.

"Proposed Federal and Municipal Scheme for Toronto." *Construction* 4 (July 1911):51.

"Proposed Henry Hudson Memorial Bridge." *Construction* 1 (March 1908):29–31.

"Provincial Board of Examiners." *Construction* 2, 4 (November 1908):30; 9 (February 1909):30.

Pugin, Augustus Welby Northmore. *An Apology for the Revival of Christian Architecture in England.* London: John Weale, 1849.

– *Contrasts: Or a Parallel Between the Noble Edifices of the Middle Ages, and Corresponding Buildings of the Present Day Showing the Present Decay of Taste.* London, 1836.

– *True Principles of Pointed or Christian Architecture.* London, 1841.

"A Question of Privilege." AABN 7 (10 April 1880):157.

"Rapid Work on Reinforced Concrete." *Construction* 2 (December 1908):60.

Ratcliffe, W.H. "Central YMCA Building, Toronto." *Construction* 7 (February 1914):51–60.

Rawlyk, G.A., ed. *Canadian Baptists and Christian Higher Education.* Montreal: McGill-Queen's University Press, 1988.

"Recent Work of the Civic Guild." *Toronto Civic Guild Monthly Bulletin* 1 (1 May 1911):6.

Regional Church Planning Office. *The Church in Akron: An Interpretive Analysis.* Cleveland, 1963.

Reid, Richard. "The Rosamond Woolen Company of Almonte: Industrial Development in a Rural Setting." *Ontario History.* 75 (September 1983):266.

"The Reinforcement of Concrete Beams." CAB 6 (November 1893):114.

"Reminiscences of Mount Allison." *Allisonia* 3 (March 1904):67–72, 78.

Rempel, John. *Building with Wood and Other Aspects of Nineteenth-Century Building in Ontario.* Toronto: University of Toronto Press, 1967.

Report of the Canadian Commission at the International Exhibition in Philadelphia, 1876. Ottawa: Government of Canada, 1877.

Reps, John. *The Making of Urban America: A History of City Planning in the United States.* Princeton: Princeton University Press, 1965.

Review of *Principles of Reinforced Concrete Construction,* by F.E. Turneaure. CAB 21 (November 1907): 25.

Richardson, Douglas. "The Glory of Toronto." Toronto: Justinia M. Barnicke Gallery, University of Toronto, 1984.

– *Gothic Revival Architecture in Ireland.* 2 vols. New York: Garland, 1983.

– "Hyperborean Gothic; or, Wilderness Ecclesiology and the Wood Churches of Edward Medley." *Architectura* 2 (January 1972):48–74.

– "The Spirit of the Place: Canadian Architecture in the Victorian Era." *Canadian Collector* 10 (September/ October 1975):20–9.

– "Wills, Frank." *Dictionary of Canadian Biography.* Toronto: University of Toronto Press, 1966– .

– ed. *Romanesque Toronto: A Photographic Exhibition of Late Nineteenth-Century Architecture.* Toronto: Hart House Art Gallery, University of Toronto, 17 May–27 June 1971.

Richardson, Margaret. *Architects of the Arts and Crafts Movement.* London: Trefoil, 1983.

Richardson, Marianna May, comp. *The Ontario Association of Architects Centennial Collection.* Pamphlet. Toronto: OAA, 1990.

Rickman, Thomas. *An Attempt to Discriminate the Styles of Architecture in England from the Conquest to the Reformation with a Sketch of the Grecian and Roman Orders.* 7th ed. London: Parker & Co., 1881.

Ritchie, T. *Canada Builds: 1867–1967.* Toronto: University of Toronto Press, 1967.

"Robert Simpson Company's Store Addition, Toronto." *Construction* 17 (March 1924):77–81.

Robertson, John Ross. *Landmarks of Toronto.* 6 vols. Toronto: J.R. Robinson, 1894–1914.

Robinson, Charles Mulford. *Modern Civic Art with*

Special Reference to the Planning of Streets and Lots. New York: Putnam 1916.

Robson, E.R. *School Architecture.* 1874. Reprint, New York: Humanities Press, 1972.

"Romance 'At Home,' Vancouver Store." *Beaver* 262, 3 (December 1931):356–60.

"Romanesque and Catholick Architecture." *Ecclesiologist* 2 (October 1842):5–16.

Rombout, Luke. "John Hammond, RCA, 1843–1939." *Canadian Collector* 4 (February 1969):24–5.

Ross, Murray G. *The YMCA in Canada: The Chronicle of a Century.* Toronto: Ryerson, 1951.

Roth, Leland. *The Architecture of McKim, Mead & White, 1870 – 1920: A Building List.* New York: Garland, 1978.

– *A Concise History of American Architecture.* New York: Icon Editions, Harper & Row, 1979.

– *McKim, Mead & White, Architects.* New York: Harper & Row, 1983.

"Royal Academy Exhibition." *CAB* 8 (May 1895):65.

"A Rural Church," *Inland Architect & News Record* 1 (1883):20–3.

Rutherford, Paul, ed. *Saving the Canadian City, the first phase, 1880–1920.* Toronto: University of Toronto Press, 1974.

S___ "Concerning 'Queen Anne.'" *AABN* 1 (16 December 1876):404.

Sackville Art Association. *John Hammond, RCA, 1843–1939: Retrospective Exhibition.* Text by Luke Rombout. Sackville: Owens Art Gallery, 1967.

Saint, Andrew. *The Image of the Architect.* New Haven: Yale University Press, 1983.

– *Richard Norman Shaw.* New Haven: Yale University Press, 1976.

St John, Judith. *Firm Foundations: A Chronicle of Toronto's Metropolitan United Church and Her Methodist Origins, 1795–1984.* Toronto: Metropolitan United Church, 1988.

Scadding, Henry. *Toronto of Old.* Ed. Frederick H. Armstrong. Toronto: Dundurn, 1987.

Schuyler, Montgomery. "Concerning Queen Anne." In *American Architecture and Other Writings,* ed. William Jordy and Frank Coe. Cambridge, MA: Belknap, 1961.

– "Last Words about the Fair." In *American Architecture and Other Writings,* ed. William Jordy and Frank Coe. Cambridge, MA: Belknap, 1961.

– "A Modern Classic." *Architectural Record* 15 (May 1904):431–44.

– "The Skyscraper Problem." In *American Architecture and Other Writings,* ed. William Jordy and Frank Coe. Cambridge, MA: Belknap, 1961.

– "The Skyscraper' Up-to-Date." *Architectural Record* 8 (January–March 1899):231–51.

– "The Works of Cram, Goodhue & Ferguson: A Record of the Firm's Most Representative Structures, 1892–1910." *Architectural Record* 29 (January 1911):18.

– "The Works of Richard Morris Hunt." In *American Architecture and Other Writings,* ed. William Jordy and Frank Coe. Cambridge, MA: Belknap, 1961.

Scott, Geoffrey. *The Architecture of Humanism: A Study in the History of Taste.* London: Constable, 1914.

Scott, Gilbert. *Personal and Professional Recollections.* London: Sampson Low, Marston, Searle & Rivington, 1879.

Scully, Vincent J., Jr. *The Shingle Style: Architectural Theory and Design from Richardson to the Origins of Wright.* New Haven: Yale University Press, 1957.

Searing, Helen, ed. *In Search of Modern Architecture: A Tribute to Henry-Russell Hitchcock.* New York: The Architectural History Foundation, 1982.

"Second Annual Exhibition of the Toronto Architectural Eighteen Club." *CAB* 15 (June 1902):71–2; 17 (November 1904):188; 18 (January 1905):2; 18 (February 1905):19; 19 (December 1906): ix; 21 (December 1907):11.

Segger, Martin. *The Buildings of Samuel MacLure.* Victoria: University of Victoria, 1986.

– *Victoria: A Primer for Regional History in Architecture.* Victoria: Pilgrim Guide to Historic Architecture, 1977.

Service, Alistair. *Edwardian Architecture.* London: Thames and Hudson, 1977.

Shaw, Richard Norman, and T.G. Jackson, eds. *Architecture, A Profession or an Art?* London: John Murray, 1892.

Shillaber, Caroline. *Massachusetts Institute of Technology School of Architecture and Planning, 1861–1961.* Cambridge, MA: Harvard University Press, 1963.

"Shillito Store." *AABN* 2 (13 October 1877):328–30.

Siddall, G. "The Advancement of Public Taste in Architecture." *CAB* 12 (February 1899):28.

"Sight-Seeing the Calgary Store." *Beaver* 262, 4 (March 1932):420.

Silver, Nathan. *Lost New York.* New York: American Legacy Press, 1967.

Simmins, Geoffrey. *Ontario Association of Architects: A*

Centennial History 1889–1989. Toronto: Ontario Association of Architects, 1989.

Simpson, Matthew, ed. *Cyclopedia of Methodism.* Philadelphia: Louis H. Everts, 1880.

"The Simpson Departmental Store." CAB 8 (October 1895):115.

Sinaiticus. "The Addition to the Robert Simpson Store, Toronto." *Construction* 22 (March 1929):72–7, 82–6.

Sinclair, Peg, and Taylor Lewis. *Victorious Victorians.* New York: Holt, Rinehart and Winston, 1985.

"Sketch for a Village Church." CAB 2 (January 1889):11.

Smith, Eden. "Architectural Education–1900." CAB 13 (June 1900):109.

– "Compulsory Architectural Education Opposed." *Construction* 2 (February 1909):67.

Smith, Robert C. "Antebellum Skyscraper." *Journal of Society of Architectural Historians* 9 (March 1950): 27–8.

Smith, St John Brock. "Children's Promotional Features– Vancouver Store." *Beaver* 262 (December 1931): 361–2.

Sobolak, Adam. "A Lennox Folly: The Beard Building." *Architectural Conservancy of Toronto NewsLetter* (November 1988):13–18.

"Some Special Features of Traders Bank Building, Toronto." CAB 20 (June 1907):91–3.

"Specialization as it Applies to Arts and Crafts." *Construction* 4 (September 1911):78–9.

Spiers, R. Phené. "Architectural Drawing." *Building News* 26 (24 April 1874):443; (1 May 1874):470.

– *Architectural Drawing.* London: Cassell & Company, 1887.

Sprague, Paul. "The Origin of Balloon Framing." *Journal of the Society of Architectural Historians* 11 (December 1981):311–19.

Stacey, Robert H., ed. *Lives and Works of the Canadian Artists.* Toronto: Dundurn, 1977.

Stamp, Gavin. "London 1900." *Architectural Design* 48, (1978):303.

Stanford, G.H. *To Serve the Community: The Story of Toronto's Board of Trade.* Toronto: University of Toronto Press, 1974.

Stanton, Phoebe. *The Gothic Revival and American Church Architecture: An Episode in Taste, 1840–56.* Baltimore: Johns Hopkins Press, 1968.

Steege, Gwen W. "The *Book of Plans* and Early Romanesque Revival in the United States: A Study in Architectural Patronage." *Journal of the Society of Architectural Historians* 46 (1987):215–27.

"Steel Joined at Bloor St Viaduct, Toronto." *Contract Record* 31 (9 May 1917):400–12.

Steiner, Frances H. *French Iron Architecture.* Ann Arbour, MI: UMI Research Press, 1984.

Stell, Christopher. *Nonconformist Chapels and Meetinghouses in Central England.* London: HMSO, 1983.

Stelter, Gilbert, and Alan Artibise. *The Canadian City: Essays in Urban and Social History.* Toronto: Oxford University Press for Carleton Library Series, 1984.

Stern, Robert A.M., Gregory Gilmartin, and John Montague Massengale. *New York 1900: Metropolitan Architecture and Urbanism 1890–1915.* New York: Rizzoli, 1983.

Stevens, John Calvin, and Albert Wimslow Cobb. *Examples of American Domestic Architecture.* New York: William T. Comstock, 1889.

Stevenson, J.J. "On the Reaction of Taste in English Architecture." *Building News* 26 (26 June 1874): 689–91.

Stokes, Leonard. "On Observation." CAB 10 (November 1897):212–13.

Stupart, R.F. "Meteorology in Canada." *Royal Astronomical Society of Canada Journal* 6 (March/ April 1912):75–87.

Sturgis, R. Clipson. "Church Architecture." CAB 11 (September 1898):153–4.

Sturgis, Russell. "The Warehouse and the Factory in Architecture." *Architectural Record* 15 (January 1904):1–17.

Sturgis, Walter Knight, ed. *The Origins of Cast Iron Architecture in America.* New York: Da Capo, 1970.

"Success of Fireproof Construction." *Real Estate Record & Guide* 62 (17 December 1898):907.

Sullivan, Louis. "The Tall Office Building Artistically Considered" (1896). In *Kindergarten Chats and Other Writings,* ed. Isabella Athey. New York: 1947.

Sward, Robert. *The Toronto Islands.* Toronto: Dreadnought, 1983.

Tallmadge, Thomas E. *The Story of Architecture in America.* New York: Norton, 1927.

Tausky, Nancy, and Lynne DiStephano. *Victorian Architecture in London and Southwestern Ontario: Symbols of Aspiration.* Toronto: University of Toronto Press, 1986.

"Terra cotta as a Building Material." CAB 1 (January 1888):15.

"Tests of Fireproofing Material." CAB 8 (June 1895): 78–9.

"Theatre Services in London." *Wesleyan Methodist Magazine* (1868):567–8.

"Thomas Ogilvie & Sons' New Warehouse." CAB 21 (December 1907):22.

Thompson, Austin Seton. *Jarvis Street: A Story of Triumph and Tragedy.* Toronto: Personal Library Publishers, 1980.

Thompson, Octavius. *Toronto in the Camera: A Series of Photographic Views.* Toronto, 1868.

Timperlake, J. *Illustrated Toronto: Past and Present.* Toronto: Peter A. Gross, 1877.

"Toronto: The Commercial Metropolis of Ontario." *Dominion Illustrated* (Montreal), Special Edition on Toronto (1892):30.

"Toronto – the Queen City of the West." *Canadian Illustrated News* 25 (28 May 1881):338–9.

Toronto and Lorne Park Summer Resort Company. *Lorne Park Illustrated.* Toronto: Bingham & Webber, c.1890.

"The Toronto Architectural Club." CAB 21 (December 1907):11.

"Toronto Architectural Eighteen Club." CAB 14 (September 1901):166; 17 (November 1904):188.

Toronto Architectural Eighteen Club (later Toronto Society of Architects). *Annual Exhibition Catalogue.* Toronto, 1901–2, 1905, 1909, and 1912.

"Toronto Architectural Eighteen Club Competition in Rendering from Photograph for Students." CAB 13 (December 1900):232.

"Toronto Architectural Eighteen Club Exhibition." CAB 14 (February 1901):29; 14 (May 1901):96; 14 (September 1901):166; 15 (May 1902):64.

"Toronto Architectural Sketch Club." CAB 3 (January 1890):6; (February 1890):17; (March 1890):26–8, 45; (May 1890):53; (September 1890):102; (October 1890):110; (November 1890):125–6; (December 1890):136, 140; 4 (January 1891):4–5; (February 1891):24; (March 1891):31; (April 1891):52; (June 1891):61, 64; (July 1891):71; (September 1891):89; (November 1891):95, 100; (December 1891):106; 5 (February 1892):ill.; (April 1892):41; (May 1892):46–8; 8 (December 1895):139, 145; 9 (June 1896):xi; (February 1896):supp. ill.; (March 1896):45, 19 (March 1906):34–5.

Toronto Board of Trade. *"A Souvenir": A History of the Queen City and Its Board of Trade and the Principal Members Thereof.* Toronto: Sabiston Lithographic & Publishing Co., 1893.

Toronto Board of Trade. *"A Souvenir": A History of the Queen City and Its Board of Trade and the Principal Members Thereof.* Toronto: Sabiston Lithographic & Publishing Co., 1893.

"Toronto Board of Trade Building Competition." CAB 1 (August 1888):4.

Toronto Civic Guild. *Report on a Comprehensive Plan for Systematic Civic Improvements in Toronto.* Toronto, 1909.

Toronto Conservatory of Music. *Twenty-Fourth Year Book, 1910–11.* Toronto, 1911.

Toronto Local Stone Cutters. *Toronto Building and Ornamental Stones.* Pamphlet. Toronto, 1914.

Toronto Mechanics Institute. *Annual Report.* Toronto, 1866 and 1867.

Toronto Society of Architects, see Toronto Architectural Eighteen Club.

"Toronto Technical School." CAB 5 (October 1892):101; 6 (November 1893):113; 7 (March 1894):39–40; 8 (November 1895):130.

Tselos, Dimitri. "The Chicago World's Fair and the Myth of the 'Lost Cause.'" *Journal of the Society of Architectural Historians* 26 (December 1967):259–68.

Turak, Theodore. "The Ecole Centrale and Modern Architecture: The Education of William Le Baron Jenney." *Journal of the Society of Architectural Historians* 29, no. 1 (1971):40–7.

– "Rememberances of the Home Insurance Building." *Journal of the Society of Architectural Historians* 44 (March 1985):60–5.

– *William Le Baron Jenney: A Pioneer of Modern Architecture.* Ann Arbour, MI: UMI Research Press, 1986.

"Twentieth Annual Convention of the Ontario Association of Architects." CAB 22 (January 1908):28.

"A Typical YMCA: The Broadview YMCA, Toronto." *Construction* 5 (January 1912):56–60.

[Ure, G.P.] *The Hand-Book of Toronto.* Toronto: Lovell & Gibson, 1858.

Van Brunt, Henry. "Greek Lines, Part 2." *Atlantic Monthly* 8 (July 1861):76–89.

"Vancouver." *Beaver* 261, 3 (December 1930):133.

"Vancouver and the Company." *Beaver* 270, 4 (March 1940):32–7.

"Vancouver Store." *Beaver* 257, 3 (December 1926):10–11.

"Victoria and Calgary Store Fronts." *Beaver* 265 (September 1934):9.

"A Victorian Style." *Building News* 33 (12 October 1877):372.

Viollet-le-Duc, Eugene-Emmanuel. *Lectures on Architecture.* 2 vols. trans. Benjamin Bucknall. New York: Dover Publications, 1987.

"WCTU Building, Toronto." *Construction* 6 (May 1913):184–7.

Walker, Byron E. "Comprehensive Plan for Toronto." In *Saving the Canadian City, the first phase 1880–1920.* Ed. Paul Rutherford. Toronto: University of Toronto Press, 1974, 221–6.

– "The Plan of Improvements to Toronto." *CAB* 19 (February 1906):18–19.

Walker, C. Howard. "The Artistic Expansion of Steel and Concrete." *CAB* 22 (February 1908):21–3.

"Watering Places of the Lower St Lawrence." *Canadian Illustrated News* 3 (9 April 1870):362; 4 (12 August 1871):97; 4 (26 August 1871):130; 6 (24 August 1872):115.

Weaver, John C. "The Modern City Realized: Toronto Civic Affairs, 1880–1915." In *Usable Urban Past: Planning and Politics in the Modern Canadian City*, ed. Alan Artibise and Gilbert Stelter. Toronto: Macmillan, 1979, 40–9.

Webster, A.E. "Canadian Dentistry and the Royal College of Dental Surgeons." *University of Toronto Monthly* 21 (1920–1):400–2.

Webster, J. Carson. "The Skyscraper: Logical and Historic Considerations." *Journal of the Society of Architectural Historians* 18 (1959):138–9.

Weir, Jean. *The Lost Craft of Ornamented Architecture: Canadian Architectural Drawing, 1850–1939.* Halifax: Dalhousie Art Gallery, Dalhousie University, 1984.

Weisman, Winston. "The Commercial Architecture of George B. Post." *Journal of the Society of Architectural Historians* 31 (October 1972):176–203.

– "New York and the Problem of the First Skyscraper." *Journal of the Society of Architectural Historians* 12 (March 1953):13–21.

– "Philadelphia Functionalism and Sullivan." *Journal of the Society of Architectural Historians* 20 (March 1961):3–19.

Werner, Hans. "Bridging Politics: A Political History of the Bloor Street Viaduct." Manuscript. Copy at CTA.

"Wesleyan Methodist Church." *Canadian Illustrated News* 5 (20 April 1872):241–3.

Westfall, William. *Two Worlds: The Protestant Culture of Nineteenth-Century Ontario.* Montreal: McGill-Queen's University Press, 1989.

"What is Fireproof Construction?" *Building News* 26 (13 March 1874):275–6.

Wheeler, Gervase. *Homes for the People in Suburb and Country; The Villa, the Mansion and the Cottage.* New York: Arno, 1972.

Whiffen, Marcus. *American Architecture since 1780: A Guide to the Styles.* Cambridge, Massachusetts: MIT Press, 1985.

White, James F. *The Cambridge Movement: The Ecclesiologists and the Gothic Revival.* Cambridge: University Press, 1962.

– *Protestant Worship and Church Architecture: Theological and Historical Considerations.* New York: Oxford University Press, 1964.

White, Murray A. "TASC Competition for a Staircase in Wood." *CAB* 4 (July 1891):ill.

"Why Not Patronize Canadian Architects?" *CAB* 22 (April 1908):18.

Willensky, Elliot, and Norval White. *AIA Guide to New York City.* New York: Harcourt Brace Jovanich, 1988.

Willett, James R. "Skeleton Structures in Building." *Inland Architect & News Record* 26 (December 1895):47–8.

Willmott, J.B. "The Royal College of Dental Surgeons of Ontario." *University of Toronto Monthly* 4 (1903–4):216–20.

Wilson, Richard Guy. *McKim, Mead & White, Architects.* New York: Rizzoli, 1983.

Wilson, William H. *The City Beautiful Movement.* Baltimore: Johns Hopkins, 1987.

Withey, Henry, and Elsie R. Withey. *Biographical Dictionary of American Architects (Deceased).* Los Angeles: Hennessey & Ingalls, 1970.

Wolfe, Jeanne. "The City Beautiful Movement in Montreal." Paper presented before the Society for the Study of Architecture in Canada, Montreal, 13 April 1989.

Wolfe, Jeanne M. "Montréal: Des plans d'embellissement." *Continuité* 31 (printemps 1986):24–7.

"Wolves in Sheep's Clothing." *Construction* 2 (April 1909):37.

Wood, Walter Mabie. "Working Plants for Young Men's Christian Associations." *Brickbuilder* 20 (August 1911):159–72.

Woodward, Geoffrey. "History." *Architectural Review.* 119 (May 1956):268–70.

"Work of the Guild." *Toronto Civic Guild Monthly Bulletin* 1 (1 March 1912):1.

"Would the Registration of Architects be a Menace to the Professions?" *Construction* 1 (January 1908):39–41.

Wright, Janet. "Thomas Seaton Scott: The Architect versus the Administrator." *Journal of Canadian Art History* 6, no. 2 (1985):202–18.

"YMCA." *Canadian Illustrated News* 6 (23 November 1872):323–4.

"YMCA Building in Bridgeport, Conn." *AABN* 24 (10 November 1888):219.

"YMCA Montreal." *Canadian Illustrated News* 6 (14 September 1872):1.

"Young Men's Christian Association Building, Utica, New York." *AABN* 23 (30 June 1888):307.

Index